Foundation Workbook

Science Companion

Book 9

CBSE ICSE NTSE High School National Boards State Boards Olympiads

Chandan Sukumar Sengupta

Creative Commons Series

Foundation Workbook Science Companion Book 2

Workbook and Activity Sheets for Students of Class 9.

Total Number of Printed Hard copies : 10,000

Place of Publication: Arabinda Nagar, Bankura, West Bengal, India – 722101

This workbook is designed for providing some time tested study materials to students aspiring for competitive examinations and Olympiads. All the question banks are from the prescribed content areas of studies duly prescribed by the National as well as State Boards of studies.

What we expect from our fellow student and what are the facilities we provide them should have proper links for ensuring the maximum return of our effort. We even come across instances during which children may revolt during repeatedly scheduled intensive learning programmes duly planned for them. For efficient handling of such job we should go on planning content delivery plan on the basis of student centred focus.

IT will even link up our plan with those of other fellow faculty members for making the effort a vibrant one. The work-book similar to this and others of similar category has a comprehensive plan of addressing content areas duly specified by the boards of studies. Answer sheets are there for some selected sheets. Rest of the other sheets kept off the side for enabling the exploratory drive of fellow students active. We are expecting their active participation in the learning and facilitation drives.

It is true that this workbook cannot follow the content areas exclusively prescribed for the aspirants of the particular age group. The purpose of the incorporations of varying types of activities is to expose the fellow students to some forthcoming challenges. It will definitely imply a sort of impression in the mind of the student and enable them to grasp through higher challenges with subtle easiness. It will also provide additional study materials to students of Class 9 -10. They even accelerate their regular studies on the basis of the scheduled worksheets and evaluation papers duly provided for them.

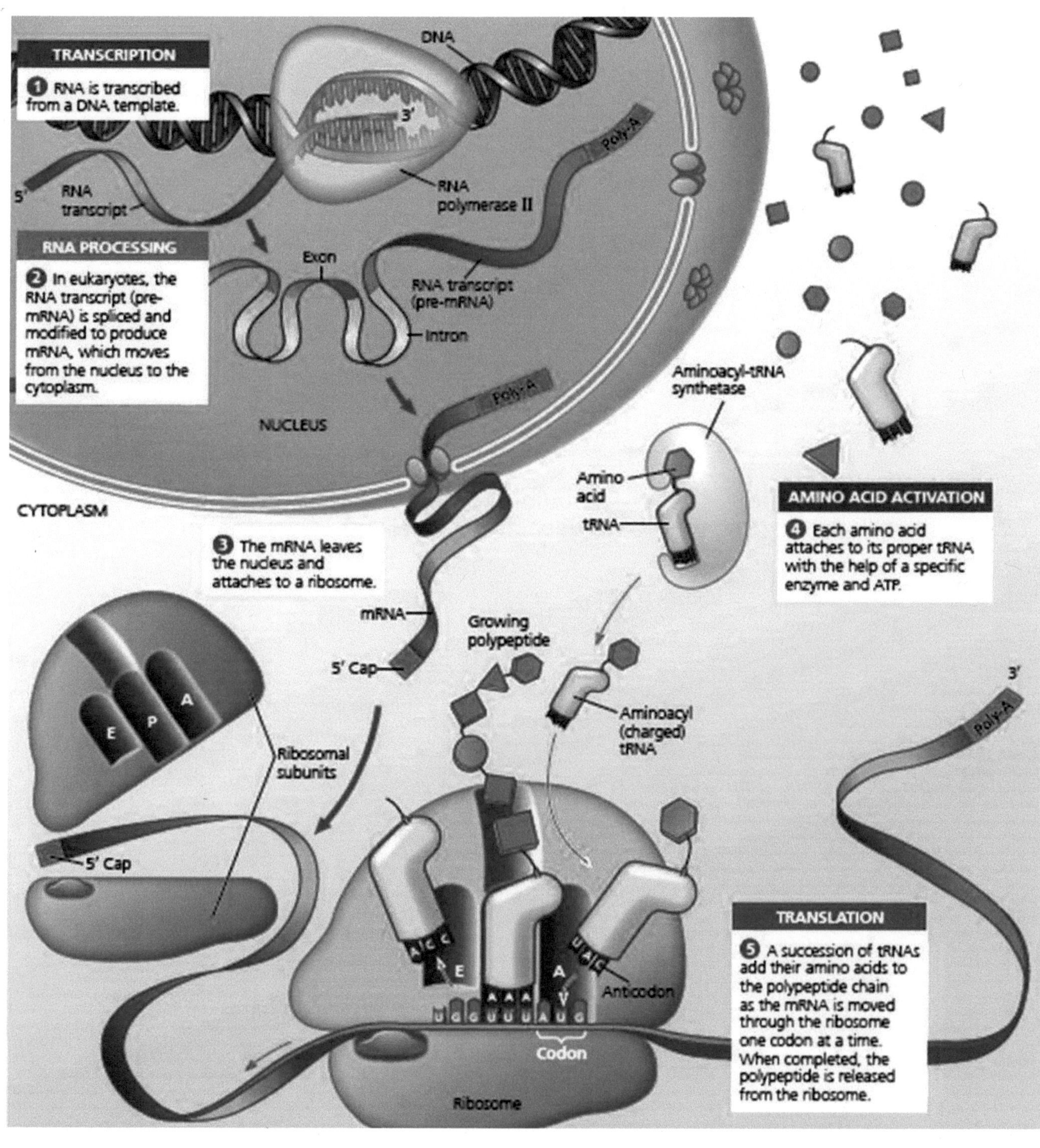

TRANSCRIPTION
1 RNA is transcribed from a DNA template.
DNA
3'
5'
RNA transcript
RNA polymerase II
Poly-A
RNA PROCESSING
2 In eukaryotes, the RNA transcript (pre-mRNA) is spliced and modified to produce mRNA, which moves from the nucleus to the cytoplasm.
Exon
RNA transcript (pre-mRNA)
Intron
Poly-A
NUCLEUS
CYTOPLASM
Aminoacyl-tRNA synthetase
Amino acid
tRNA
AMINO ACID ACTIVATION
4 Each amino acid attaches to its proper tRNA with the help of a specific enzyme and ATP.
3 The mRNA leaves the nucleus and attaches to a ribosome.
mRNA
Growing polypeptide
5' Cap
Aminoacyl (charged) tRNA
3'
Poly-A
E
P
A
Ribosomal subunits
5' Cap
TRANSLATION
5 A succession of tRNAs add their amino acids to the polypeptide chain as the mRNA is moved through the ribosome one codon at a time. When completed, the polypeptide is released from the ribosome.
A C C
E
A A A
A
U A C
Anticodon
U G G U U U A U G
Codon
Ribosome

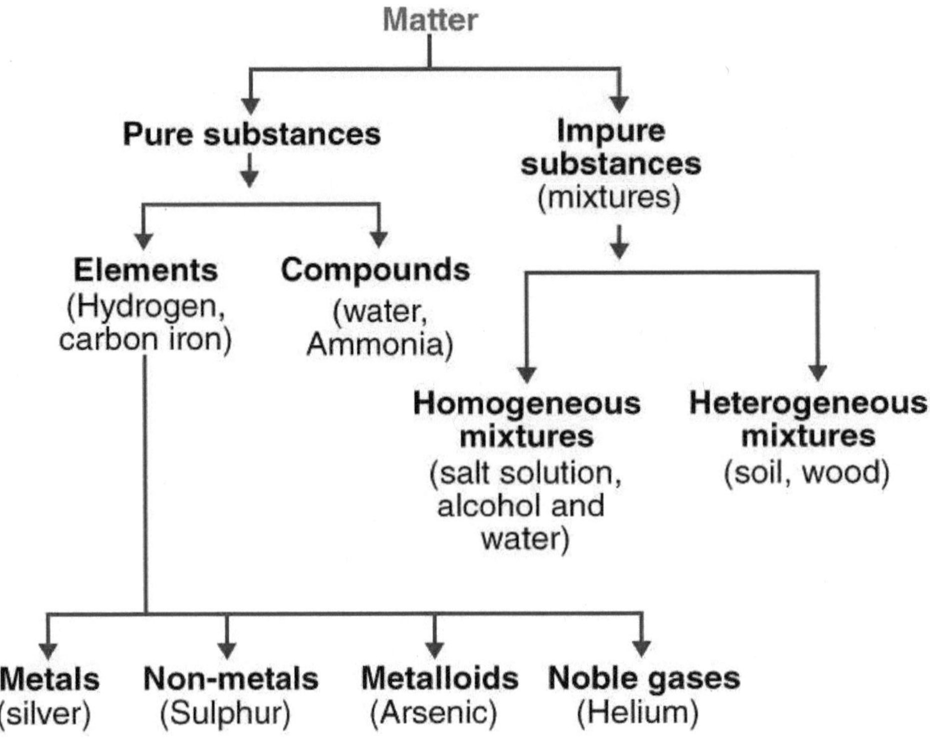

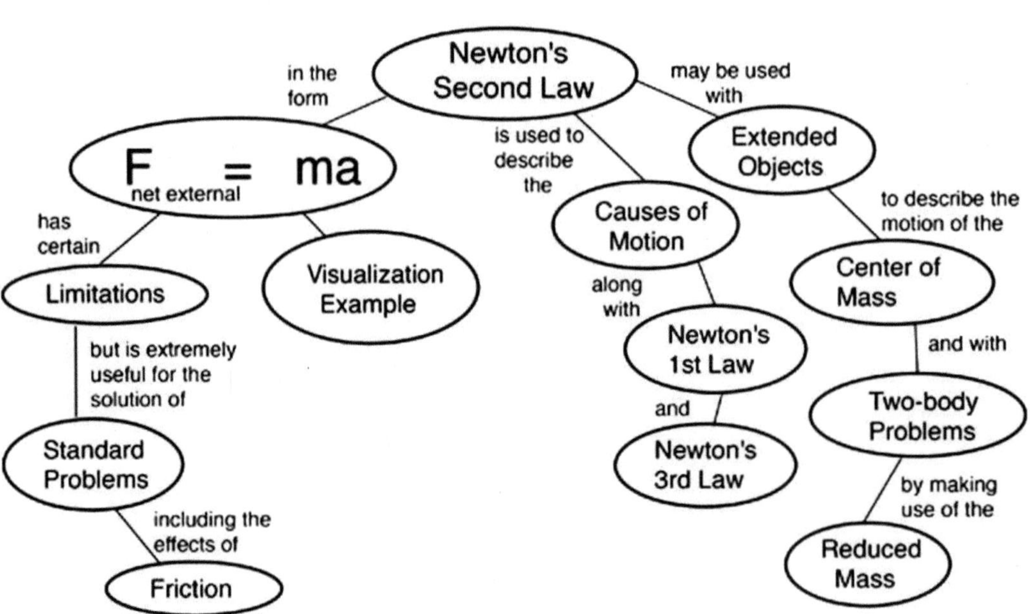

This Workbook is dedicated to Students having affinity towards moving through advanced studies.

Contents

Basics

Learning is a continuous process. Even this process may continue for life time. These days learning has become an effort to fit oneself for desired competitive examinations. Aspirants are more in number than compared to number of seats available for them. We learn many things which have no linkage with the content areas specified for the specific level of the prescribed curriculum. We also learn many things which have multifarious relations with the content areas duly specified for the forthcoming examinations. It would be better if we fix our sets of curriculum definitely for definite sets of examinations.

We learn many things and also come across many experiences in our daily life. Some of such experiences strike our mind to a greater extent and some of the gained experiences remain as an off-sided thing because of the ignorance of our mind.

Learning, as one can go through in life, is not any forceful effort of the mind. It should have a support of mind, body and intellect. Then only it can bring variations in our thought process. There are so many faculties through which the learning of a student might move on. It may be a hybrid faculty combining some of the inter-related streams of study; such as Astronomy and Physics will jointly make the faculty of Astro-Physics; Geology and Information Technology will make the faculty of Geo-Informatics and many more.

Parents often claim that their ward is proficient in some of the selected faculties and work with limitations in some other. Actually the trend of the study of a learner is a non-identifiable trend because of the chance of its alterations in relation to time. One cannot guess about the affinity of the brain before the age of 13 of a student. Learning affinity and allied success largely depends upon the combination of parenting and related service linings. Only parenting and any service lining without parenting may not bring any desired result in time. Combination of both the factor can link up the milestones leading ultimately towards success.

India Government has decided to centralise the process of admissions to various Graduate level Medical Colleges. This admission process will be accomplished by the entrance examinations taken up by National Testing Agency (or NTA). Aspirants having a willingness to attain the Entrance Examination conducted by NTA or other such testing agency should have access to the knowledge system duly prescribed for the prevalent knowledge drilling and information delivery pattern. Preparation for such kind of testing is also a job which requires prolonged involvement of the fellow learner. The learner with such willingness should have a strong base of knowledge which will ensure the smooth and swift propagation of mind and intellect through the definite path of success.

We restrict our discussion to the limit of the content areas for which the present workbook is having some inputs. Students of class six should have a proper understanding of basic shapes, number system, daily life problems and ecological concerns. Most of the problems are related to daily experiences and normal operational concerns.

It is expected that students should go on facing day to day problems from science, mathematics and humanities. They should also address problems related to high order thinking skills. They also participate in online digital classes and social media platforms for exploring relevant information on certain topic. Hunting merely for information may not fulfil the purpose in particular. Information duly collected should have adequate alignment with facts and figures for ensuring the process of remembering and recollecting such kinds of learning during need.

We are also incorporating few words from the faculty of mathematics. Most of the part of publication is based on the pattern of questions people select for Olympiads, Talent Search Examinations and other competitive examinations of similar nature. This publication also introduces a learner with some apprehensions of Critical thinking.

Mathematics deals with some fundamental aspects related to time and space. We all learn different rules and related operations starting from our elementary stage of schooling. Different students take the subject differently as per their interest and willingness. Some students calculate values with adequate speed and some other students do the same with lot of difficulties. We also point out the development of fear related to Mathematics in the mind of some of the fellow students.

We cannot analyse the possible reasons of the development of such fear in the mind of students. This development cannot be generalised. It is not developed in the minds of all the fellow students. Things often become difficult when our fellow ward fail to correlate the linkages of real life problems with that of mathematical ones. It is the main reason of the lack of proper orientation in the process of the development of mathematical skills. A skilful student can correlate both the aspects of mathematics and real life problems with much efficiency. A skilful student of mathematics should be a good observer, a perfect planner, optimum analyser and abled calculator. Some students can take much time in solving any individual mathematical problem that compared to the time taken by the other fellow from the same peer group. This book is designed to expose a student to different types of mathematical problems from the allied fields of the curriculum specified for the middle school. It is expected that this workbook can equip a student in different ways and enable them to acquire mathematical skills with a long lasting impression in mind.

Author

February 2022

Basics of Study

A book can provide timely relevant support to students. It can even equip a student differently for making oneself fit for accepting challenges of some broad spectrum. This collection is exclusively meant for students aspiring for examinations of Standard 9th of National as well as State Boards. It can also provide adequate references to students aspiring for various competitive examinations. The collection of this series is coming in accord to the subject areas.

Basic Science is the field of study which is common for most of the competitive examinations. The general understanding on the theories and their applications is the general expectation of examiners from a student of school education. One should understand the application of scientific temperaments for solving day to day problems. Ecology and environment is the common core of content areas for all possible levels of discussions related to science and scientific observations.

We expect a kind of understanding from students of Grade 9 to 12 of the National Curriculum. The fellow student should understand the number system and related operations. There are some relationships exist in between number systems of various types. We often come across four different number systems in computer Science. For the class works and mathematical operations as mentioned in their respective workbooks meant for school students we restrict our discussion to decimal system only.

I hope the kind of effort and combination of problems might enhance the knowledge base of our fellow students.

Questions are there without respective answers. It can be obtained from the source. There exists a plan of fulfilling dual purpose of the effort. These sets can be utilized to engage a student for working out the possible outputs without being inflicted primarily with answers.

If answers are provided alongside the questions then the material will fulfill half of the purpose. It cannot contingent for overcoming the problems and also cannot facilitate in skill enhancement efforts.

Set of questions can be used for the purpose of assessing skill acquisition process and also can be assigned to the ward by parents and guides.

It is not mandatory to go through all sets of problems, but not to skip any of the problems is recommended for assuring the perfect skill acquisition.

Science is the ever-growing field of knowledge. Most of the human activities depend directly or indirectly on the proposals of science. It also increases the basic understanding of a person regarding the day to day events and related concerns. We can even describe most of the daily events on the basis of our scientific observations.

Whenever we come across any new events then our mind start recollecting different ideas related to our knowledge base. We also start correlating the reported events for assuring applicability of such knowledge base. Some of the events from our daily life often strike our mind differently. Why tooth pastes are basic in nature? Why room cleaners are acidic? Why metallic copper cannot react with salt solution of iron, zinc or sodium? Other such questions of particular types can be advanced to ascertain the need of intensive studies of the related areas of science for making oneself adequately equipped for accepting some higher challenges.

This activity book can provide an ample scope of learning to the fellow learners which are needed for improving their skills and competences related to science and technology. Extended worksheets and self-evaluation modules can be used for assessing the progress of the individual learner. Chapters are grouped on the basis of their inter-relations. These are also grouped on the basis of their subject areas.

Learning by doing will be the best approach of acquiring skills in the field of Science and Technology. One can move through experience sharing to enhance one's skills and competence related to science and technology. Learning with understanding is a participatory process of interaction through which information flows from experts to the learners. It is also a process of sharing experiences and concerns. It will equip both the learners and facilitators in enhancing their skills of participatory learning.

Selected Content areas:

1: Tissues

2: Diversity in Living Organisms

3: Motion and related rules.

4: Force and Laws of Motion

5: Gravitation

Some of the worksheets duly incorporated in forthcoming chapters are from one two or all of the aforesaid content areas. Activity sheets are also of the same combination. Some enrichment activities are incorporated in this workbook to equip the fellow learner with some higher level practice works.

A Study guide

Charts and References:

Chart to show different types of Animal Tissue.

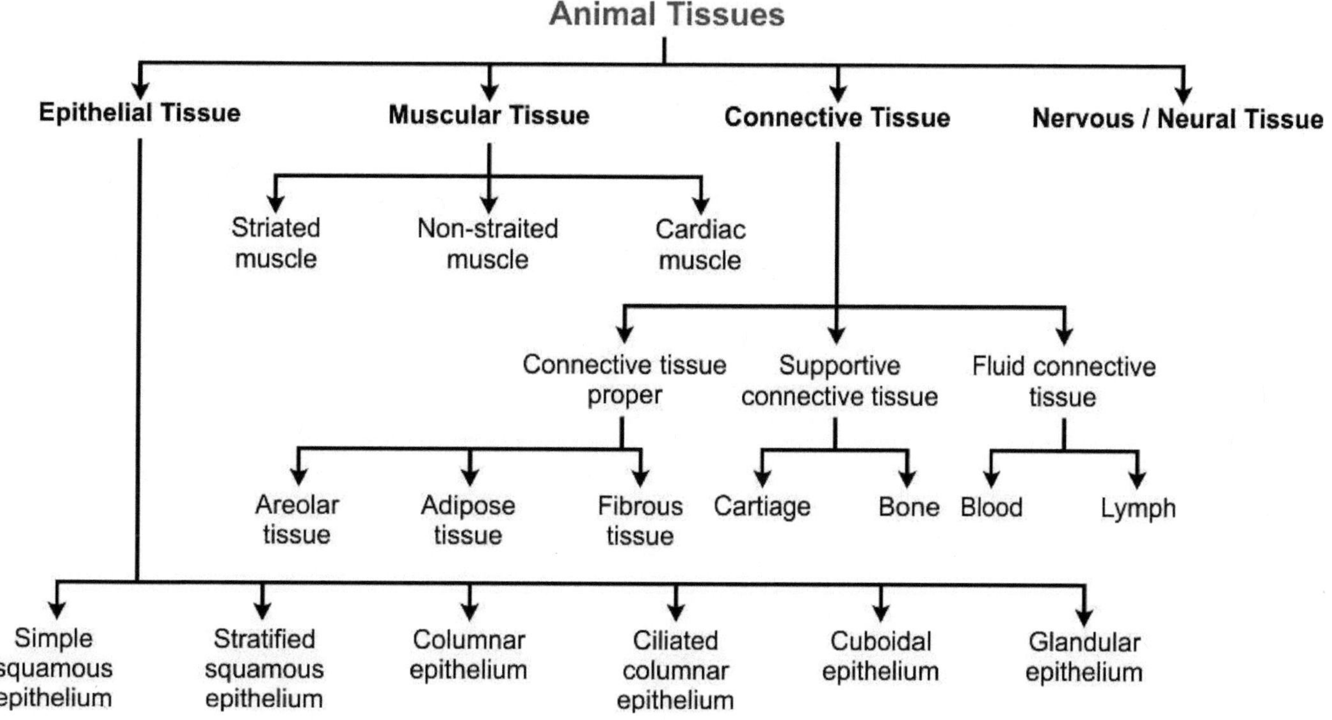

Different types of Plant Tissue are represented below …

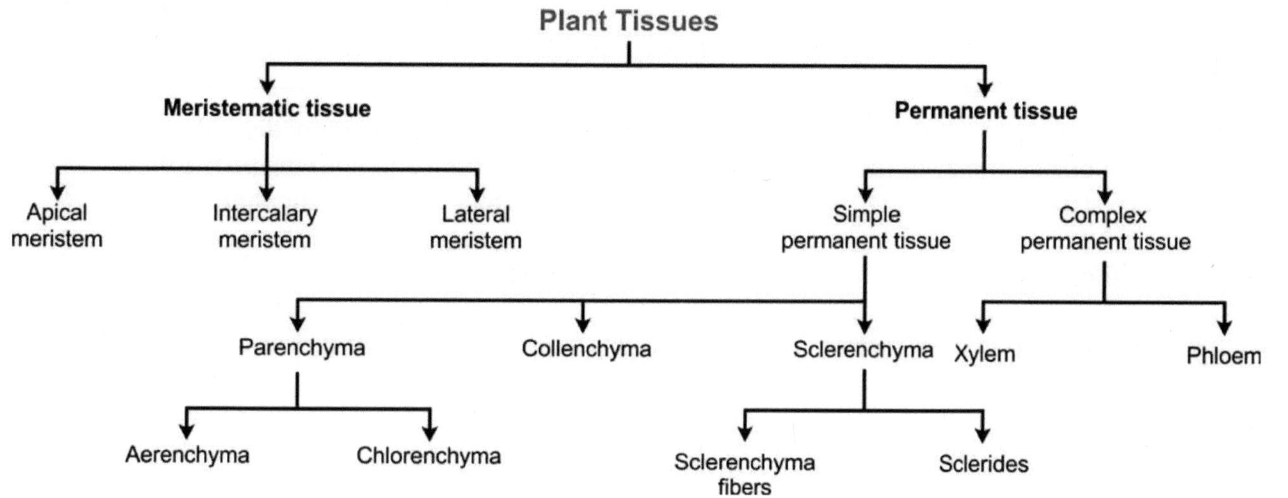

Laws of Universal Gravity can be elaborated through the following flow chart.

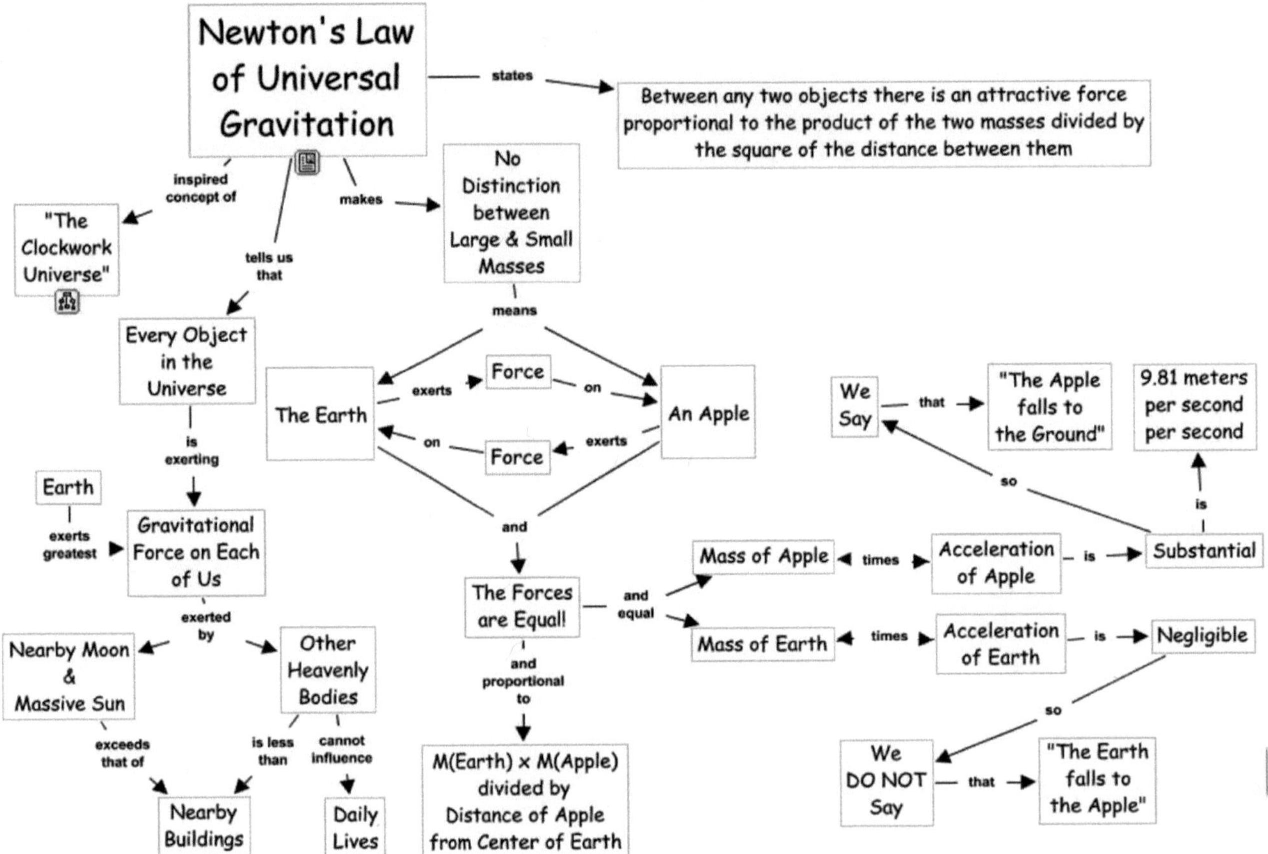

Difference between Distance and Displacement

Distance	Displacement
(i) Distance is the length of the actual path travelled by an object. It may or may not be measured in a straight line. (ii) It is a scalar quantity. (iii) It is either equal to or greater than displacement. (iv) Distance travelled is always positive.	(i) Displacement is the minimum distance between the starting and finishing points that the object has marked during the motion. (ii) It is a vector quantity. (iii) It is either equal to or less than distance. (iv) Displacement may be positive or negative or zero.

Tips for Students

Preparation for any examination or for any targeted entrance requires planning. Such kind of specific planning requires proper understanding of the content areas and related framework of curriculum. All kinds of examinations have a definite pattern of questions and proper settings of content areas specified for designing test papers. Students are expected to attend that definite pattern of questions for gaining a desirable score.

Things to be avoided while preparing for an examination:

a. Fear is our enemy. It hampers the intellect. That is why one should not allow oneself to be trapped in fear.

b. Overlooking any content areas may not give adequate mastery of any subject. One should go on exploring minute details of the content areas meant for the test.

c. Indulgence in so many subjects cannot give mastery of any subject. One should avoid unwanted indulgence in subject areas which are not relevant.

d. Overconfidence is another problem which hampers the growth of skills. Students gaining higher score in a small group may not be capable of gaining such mastery in any higher group. That is why one should not get inflicted with overconfidence.

e. Small things which are often neglected by a student may put the fellow in trouble. Small and easy questions often become challenging.

Assets of a Student:

a. Books, exam papers, previous year papers, quality guidance of teachers and good associations are very importance assets.

b. One should keep all sorts of information properly arranged and indexed.

c. All schedules of a student meant for the preparation for the test should be maintained properly.

d. One should maintain confidence upon oneself. Such confidence will enhance skill of the individual and equip the mind and intellect with readiness.

e. Regularity of study is another important factor that makes the student contented.

f. Quick recap of syllabus is most important for preparing oneself for higher challenges.

g. Regular classroom study along with some higher challenges will make the ward fit for higher level examinations.

There are several other factors which can be considered before moving on for preparing oneself for some higher challenges. None of the parts of content areas duly prescribed for a test should be avoided. Preparation for any exam does not mean limiting oneself up to the final content area duly prescribed for the test. Grasping through some higher level content areas may also equip oneself for the test. Studies related to cell and molecular biology, for an example, should not be limited only up to the level of the specified classroom. It should have some higher level inputs in it.

One should go on analyzing the patterns of test paper, model papers and other references for giving extra touch to the preparatory efforts. One should go on examining updates periodically for making oneself acquainted with changes of different types.

Working in a group will give additional advantage as such kinds of association will equip the student with doubt clearing initiatives. Group discussion will also increase the levels of confidence of the fellow student.

Merely learning without getting involved in regular practice cannot bring fruitful results of desired type. We must go on practicing test papers regularly for removing our doubts.

We cannot claim that this activity book will equip a student with all such skills which are needed for facing challenges like Olympiads, medical entrance examinations or exam for gaining scholarships. But it is confirmed that this workbook will open up a horizon of interactive study through which the fellow student will gain adequate confidence.

1. Work Energy and Power

If any force brings any change in the momentum of an object then only we can say that the work is done. If a car is moving with a uniform velocity along a straight path then from the law of the work done we can say that the force applied upon the moving car is not doing any work. The force applied during its stationary movement is actually utilised by the car for balancing the frictional force implied upon it by the road.
Mathematical expression of Work Done W= F X D; [W = work Done; F = Force and D = Displacement]
The change in kinetic energy of an object is equal to the work done on it by the net force.

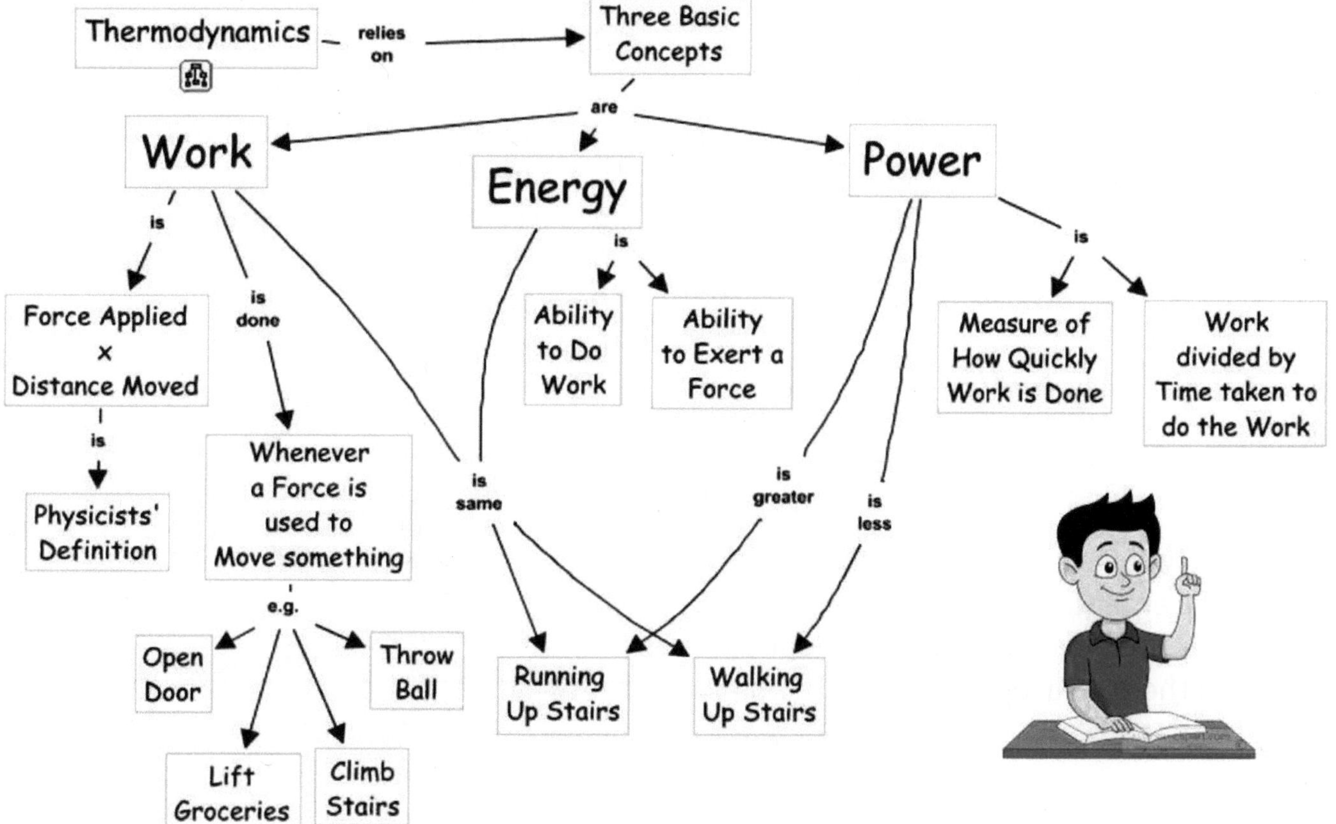

Energy can do work through objects. It can also gain capability to exert force. No work is done by the force if it acts perpendicular to the displacement of the body. The total mechanical energy of a system is conserved if the forces doing work on it are conservative. Energy can exist in various forms such as mechanical energy, heat energy, light energy, sound energy, etc. The motion of a simple pendulum is an example of the conversion of P.E. into K.E. and vice-versa.
For our better understanding we prefer moving through some common examples from our study table. All such examples will be periodically asked to examine understanding of the topic.

Work done in Physics is absolutely a concern of displacement caused by the force. If we lift a load and again keep it back to the same position from which it was lifted up then work done will be absolutely zero.

Some of the common formulas related to work energy and power we apply are as follows ...

$$W = \mathbf{F} \bullet \mathbf{s} = (F \cos\theta)s$$

$$KE = \frac{1}{2}mv^2$$

$$W = KE_f - KE_0 = \frac{1}{2}mv_f^{\ 2} - \frac{1}{2}mv_0^{\ 2}$$

$$PE = mgh$$

$$W_g = \Delta PE_g = mg(h_0 - h_f)$$

$$PE_0 + KE_0 = PE_f + KE_f$$

$$P = \frac{W}{t}$$

$$P = \mathbf{F} \bullet \mathbf{v} = (F \cos\theta)v$$

where
W = work
F = force
s = displacement
F • s = scalar product of force and displacement
KE = kinetic energy
v = velocity or speed
m = mass
PE = potential energy (denoted as *U* on the AP Physics exam)
g = acceleration due to gravity
h = height above some reference point
P = power
t = time

work is defined as the scalar product of force and displacement.
where θ is the angle between the applied force and the displacement

W = **F·s** = $Fs\cos\theta$

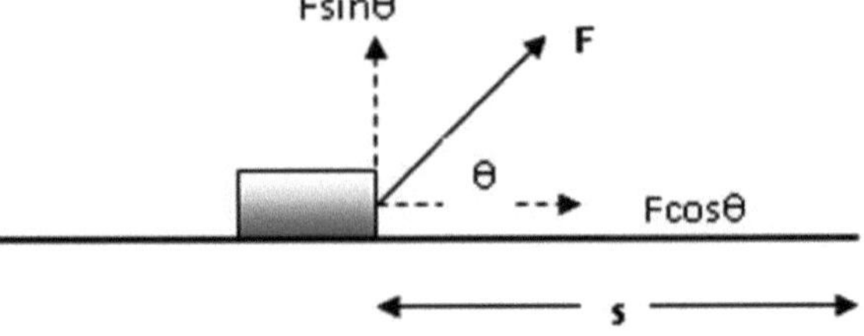

Our perception of Work , Energy and Power on the basis of Physics will be on the basis of above mentioned theoretical perspectives.

Force may be conservative or non-conservative type. It may be contact or non-contact type. Force can bring change in momentum. Gravitational, Electrostatic and Magnetic Forces will be of Non-contact type. It can work on any object from a distant location. Force makes body accelerate. It can even intend to stop a moving object. When work done in a system then total energy used and total energy liberated will be equal to each other. Energy balance is maintained in a system. It cannot be created or destroyed during any type of physical or chemical change. Energy matter inters exchange and inter-conversion is the subject of Nuclear Reaction. It cannot be the subject of any other physical or chemical change.

Kinetic energy is the energy an object has because it is moving. In order for a mass to gain kinetic energy, work must be done on the mass to push it up to a certain speed, or to slow it down. The work-energy theorem states that the change in kinetic energy of an object is exactly equal to the work done on it, assuming there is no change in the object's potential energy.

The work done on a system can also be converted into heat energy, and usually some of the work is.

$$W = \Delta KE = \frac{1}{2}mv_f^{\ 2} - \frac{1}{2}mv_o^{\ 2}$$

Potential energy is the energy a system has because of its position or configuration. When you stretch a rubber band, you store energy in the rubber band as elastic potential energy. When you lift a mass upward against gravity, you do work on the mass and therefore change its energy.

$W = Fs = (mg)h$ which must also equal its potential energy $PE = mgh$

A Simple Example:
A man carrying a box on his head:In this case, the force acting on the man is the weight of the box, which is acting downwards.
The displacement of the man is along the horizontal direction.
Therefore, the force and the displacement are perpendicular to each other.
So there is no work involved in this process.

Conservative or Non-Conservative!

A force is said to be conservative if the work done by the force does not depend on the path taken between any two points. The gravitational force and the spring force are two examples of conservative forces. These two forces conserve energy during a round trip. A force is said to be nonconservative if the work done by the force depends on the path taken. Friction is the most common example of a nonconservative force
since a taking longer path will dissipate more heat energy.
Work done by a nonconservative force generally cannot be recovered as usable energy.

Recap 1

A 10 kg block placed on a rough horizontal floor is being pulled by a constant force 50 N. Coefficient of kinetic friction between the block and the floor is 0.4. Find work done by each individual force acting on the block over displacement of 5 m.

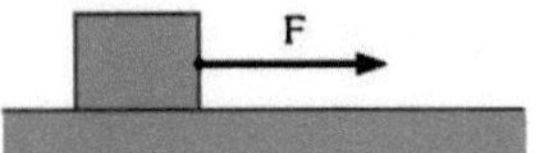

Solution.

Forces acting on the block are its weight (mg = 100 N), normal reaction (N = 100 N) from the ground, force of kinetic friction (f = 40 N) and the applied force (F = 50 N) and displacement of the block are shown in the given figure.

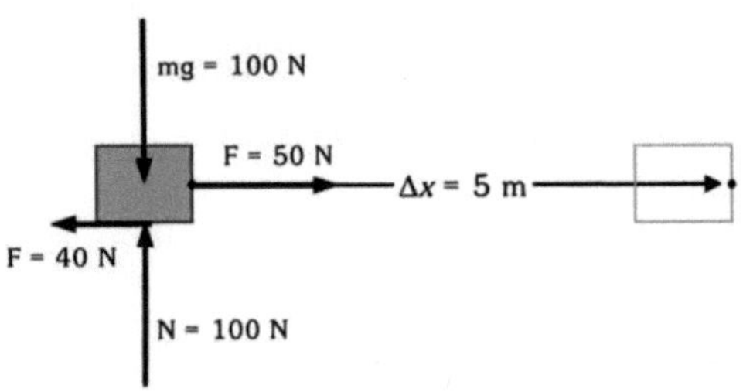

All these force are constant force, therefore we use equation $W_{i\to f} = \vec{F}\cdot\Delta\vec{r}$.

Work done W_g by the gravity i.e. weight of the block $W_g = 0$ J $(\because m\vec{g} \perp \Delta\vec{x})$

Work done W_N by the normal reaction $W_N = 0$ J $(\because \vec{N} \perp \Delta\vec{x})$

Work done W_F by the applied force $W_F = 250$ J $(\because \vec{F} \parallel \Delta\vec{x})$

Work done W_f by the force of kinetic friction $W_f = -200$ J $(\because \vec{f} \uparrow\downarrow \Delta\vec{x})$

Recap 2

A 10 kg block placed on a rough horizontal floor is being pulled by a constant force 100 N acting at angle 37 . Coefficient of kinetic friction between the block and the floor is 0.4. Find work done by each individual force acting on the block over displacement of 5 m.

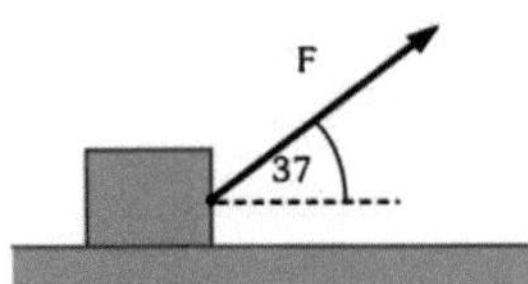

Solution.

Forces acting on the block are its weight (mg = 100 N), normal reaction (N = 40 N) from the ground, force of kinetic friction (f = 16 N) and the applied force (F = 100 N) and displacement of the block are shown in the given figure.

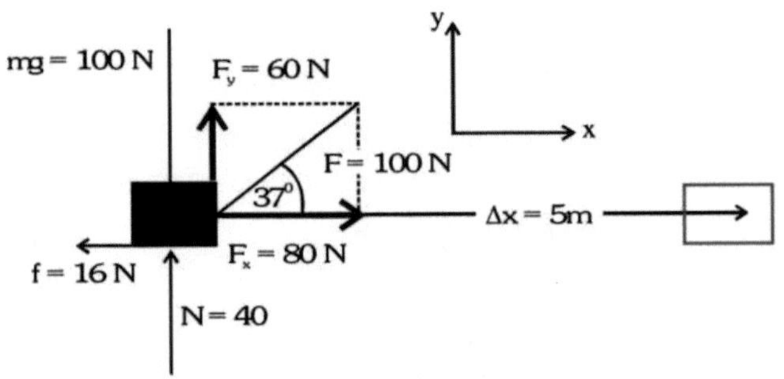

All these force are constant force, therefore we use equation $W_{i\to f} = \vec{F}\cdot\Delta\vec{r}$.

Work done W_g by the gravity i.e. weight of the block $W_g = 0$ J $(\because m\vec{g} \perp \Delta\vec{x})$

Work done W_N by the normal reaction $W_N = 0$ J $(\because \vec{N} \perp \Delta\vec{x})$

Work done W_F by the applied force $W_F = \vec{F}\cdot\Delta\vec{x} = F_x\Delta x = 400$ J

Work done W_f by the force of kinetic friction $W_f = -80$ J $(\because \vec{f} \uparrow\downarrow \Delta\vec{x})$

Recap 3

A block of mass 2 kg is dragged by a force of 20 N on a smooth horizontal surface. It is observed from three reference frames ground, observer A and observer B. Observer A is moving with constant velocity of 10 m/s and B is moving with constant acceleration of 10 m/s^2. The observer B and block starts simultaneously at t =0.

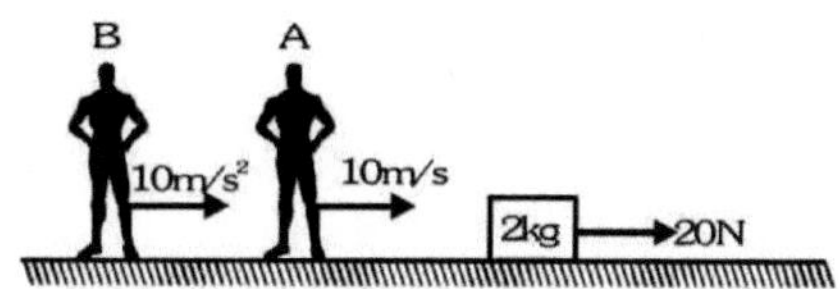

Column I	Column II
(A) Work energy theorem is applicable in	(P) 100 J
(B) Work done on block in 1s as observed by ground is	(Q) – 100 J
(C) Work done on block is 1 s as observed by observer A is	(R) zero
(D) Work done on block in 1 s as observed by observer B is	(S) only ground & A
	(T) all frames ground, A & B

Solution **Ans. (A) →(T); (B) →(P); (C) →(Q); (D) →(R)**

For (A) : Work energy theorem is applicable in all reference frames.

For (B) : w.r.t. ground : At t =0, u =0 and t = 1 s, $v = at = \left(\frac{20}{2}\right)(1) = 10$ m/s

Work done = change in kinetic energy = $\frac{1}{2}(2)(10)^2 - \frac{1}{2}(2)(0)^2 = 100$ J

For (C) : w.r.t. observer A : Initial velocity = 0 – 10 = – 10 m/s, Final velocity = 10 – 10 = 0

Work done = $\frac{1}{2}(2)(0)^2 - \frac{1}{2}(2)(-10)^2 = -100$ J

For (D) : w.r.t. observer B : Initial velocity = 0 – 0 = 0

Final velocity = 10 – 10 = 0; Work done = 0

Worksheet 1

Q1. An electron and a proton are moving under the influence of mutual forces. In calculating the change in the kinetic energy of the system during motion, one ignores the magnetic force of one on another. This is, because
(a) the two magnetic forces are equal and opposite, so they produce no net ' effect
(b) the magnetic forces do not work on each particle
(c) the magnetic forces do equal and opposite (but non-zero) work on each particle
(d) the magnetic forces are necessarily negligible

Q2. A proton is kept at rest. A positively charged particle is released from rest at a distance d in its field. Consider two experiments; one in which the charged particle is also a proton and in another, a positron. In the same time t, the work done on the two moving charged particles is
(a) same as the same force law is involved in the two experiments
(b) less for the case of a positron, as the positron moves away more rapidly and the force on it weakens
(c) more for the case of a positron, as the positron moves away a larger distance
(d) same as the work done by charged particle on the stationary proton

Q3. A man squatting on the ground gets straight up and stand. The force of reaction of ground on the man during the process is
(a) constant and equal to mg in magnitude
(b) constant and greater than mg in magnitude
(c) ' variable but always greater than mg
(d) at first greater than mg and later becomes equal to mg

Q4. A bicyclist comes to a skidding stop in 10 m. During this process, the force on the bicycle due to the road is 200 N and is directly opposed to the motion. The work done by the cycle on the road is
(a) +2000 J (b) -200 J (c) zero (d) -20,000 J

Q5. A body is falling freely under 'the action of gravity alone in vacuum. Which of the following quantities remain constant during the fall?
(a) Kinetic energy (b) Potential energy
(c) Total mechanical energy (d) Total linear momentum

Q6. During inelastic collision between two bodies, which of the following quantities always remain conserved?
(a) Total kinetic energy (b) Total mechanical energy
(c) Total linear momentum (d) Speed of each body

7: A body possesses ____________ energy due to the chemical bonding of its atoms. A body possesses _______ energy due to the disorderly motion of its molecules.

8: _______________ by force acting on an object is equal to the magnitude of the force multiplied by the distance moved in the direction of the application of force.

9: A moving block having mass m, collides with another stationary block having mass 4m. The lighter block comes to rest after collision. When the initial velocity of the lighter block is v, then the value of coefficient of restitution (e) will be (a) 0.5 (b) 0.25 (c) 0.8 (d) 0.4

10: __________ of a body is defined as the capacity or ability of the body to do some work.

11: ___________ _____________ of a body is the sum of its kinetic energy and potential energy. Kinetic energy: The energy possessed by a body by the virtue of its motion.

12:: _____________ ______________ is the energy possessed by a body due to its position or configuration.

13: ___________________________________ states that Energy can neither be created nor be destroyed, it can only be transformed from one form to another.

14: ________________________________ : If there is no loss of energy, then mechanical energy of a system is always constant.

15: ___________ is defined as the rate of doing work or rate of transfer of energy.
16: _______________________ describes energies to all masses ($E = mc^2$) and masses to all energies ($Ec^2 = m$)
17: 1 kilowatt hour is the energy produced by 1 kilowatt power source in ____________.

Solution : 1: b; 2: c; 3: d; 4: c; 5: c; 6: c;
Ans 7: chemical; heat/ thermal;
Ans 8: Work done;
Ans : b;
Ans 10: Energy;
Ans 11: Mechanical energy;
Ans 12: Potential energy;
Ans 13: Law of conservation of energy;
Ans 14: Conservation of mechanical energy;
Ans 15: Power
Ans 16: The mass-energy equivalence formula; 17: 1 hour;

Worksheet 2

1: Observe the data table and answer the questions as follows.

Two types of units of Work done are as follows ---

Absolute units	Gravitational units
Joule [S.I.]: Work done is said to be one *Joule*, when 1 *Newton* force displaces the body through 1 *meter* in its own direction. From $W = F.s$ $1\ Joule = 1\ Newton \times 1\ metre$	*kg-m* [S.I.]: 1 *Kg-m* of work is done when a force of 1*kg-wt*. displaces the body through 1*m* in its own direction. From $W = F s$ $1\ kg\text{-}m = 1\ kg\text{-}wt \times 1\ metre$ $= 9.81\ N \times 1\ metre = 9.81\ Joule$
Erg [C.G.S.] : Work done is said to be one *erg* when 1 *dyne* force displaces the body through 1 *cm* in its own direction. From $W = F s$ $1\ Erg = 1 Dyne \times 1 cm$ *Relation between Joule and erg* $1\ Joule = 1\ N \times 1\ m = 10^5\ dyne \times 10^2\ cm$ $= 10^7\ dyne \times cm = 10^7\ Erg$	*gm-cm* [C.G.S.] : 1 *gm-cm* of work is done when a force of 1*gm-wt* displaces the body through 1*cm* in its own direction. From $W = F s$ $1\ gm\text{-}cm = 1gm\text{-}wt \times 1cm. = 981\ dyne \times 1cm$ $= 981\ erg$

A: 100 Joule = __________ Erg;

B: Work done by a force to raise a box of mass 20 kg up to 50 m height = __________Joule.

Q 2. Two inclined frictionless tracks, one gradual and the other steep meet at A from where two stones are allowed to slide down from rest, one on each track as shown in figure.
Which of the following statement is correct?

(a) Both the stones reach the bottom at the same time but not with the same speed.

(b) Both the stones reach the bottom with the same speed and stone I reaches the bottom earlier than stone II.

(c) Both the stones reach the bottom with the same speed and stone II reaches the bottom earlier than stone I.

(d) Both the stones reach the bottom at different times and with different speeds.

Q 3 . Two identical balls A and B having velocities of 0.5 m s^{-1} and –0.3 m s^{-1} respectively collide elastically in one dimension. The velocities of B and A after the collision respectively will be ________________.

Q 4: A man of mass m, standing at the bottom of the staircase, of height h climbs it and stands at its topmost position.

(a) Work done by all forces on man is equal to the rise in potential energy mgh.

(b) Work done by all forces on man is zero.

(c) Work done by the gravitational force on man is mgh.

(d) The reaction force from a step does not do work because the point of application of the force does not move while the force exists.

Q 5. Two identical ball bearings in contact with each other frictionless table are hit head-on by another ball bearing of the same mass moving initially with a speed v as shown in figure. If the collision is elastic, which of the following (figure) is a possible result after collision?

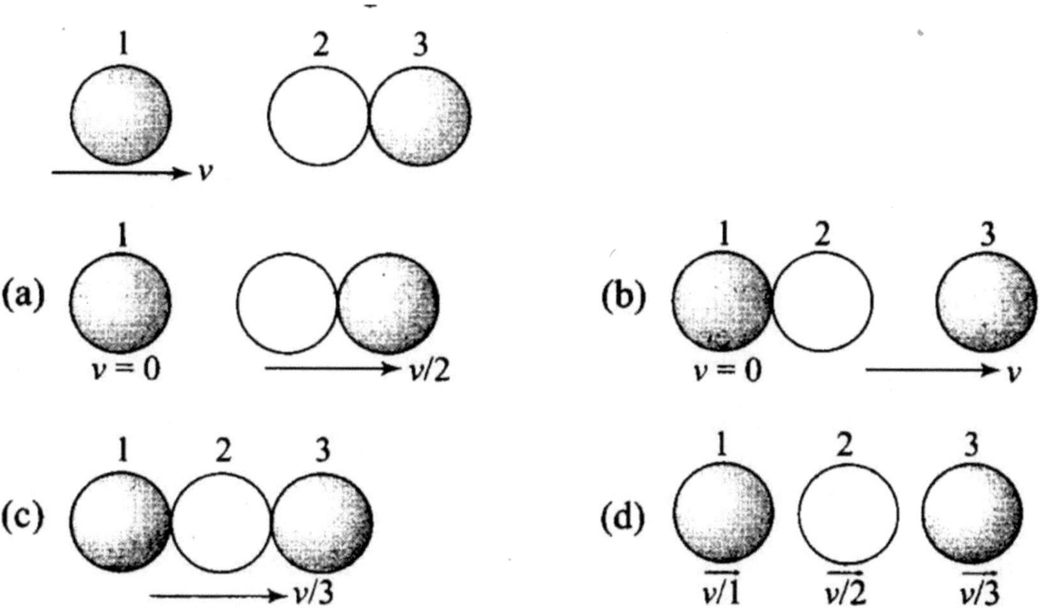

Q 6: Solve the following ---

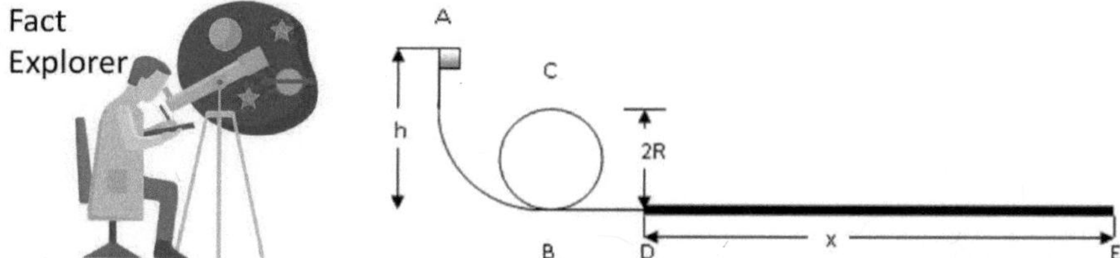

A small block of mass m begins from rest at the top of a curved track at a height h and travels around a circular loop of radius R. There is negligible friction between the block and the track between points A and D, but the coefficient of kinetic friction on the horizontal surface between points D and E is μ. The distance between points D and E is x.

(a) Determine the speed of the block at point B, at the bottom of the loop.
(b) Determine the kinetic energy of the block at point C, at the top of the loop.

After the block slides down the loop from point C to point D, it enters the rough portion of the track. The speed of the block at point E is half the speed of the block at point D.

(c) Determine the speed of the block at point D, just before it enters the rough portion of the track.
(d) Determine the amount of work done by friction between points D and E.
(e) Find an expression for the coefficient of kinetic friction μ.

Solutions:

1: A = 10^9 Erg; B: Work done = 981 Joule; [g = 9.81 ms^{-2}]

2: c;

3: 4: c; 0.5 m s^{-1} and -0.3 m s^{-1} ; 5: b; [When two bodies of equal masses collides elastically, their velocities are interchanged. Kinetic energy and linear momentum remains conserved Total kinetic energy of the system before collision.]

6:

Since there is no friction on the track between points A and B, there is no loss of energy. Thus,

$$U_A = K_B$$

$$mgh = \frac{1}{2}mv_B^{\ 2}$$

Solving for v_B, $v_B = \sqrt{2gh}$

(b) Conservation of energy:

$$U_A = U_C + K_C$$
$$mgh = mg(2R) + K_C$$
$$K_C = mgh - 2mgR$$

(c) There is no energy lost on the track between points A and D, so the speed of the block at point D is the same as the speed at point B:

$$v_D = \sqrt{2gh}$$

(d) The work done by friction is the product of the frictional force and the displacement through which it acts.

$$W_f = fx = \mu F_N x = \mu mgx$$

(e) The frictional force causes the block to have a negative acceleration according to Newton's second law:

Using a kinematic equation, $a = \frac{f}{m} = \frac{-\mu mg}{m} = -\mu g$

$$v_E^{\ 2} = v_D^{\ 2} + 2ax$$

$$0 = \left(\sqrt{2gh}\right)^2 + 2(-\mu g)x$$

$$\mu = \frac{2gh}{2gx} = \frac{h}{x}$$

Self Study:

I: A 75.0 kg man pushes on a 500,000 kg wall for 250 s but it does not move.

a. How much work does he do on the wall? ____________

b. How much energy is used?__________

c. How much power is exerted?_______________

II: If a small motor does 520 J of work for 10seconds, how much power is exerted?__________

III: A body of mass 10 g is attached to a hanging spring whose force constant is 10 N/m. The body is lifted until the spring is in its unstretched state. The body is then released. Calculate the speed of the body when it strikes a table 15 cm below the release point.

Worksheet 3

1: A particle of mass 10 g moves along a circle of radius 6.4 cm with a constant tangential acceleration. What is the magnitude of this acceleration if the kinetic energy of the particle becomes equal to 8×10^{-4} J by the end of the second revolution after the beginning of the motion?

(a) 0.18 m/s^2 (b) 0.2 m/s^2 (c) 0.1 m/s^2 (d) 0.15 m/s^2

2: A bullet of mass 10 g moving horizontally with a velocity of 400 m s–1 strikes a wood block of mass 2 kg which is suspended by light inextensible string of length 5 m. As a result, the centre of gravity of the block found to rise a vertical distance of 10 cm. The speed of the bullet after it emerges out horizontally from the block will be ___.

3: When a very light body in motion collides with a heavy stationary body in an elastic collision, the lighter one ____________ __________with the same speed without the heavy body being displaced.

4: When a body moving with some velocity undergoes elastic collision with another similar body at rest, then there is ______________their velocities after collision

5: 2001/107 J = ___________ erg.

6: The law of conservation of ___________ states that the total energy of an isolated system remains constant, it is said to be conserved over time. This law means that energy can neither be created nor destroyed; rather, it can only be ________________ from one form to another. [Complete the statement]

7: The ________ is calculated by multiplying the force (F) by the amount of movement (d) of an object.
W = F * d . For an example, a force of 10 Newton move an object 3 meters, does 30 N-m of work.
A _______________ is the same thing as a joule.

8: __________ and _________ are the S.I. and C.G.S. units of work and energy. Energy is the capacity of the body to do the work.

9: Observe the following Force – Displacement Graph ---

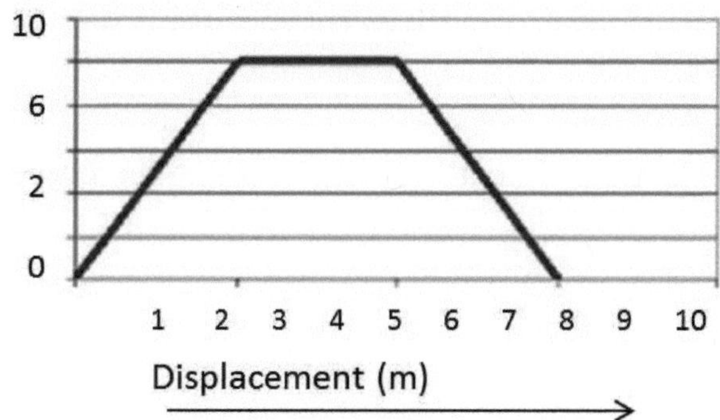

The ___________under the force-displacement graph is equal to the work done.

10: Work done by the gravitational or electric force does not depend on the nature of the ________followed.

11: Force of ___________worked on any object depends only on the initial and final positions of the path of the body during motion.

12: Solve the following:

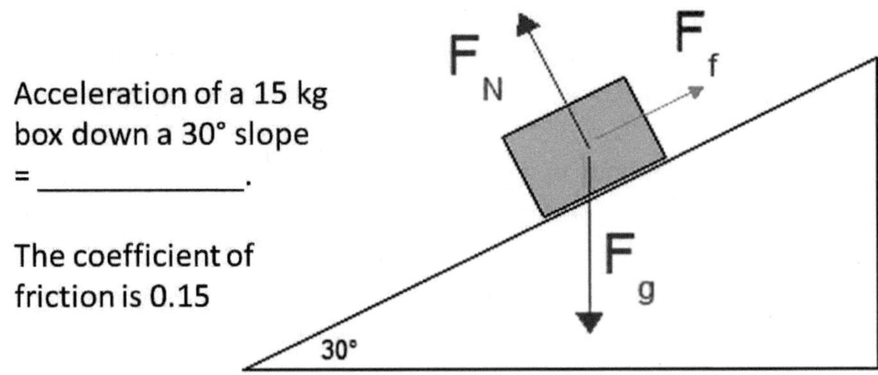

13: Last winter my car got caught in a snow bank. I promise a couple of my friends that if he comes over to do some work for me I'll buy each of them a Cake (with extra cream on it). We get behind the car and push it out of the snow. Explain if we did any work.

14: Select the correct option:

(a)
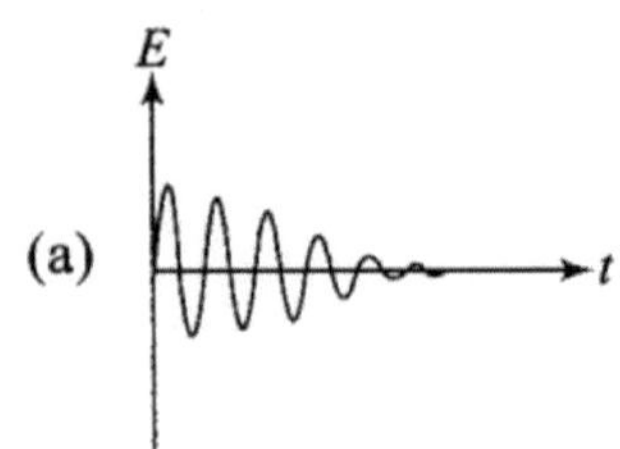

(b) E, t

(c) E, t

(d)
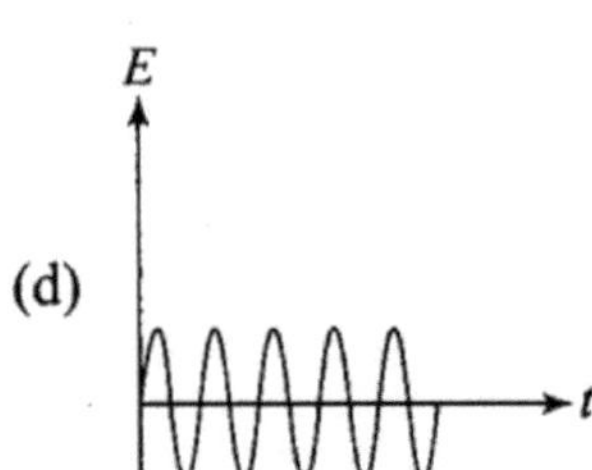

The diagram ______in the given figure represents variation of total mechanical energy of a pendulum oscillating in air as function of time.

Aid Box

When a pendulum oscillates in air, its total mechanical energy decreases continuously in overcoming resistance due to air. Therefore, total mechanical energy of the pendulum decreases exponentially with time.

Solutions/Answers:

1: c; 2: (c) 120 m s^{-1}; 3: rebounds back; an exchange of; 5: 2001; 6: energy; transformed; 7: work; Newton-meter ;

8: Joule (J) ; erg ; 9: area; 10: path; 11: Gravity; 12: acceleration = 3.6 ms^{-2} ;

13: In this situation, we all were pushing in the same direction (parallel to each other) and the car moved in that direction. So the answer would be "Yes!"

14: Option c is correct;

Different Instances of Work Done ....

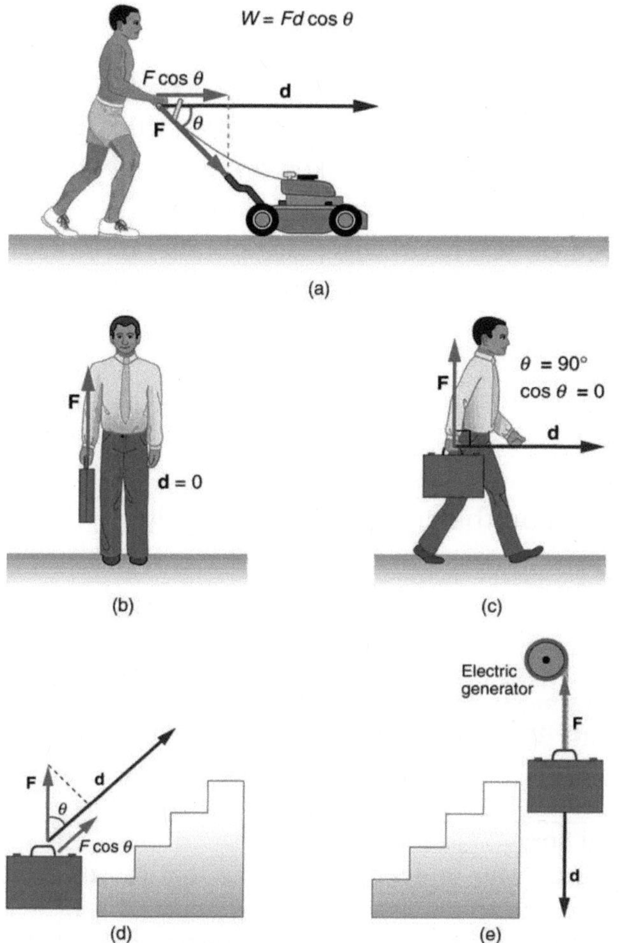

The work done on a system by a constant force is the product of the component of the force in the direction of motion times the distance through which the force acts. For one-way motion in one dimension, this is expressed in equation form as

W = F. dcosθ

where W is work, F is the magnitude of the force on the system, d is the magnitude of the displacement of the system, and θ is the angle between the force vector $\vec{F}$ and the displacement vector d.

Examples of work.

(a) The work done by the force F on this lawn mower is Fd cosθ. Note that F cosθ is the component of the force in the direction of motion.

(b) A person holding a briefcase does no work on it, because there is no displacement. No energy is transferred to or from the briefcase.

(c) The person moving the briefcase horizontally at a constant speed does no work on it, and transfers no energy to it.

(d) Work is done on the briefcase by carrying it up stairs at constant speed, because there is necessarily a component of force F in the direction of the motion. Energy is transferred to the briefcase and could in turn be used to do work.

(e) When the briefcase is lowered, energy is transferred out of the briefcase and into an electric generator. Here the work done on the briefcase by the generator is negative, removing energy from the briefcase, because F and d are in opposite directions.

How much work is done on the lawn mower by the person in Option (a) if he exerts a constant force of 40.0 N at an angle 30° below the horizontal and pushes the mower 25.0 m on level ground?

Hints:

The equation for the work is

W = Fdcosθ.W=Fdcosθ.

W = (40.0 N)(25.0 m)cos30^0

W = 1000X 0.866 N

W = 866 N

Aid Box:

I: How much work does a Market Complex checkout attendant do on a can of soup that is pushed by him 0.600 m horizontally with a force of 5.00 N?

II: A 75 kg person climbs stairs, gaining 4 meters in height. Find the work done by him to accomplish this task.

III:

Worksheet 4

1: Observe the diagram given below ...

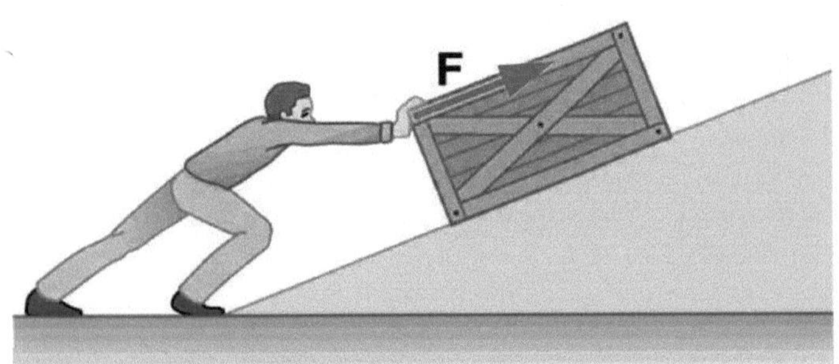

Calculate the work done by an 85.0-kg man who pushes a crate 4.00 m up along a ramp that makes an angle of 20.0° with the horizontal. He exerts a force of 500 N on the crate parallel to the ramp and moves at a constant speed.

a) What is the work done on the crate ?
b) What is the work done on himself to lift him up ?
c) What is the total work = a + b? This is the work he does on the crate *and* on his body to get up the ramp.

2: A boy is pulling his sister in a wagon.

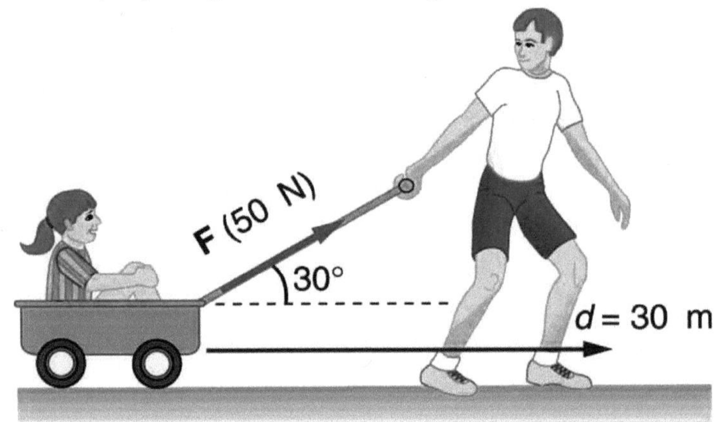

How much work is done by the boy pulling his sister 30.0 m in a wagon as shown in the given figure? Assume no friction acts on the wagon.

Aid Box:
The transfer of energy by a force that causes an object to be displaced; the product of the component of the force in the direction of the displacement and the magnitude of the displacement.

3:

Answer:

1: a) work = force x distance = 2000 J as angle between force and 4 m is 0 degrees b) m g h where h = 4m sin 20.0 = 1140 c) 3140 J in total;

2: Fd Cos 30^0 = 50 X 30 X 0.866 N = _______ N;

3:

→ If the rails are on a plane surface and there is no friction, the power dissipated by the engine is zero.

Worksheet 5

Power

Work can be done slowly or quickly, but the time taken to perform the work doesn't affect the amount of work which is done, since there is no element of time in the definition for work. However, if you do the work quickly, you are operating at a higher power level than if you do the work slowly. *Power is defined as the rate at which work is done.* Oftentimes we think of electricity when we think of power, but it can be applied to mechanical work and energy as easily as it is applied to electrical energy. The equation for power is

$$P = \frac{Work}{time}$$

and has units of joules/second or *watts* (W). A machine is producing one watt of power if it is doing one joule of work every second. A 75-watt light bulb uses 75 joules of energy each second.

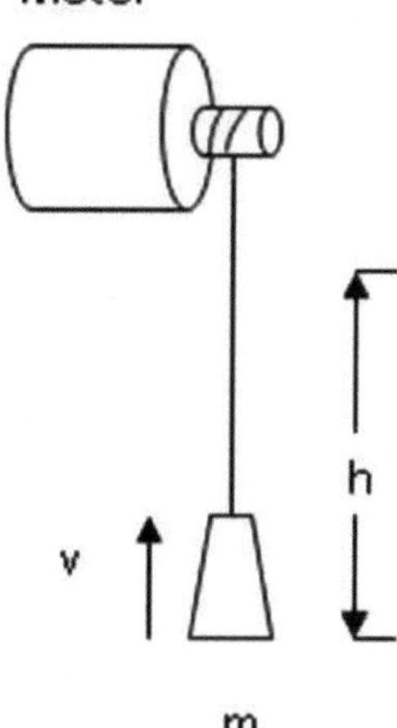

A motor raises a mass of 3 kg to a height *h* at a constant speed of 0.05 m/s. The battery (not shown) which provides energy to the motor originally stores 4 J of energy, all of which can be used to lift the mass.

(a) What is the power developed in the motor?
(b) To what maximum height can the motor lift the mass using its stored energy?

(a) $$P = \frac{W}{t} = \frac{Fh}{t} = \frac{(mg)h}{t} = (mg)v = (3kg)(10\,m/s^2)(0.05\,m/s) = 1.5\ Watt$$

(b) $$W = mgh$$
$$h = \frac{W}{mg} = \frac{4\,J}{(3kg)(10\,m/s^2)} = 0.13\,m$$

We calculate power of an engine on the basis of Work done by it in a unit time. When work is done by a body, its either P.E. or K.E. decreases. Mass and energy are interconvertible For any free falling object Energy budget is equivalent to product of mass and acceleration due to gravity. In any system having no influence of other types K.E. can change into P.E. and vice-versa keeping the net energy constant. One form of energy in a system of moving particle can be changed into other forms according to the law of conservation of energy. When a body falls down under the influence of the force of gravity, its P.E. is gradually converted into its K.E. letting it gain a maximum amount of K.E. just before touching ground.

1: Compare the kinetic energy of a 20,000-kg truck moving at 110 km/h with that of an 80.0-kg astronaut in orbit moving at 27,500 km/h.

2: (a) How fast must a 3000-kg elephant move to have the same kinetic energy as a 65.0-kg sprinter running at 10.0 m/s? (b) Discuss how the larger energies needed for the movement of larger animals would relate to metabolic rates.

3: Confirm the value given for the kinetic energy of an aircraft carrier in Chapter 7.6 Table 1. You will need to look up the definition of a nautical mile (1 knot = 1 nautical mile/h).

4: (a) Calculate the force needed to bring a 950-kg car to rest from a speed of 90.0 km/h in a distance of 120 m (a fairly typical distance for a non-panic stop). (b) Suppose instead the car hits a concrete abutment at full speed and is brought to a stop in 2.00 m. Calculate the force exerted on the car and compare it with the force found in part (a).

5: A car's bumper is designed to withstand a 4.0-km/h (1.1-m/s) collision with an immovable object without damage to the body of the car. The bumper cushions the shock by absorbing the force over a distance. Calculate the magnitude of the average force on a bumper that collapses 0.200 m while bringing a 900-kg car to rest from an initial speed of 1.1 m/s.

6: Boxing gloves are padded to lessen the force of a blow. (a) Calculate the force exerted by a boxing glove on an opponent's face, if the glove and face compress 7.50 cm during a blow in which the 7.00-kg arm and glove are brought to rest from an initial speed of 10.0 m/s. (b) Calculate the force exerted by an identical blow in the gory old days when no gloves were used and the knuckles and face would compress only 2.00 cm. (c) Discuss the magnitude of the force with glove on. Does it seem high enough to cause damage even though it is lower than the force with no glove?

7: Using energy considerations, calculate the average force a 60.0-kg sprinter exerts backward on the track to accelerate from 2.00 to 8.00 m/s in a distance of 25.0 m, if he encounters a headwind that exerts an average force of 30.0 N against him.

8: A 60.0-kg person jumps onto the floor from a height of 3 m. If he lands stiffly (with his knee joints compressing by 0.500 cm), calculate the force exerted on the knee joints.

Answers:

Problems & Exercises

1: 1/250

3: 1.1×10^{10} J1.1×10^{10} J

5: 2.8×10^{3} N2.8×10^{3} N

7: net force = 72 N so the person force = 72 + 30 = 10^2 N net force = change in kinetic energy = 1/2 m (v final)^2 – 1/2 m (v initial)^2

8: Force = 3.53×10^5 N;

Worksheet 6

1: Solve the following:

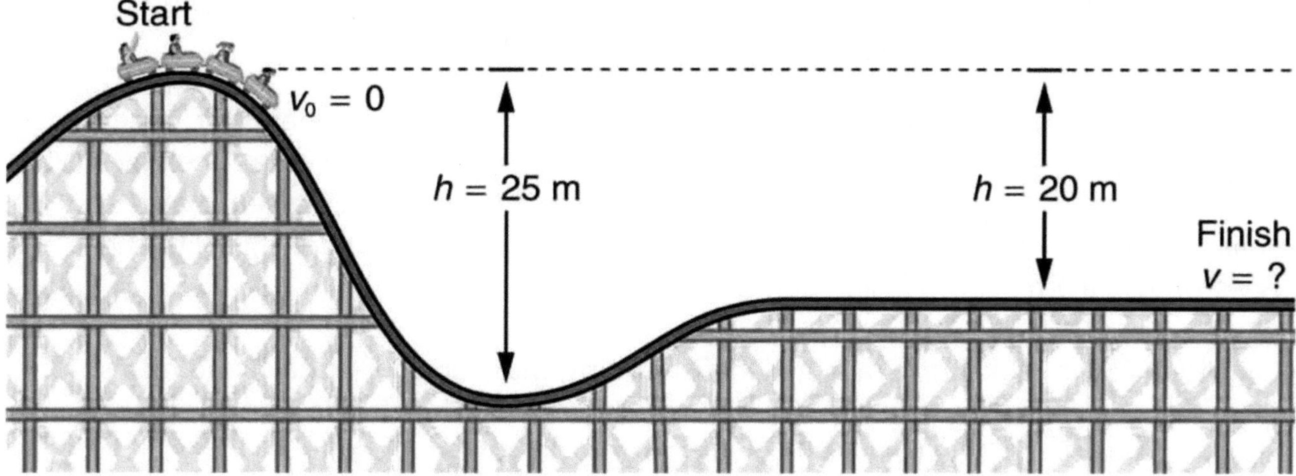

The speed of a roller coaster increases as gravity pulls it downhill and is greatest at its lowest point. Viewed in terms of energy, the roller-coaster-Earth system's gravitational potential energy is converted to kinetic energy. If work done by friction is negligible, all ΔPEg is converted to KE.

(a) What is the final speed of the roller coaster shown in Figure if it starts from rest at the top of the 20.0 m hill and work done by frictional forces is negligible? (b) What is its final speed (again assuming negligible friction) if its initial speed is 5.00 m/s?

Aid Box:
The roller coaster loses potential energy as it goes downhill. We neglect friction, so that the remaining force exerted by the track is the normal force, which is perpendicular to the direction of motion and does no work. The net work on the roller coaster is then done by gravity alone. The *loss* of gravitational potential energy from moving *downward* through a distance *h* equals the *gain* in kinetic energy. This can be written in equation form as -ΔPEg = ΔKE. Using the equations for PE_g and KE, we can solve for the final speed *v*, which is the desired quantity.

2: In a downhill ski race, surprisingly, little advantage is gained by getting a running start. (This is because the initial kinetic energy is small compared with the gain in gravitational potential energy on even small hills.) To demonstrate this, find the final speed and the time taken for a skier who skies 70.0 m along a 30° slope neglecting friction. Hint: you have to use trigonometry to find the height of the hill first. (a) Starting from rest. (b) Starting with an initial speed of 2.50 m/s. (c) Does the answer surprise you? Discuss why it is still advantageous to get a running start in very competitive events.

3: Solve the following ----
How much gravitational potential energy (relative to the ground on which it is built) is stored in the Great Pyramid of Cheops, given that its mass is about 7×10^9 kg and its center of mass is 36.5 m above the surrounding ground?

4: A hydroelectric power facility converts the gravitational potential energy of water behind a dam to electric energy. (a) What is the gravitational potential energy relative to the generators of a lake of volume 50.0 km^3 mass = 5.00×10^{13} kg, given that the lake has an average height of 40.0 m above the generators? (b) Compare this with the energy stored in a 9-megaton fusion bomb.

5: Suppose a 350-g kookaburra (a large kingfisher bird) picks up a 75-g snake and raises it 2.5 m from the ground to a branch. (a) How much work did the bird do on the snake? (b) How much work did it do to raise its own center of mass to the branch?

6: In a downhill ski race, surprisingly, little advantage is gained by getting a running start. (This is because the initial kinetic energy is small compared with the gain in gravitational potential energy on even small hills.) To demonstrate this, find the final speed and the time taken for a skier who skies 70.0 m along a 30° slope neglecting friction. Hint: you have to use trigonometry to find the height of the hill first. (a) Starting from rest. (b) Starting with an initial speed of 2.50 m/s. (c) Does the answer surprise you? Discuss why it is still advantageous to get a running start in very competitive events.

7: Statement related to Conservative Force are as follows:

A. A conservative force is one for which work depends only on the starting and ending points of a motion, not on the path taken.
B. We can define potential energy **(PE)** for any conservative force, just as we defined $\mathbf{PE_g}$ for the gravitational force.
C. The potential energy of a spring is PEs=(1/2)kx^2,, where ***k*** is the spring's force constant and ***x*** is the displacement from its undeformed position.
D. Mechanical energy is defined to be **KE+PE** for a conservative force.

Identify if any of the statement is not explaining characteristics of Conservative Force properly. Wrong statements are : ____________________.

8: ____________energy is the energy a system has due to position, shape, or configuration. It is stored energy that is completely recoverable.

Solution:

1:

Solution for (a)

Here the initial kinetic energy is zero, so that $\Delta \mathbf{KE} = \frac{1}{2} m v^2$. The equation for change in potential energy states that $\Delta \mathbf{PE_g} = mgh$. Since h is negative in this case, we will rewrite this as $\Delta \mathbf{PE_g} = -mg|h|$ to show the minus sign clearly. Thus,

$$-\Delta \mathbf{PE_g} = \Delta \mathbf{KE}$$

becomes

$$mg|h| = \frac{1}{2} m v^2.$$

Solving for v, we find that mass cancels and that

$$v = \sqrt{2g|h|}.$$

Substituting known values,

$$\begin{aligned} v &= \sqrt{2(9.80 \text{ m/s})(20.0 \text{ m})} \\ &= 19.8 \text{ m/s}. \end{aligned}$$

Solution for (b)

Again $-\Delta \mathbf{PE_g} = \Delta \mathbf{KE}$. In this case there is initial kinetic energy, so $\Delta \mathbf{KE} = \frac{1}{2} m v^2 - \frac{1}{2} m v_0^2$. Thus,

$$mg|h| = \frac{1}{2} m v^2 - \frac{1}{2} m v_0^2.$$

Rearranging gives

$$\frac{1}{2} m v^2 = mg|h| + \frac{1}{2} m v_0^2.$$

This means that the final kinetic energy is the sum of the initial kinetic energy and the gravitational potential energy. Mass again cancels, and

$$v = \sqrt{2g|h| + v_0^2}.$$

This equation is very similar to the kinematics equation$v = \sqrt{v_0^2 + 2ad}$,but it is more general—the kinematics equation is valid only for constant acceleration, whereas our equation above is valid for any path regardless of whether the object moves with a constant acceleration. Now, substituting known values gives

$$\begin{aligned} v &= \sqrt{2(9.80 \text{ m/s}^2)(20.0 \text{ m}) + (5.00 \text{ m/s})^2} \\ &= 20.4 \text{ m/s}. \end{aligned}$$

Solution 2: h = 35.0 m = (70 m) sin 30.0^{o} m g h = 1/ 2 m v^{2} so v = 26.2 m/s;

3: Calculate : m X g X h = __________ N-m;

4: (a) 1.96 x 10^{16} J (b) The ratio of gravitational potential energy in the lake to the energy stored in the bomb is 0.52. That is, the energy stored in the lake is approximately half that in a 9-megaton fusion bomb.

5: (a) 1.8 J (b) 8.6 J; 6: h = 35.0 m = (70 m) sin 30.0° m g h = 1/ 2 m v^{2} so v = 26.2 m/s;

7: all are correct; 8: Potential;

Conservation of Mechanical Energy:

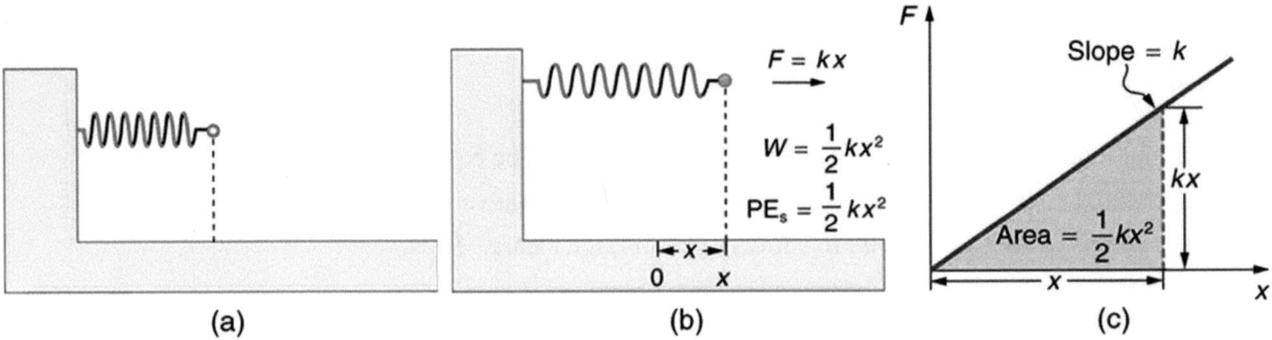

(a) An undeformed spring has no ***PE_s*** *stored in it. (b) The force needed to stretch (or compress) the spring a distance* ***x*** *has a magnitude* ***F=kx****, and the work done to stretch (or compress) it is* ***1/2 kx²****. Because the force is conservative, this work is stored as potential energy* ***(PE_s)*** *in the spring, and it can be fully recovered. (c) A graph of* ***F*** *vs.* ***x*** *has a slope of* ***k****, and the area under the graph is* ***1/2 kx²****. Thus the work done or potential energy stored is* ***1/2 kx²****.*

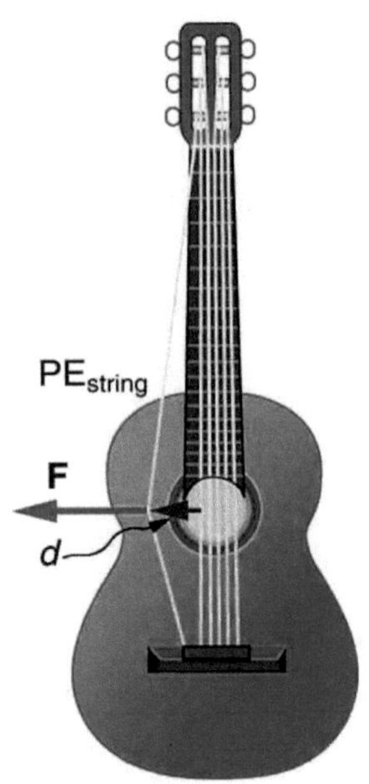

Work is done to deform the guitar string, giving it potential energy. When released, the potential energy is converted to kinetic energy and back to potential as the string oscillates back and forth. A very small fraction is dissipated as sound energy, slowly removing energy from the string.

The work-energy theorem states that the net work done by all forces acting on a system equals its change in kinetic energy. In equation form, this is
Wnet=1/2 $(mv^2- mv_0^2)$ = ΔKE.mv02=ΔKE.
If only conservative forces act, then $W_{net}=W_c$,,
where $\boldsymbol{W_c}$ is the total work done by all conservative forces. Thus,
Wc=ΔKE..
Now, if the conservative force, such as the gravitational force or a spring force, does work, the system loses potential energy. That is, $\boldsymbol{W_c}$ **= -ΔPE**. Therefore,
−ΔPE=ΔKE
or
ΔKE+ΔPE=0.ΔKE+ΔPE=0.
This equation means that the total kinetic and potential energy is constant for any process involving only conservative forces. That is,
KE+PE=constantorKEi+PEi=KEf+PEfKE+PE=constantorKEi+PEi=KEf+PEf}}
(conservative forces only),(conservative forces only),
where i and f denote initial and final values. This equation is a form of the work-energy theorem for conservative forces; it is known as the **conservation of mechanical energy** principle.

.

Worksheet 7

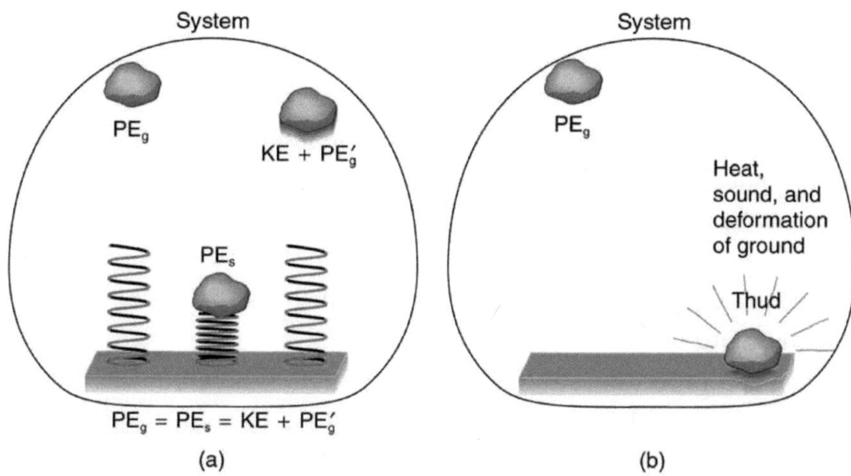

Comparison of the effects of conservative and nonconservative forces on the mechanical energy of a system. (a) A system with only conservative forces. When a rock is dropped onto a spring, its mechanical energy remains constant (neglecting air resistance) because the force in the spring is conservative. The spring can propel the rock back to its original height, where it once again has only potential energy due to gravity. (b) A system with nonconservative forces. When the same rock is dropped onto the ground, it is stopped by nonconservative forces that dissipate its mechanical energy as thermal energy, sound, and surface distortion. The rock has lost mechanical energy.

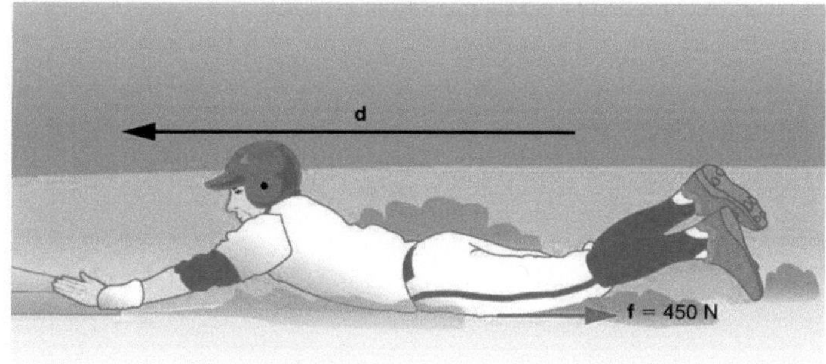

Consider the situation shown in the adjoining, where a baseball player slides to a stop on level ground. Using energy considerations, calculate the distance the 65.0-kg baseball player slides, given that his initial speed is 6.00 m/s and the force of friction against him is a constant 450 N.

Friction stops the player by converting his kinetic energy into other forms, including thermal energy. In terms of the work-energy theorem, the work done by friction, which is negative, is added to the initial kinetic energy to reduce it to zero. The work done by friction is negative, because ***f*** is in the opposite direction of the motion (that is, $\boldsymbol{\vartheta} = \mathbf{180°}$, and so $\mathbf{\cos \vartheta = -1}$). Thus $\boldsymbol{W_{nc} = -fd}$. The equation simplifies to $\frac{1}{2} mv_i^2 - fd = 0$

I: Provide Key Words for the following:

a) ______________________________ : : the general law which states that total energy remains constant in any process; energy may change in form or can be transferred from one system to another, but the total remains the same throughout the instances.

b) _______________ : the type of energy carried by conductor wires against the flow of charge through it.

c) _______________: the energy in a substance stored in the form of bonds between atoms and molecules that can be released during a chemical reaction. Because of that reason energy giving nurtrients carry such kind of energy from producer plants to consumer animals.

d) _______________: the energy carried by any kind of electromagnetic waves. Light rays also radiate such kind of energy as we receive it from the sun.

e) _______________: energy released by changes within atomic nuclei, such as the fusion of two light nuclei or the fission of a heavy nucleus into two or more smaller nuclei.

f) _______________: the energy within an object due to the random motion of its atoms and molecules that accounts for the increase in object's temperature.

g) _______________: a measure of the effectiveness of the input of energy duly required to do work; useful energy or work divided by the total input of energy.

II: Power Calculation:

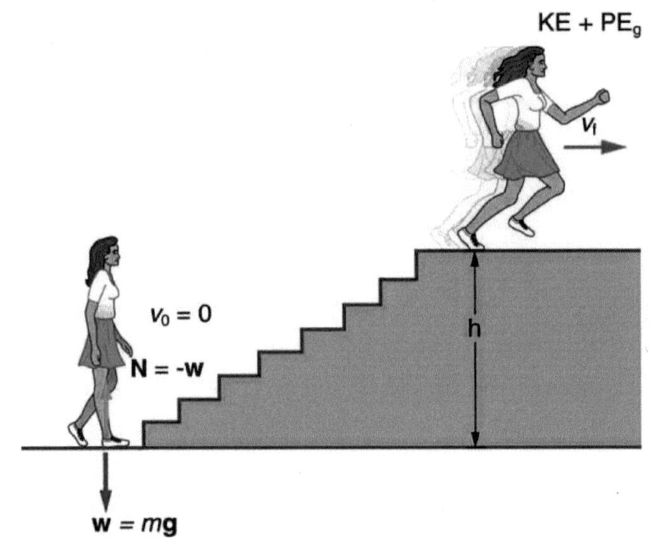

What is the power output for a 60.0-kg woman who runs up a 3.00 m high flight of stairs in 3.50 s, starting from rest but having a final speed of 2.00 m/s?

Aid Box

The work going into mechanical energy is ***W* = KE + PE**. At the bottom of the stairs, we take both **KE** and **PE$_{gas}$** initially zero; thus,

$W = KE_f + PE_g = ½\ mv_f^2 + mgh$,
where ***h*** is the vertical height of the stairs. Because all terms are given, we can calculate ***W*** and then divide it by time to get power.

IV = 10 Horse Power = _________________ Watt;

V:

Solution:

I: a) law of conservation of energy; b) electrical energy; c) chemical energy; d) radiant energy; e) nuclear energy; f) thermal energy; g) efficiency; II: Work done in unit time (Power) = 538 J/s = 538 Watt;

III: 7460 Watt; IV:

Worksheet 8

1: _________________: It is defined as the energy possessed by a body due to its motion.

Table displaying Power estimation in Watt.

Object or Phenomenon	Power in Watts
Supernova (at peak)	5×10^{37}
Milky Way galaxy	10^{37}
Crab Nebula pulsar	10^{28}

2: Suppose a star 1000 times brighter than our Sun (that is, emitting 1000 times the power) suddenly goes supernova. Using data from the above table. (a) By what factor does its power output increase? (b) How many times brighter than our entire Milky Way galaxy is the supernova? (c) Based on your answers, discuss whether it should be possible to observe supernovas in distant galaxies. Note that there are on the order of 10^{11} observable galaxies, the average brightness of which is somewhat less than our own galaxy.

3: A person in good physical condition can put out 100 W of useful power for several hours at a stretch, perhaps by pedalling a mechanism that drives an electric generator. Neglecting any problems of generator efficiency and practical considerations such as resting time: (a) How many people would it take to run a 4.00-kW electric clothes dryer? (b) How many people would it take to replace a large electric power plant that generates 800 MW?

4: What is the cost of operating a 3.00-W electric clock for a year if the cost of electricity is $0.0900 per kW • h?

5: A large household air conditioner may consume 15.0 kW of power. What is the cost of operating this air conditioner 3.00 h per day for 30.0 d if the cost of electricity is $0.110 per kW • h?

6: (a) What is the average power consumption in watts of an appliance that uses 5.00 kW • h of energy per day? (b) How many joules of energy does this appliance consume in a year?

7: (a) What is the average useful power output of a person who does 6.00×10^{6} J of useful work in 8.00 h? (b) Working at this rate, how long will it take this person to lift 2000 kg of bricks 1.50 m to a platform? (Work done to lift his body can be omitted because it is not considered useful output here.)

8: A 500-kg dragster accelerates from rest to a final speed of 110 m/s in 400 m (about a quarter of a mile) and encounters an average frictional force of 1200 N. What is its average power output in watts and horsepower if this takes 7.30 s?

9: (a) How long will it take an 850-kg car with a useful power output of 40.0 hp (1 hp = 746 W) to reach a speed of 15.0 m/s, neglecting friction? (b) How long will this acceleration take if the car also climbs a 3.00-m-high hill in the process?

10: (a) Find the useful power output of an elevator motor that lifts a 2500-kg load a height of 35.0 m in 12.0 s, if it also increases the speed from rest to 4.00 m/s. Note that the total mass of the counterbalanced system is 10,000 kg—so that only 2500 kg is raised in height, but the full 10,000 kg is accelerated. (b) What does it cost, if electricity is $0.0900 per kW • h?

11: (a) What is the available energy content, in joules, of a battery that operates a 2.00-W electric clock for 18 months? (b) How long can a battery that can supply 8.00×10^{4} J run a pocket calculator that consumes energy at the rate of 1.00×10^{-3} W?

12: (a) How long would it take a 1.50×10^{5}-kg airplane with engines that produce 100 MW of power to reach a speed of 250 m/s and an altitude of 12.0 km if air resistance were negligible? (b) If it actually takes 900 s, what is the power? (c) Given this power, what is the average force of air resistance if the airplane takes 1200 s? (Hint: You must find the distance the plane travels in 1200 s assuming constant acceleration.)

13: Calculate the power output needed for a 950-kg car to climb a 2.00° slope at a constant 30.0 m/s while encountering wind resistance and friction totaling 600 N.

14.: It is defined as the energy possessed or gained by a body due to its raised position above the surface of earth.

15: ____________________: It is the limiting value of the average power of an agent in a small time interval tending to zero.

Solution:

1: 2×10^{-10}; **3:** (a) 40 (b) 8 million; **5:** \$149; **7:** (a) 208 W (b) 141 s; **9:** (a) 3.20 s (b) 4.04 s

11: (a) 9.46×10^7 J (b) 2.54 y;

13: Identify knowns:

$$m = 950\text{ kg},\ \text{slope angle } \theta = 2.00^0,\ v = 3.00\text{ m/s},\ f = 600\text{ N}$$

Identify unknowns: power P of the car, force F that car applies to road

Solve for unknown:

$$P = \frac{W}{t} = \frac{Fd}{t} = F\left(\frac{d}{t}\right) = Fv,$$

where F is parallel to the incline and must oppose the resistive forces and the force of gravity:

$$F = f + w = 600\text{ N} + mg\sin\theta$$

Insert this into the expression for power and solve:

$$\begin{aligned} P &= (f + mg\sin\theta)v \\ &= [600\text{ N} + (950\text{ kg})(9.80\text{ m/s}^2)\sin 2^0](30.0 m/s) \\ &= 2.77 \times 10^4\text{ W} \end{aligned}$$

About 28 kW (or about 37 hp) is reasonable for a car to climb a gentle incline.

14: Gravitational P.E; It is also defined as the energy possessed by a body due to its position or configuration.
15: Instantaneous Power;

Worksheet 9 [Unsolved]

1 How much work does a pulling force of 40 N do on the 20 kg box in pulling it 8 m across the floor at a constant speed. The pulling force is directed at 60° above the horizontal

(a) 160 J (b) 277 J

(c) 784 J (d) None of the above

2 A horizontal force of 5 N is required to maintain a velocity of 2 m/s for a block of 10 kg mass sliding over a rough surface. The work done by this force in one minute is

(a) 600 J (b) 60 J

(c) 6 J (d) 6000 J

3 Work done in time t on a body of mass m which is accelerated from rest to a speed v in time t_1 as a function of time t is given by

(a) $\frac{1}{2} m \frac{v}{t_1} t^2$ (b) $m \frac{v}{t_1} t^2$

(c) $\frac{1}{2}\left(\frac{m v}{t_1}\right)^2 t^2$ (d) $\frac{1}{2} m \frac{v^2}{t_1^2} t^2$

4 What is the shape of the graph between the speed and kinetic energy of a body

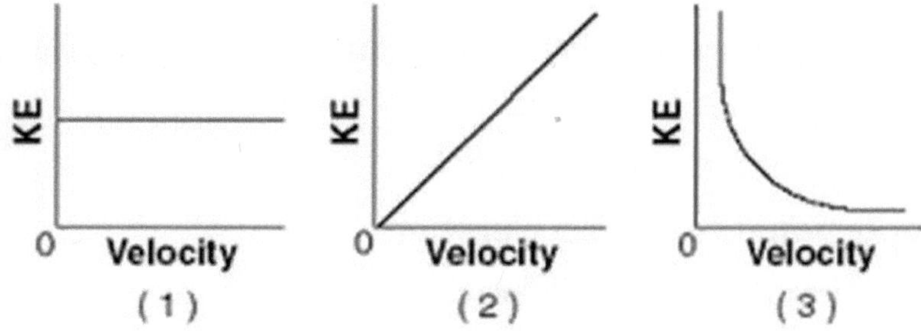

5 When a body moves with some friction on a surface

(a) It loses kinetic energy but momentum is constant
(b) It loses kinetic energy but gains potential energy
(c) Kinetic energy and momentum both decrease
(d) Mechanical energy is conserved

6 A bullet of mass m moving with velocity v strikes a suspended wooden block of mass M. If the block rises to a height h, the initial velocity of the block will be

(a) $\sqrt{2gh}$
(b) $\frac{M+m}{m}\sqrt{2gh}$
(c) $\frac{m}{M+m}2gh$
(d) $\frac{M+m}{M}\sqrt{2gh}$

8 There will be decrease in potential energy of the system, if work is done upon the system by

(a) Any conservative or non-conservative force
(b) A non-conservative force
(c) A conservative force
(d) None of the above

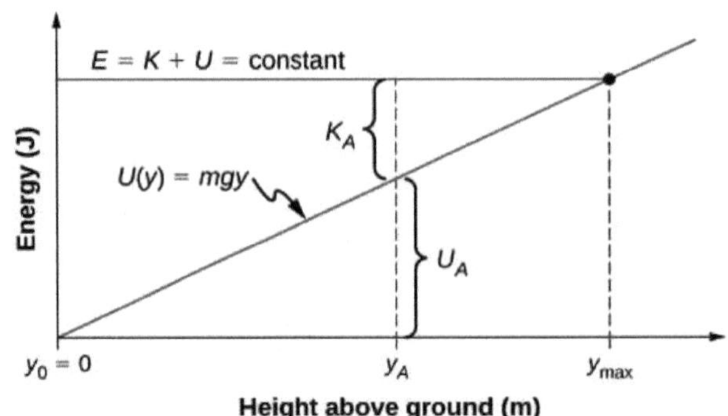

9 The slope of kinetic energy displacement curve of a particle in motion is

(a) Equal to the acceleration of the particle
(b) Inversely proportional to the acceleration
(c) Directly proportional to the acceleration
(d) None of the above

10 A body of mass 2 *kg* slides down a curved track which is quadrant of a circle of radius 1 *metre*. All the surfaces are frictionless. If the body starts from rest, its speed at the bottom of the track is

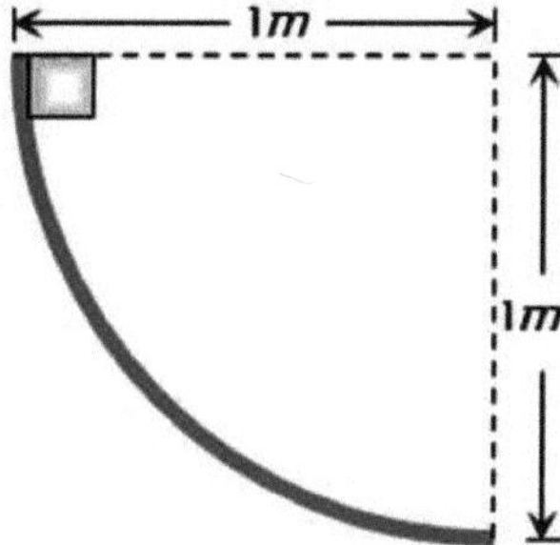

(a) 4.43 *m/sec*

(b) 2 *m/sec*

(c) 0.5 *m/sec*

(d) 19.6 *m/sec*

11 A bomb of mass 3*m kg* explodes into two pieces of mass *m kg* and 2*m kg*. If the velocity of *m kg* mass is 16 *m/s*, the total kinetic energy released in the explosion is

(a) 192 *mJ* (b) 96 *mJ*

(c) 384 *mJ* (d) 768 *mJ*

12 Which one of the following statement does not hold good when two balls of masses m_1 and m_2 undergo elastic collision

(a) When $m_1 << m_2$ and m_2 at rest, there will be maximum transfer of momentum

(b) When $m_1 >> m_2$ and m_2 at rest, after collision the ball of mass m_2 moves with four times the velocity of m_1

(c) When $m_1 = m_2$ and m_2 at rest, there will be maximum transfer of K.E.

(d) When collision is oblique and m_2 at rest with $m_1 = m_2$, after collision the balls move in opposite directions

13 The kinetic energy of a body decreases by 36%. The decrease in its momentum is

(a) 36% (b) 20%

(c) 8% (d) 6%

14 A neutron travelling with a velocity v and K.E. E collides perfectly elastically head on with the nucleus of an atom of mass number A at rest. The fraction of total energy retained by neutron is

(a) $\left(\frac{A-1}{A+1}\right)^2$ (b) $\left(\frac{A+1}{A-1}\right)^2$

(c) $\left(\frac{A-1}{A}\right)^2$ (d) $\left(\frac{A+1}{A}\right)^2$

15 A body of mass m_1 moving with uniform velocity of 40 m/s collides with another mass m_2 at rest and then the two together begin to move with uniform velocity of 30 m/s. The ratio of their masses $\frac{m_1}{m_2}$ is

(a) 0.75 (b) 1.33

(c) 3.0 (d) 4.0

16 Six identical balls are lined in a straight groove made on a horizontal frictionless surface as shown. Two similar balls each moving with a velocity v collide elastically with the row of 6 balls from left. What will happen

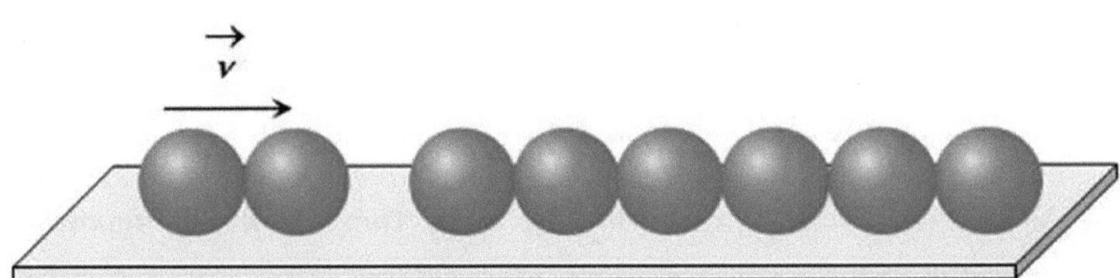

(a) One ball from the right rolls out with a speed $2v$ and the remaining balls will remain at rest

(b) Two balls from the right roll out with speed v each and the remaining balls will remain stationary

(c) All the six balls in the row will roll out with speed $v/6$ each and the two colliding balls will come to rest

(d) The colliding balls will come to rest and no ball rolls out from right

17 A wooden block of mass M rests on a horizontal surface. A bullet of mass m moving in the horizontal direction strikes and gets embedded in it. The combined system covers a distance x on the surface. If the coefficient of friction between wood and the surface is μ, the speed of the bullet at the time of striking the block is (where m is mass of the bullet)

(a) $\sqrt{\frac{2Mg}{\mu m}}$ (b) $\sqrt{\frac{2\mu mg}{Mx}}$

(c) $\sqrt{2\mu gx}\left(\frac{M+m}{m}\right)$ (d) $\sqrt{\frac{2\mu mx}{M+m}}$

18 A ball moving with speed v hits another identical ball at rest. The two balls stick together after collision. If specific heat of the material of the balls is S, the temperature rise resulting from the collision is

(a) $\frac{v^2}{8S}$ (b) $\frac{v^2}{4S}$

(c) $\frac{v^2}{2S}$ (d) $\frac{v^2}{S}$

19 A bag of sand of mass M is suspended by a string. A bullet of mass m is fired at it with velocity v and gets embedded into it. The loss of kinetic energy in this process is

(a) $\frac{1}{2}mv^2$ (b) $\frac{1}{2}mv^2 \times \frac{1}{M+m}$

(c) $\frac{1}{2}mv^2 \times \frac{M}{m}$ (d) $\frac{1}{2}mv^2\left(\frac{M}{M+m}\right)$

20: The potential energy of a system increases if work is done
(a) upon the system by a nonconservative force.
(b) by the system against a conservative force.
(c) by the system against a nonconservative force.
(d) upon the system by a conservative force.

Worksheet 10

1: Capacity of doing work is called *Energy*[1] and rate of doing work is called *power*. Look at some of selected activities listed below. Reason out whether work is done or not done in the light of your understanding of the 'work done' in the context of Physics.

(a) Suma, Nikita nad Rikin are swimming in a pond. (b) A donkey is carrying a bulk of heavy load on its back.
(c) A windmill is used in lifting water from a dug well. (d) A green plant is carrying out photosynthesis by trapping Sunlight.
(e) An engine is pulling a goods train and gaining acceleration.
(f) Harvested food grains are getting dried in the sun. (g) A sailboat is moving under the influence of wind energy.

2: Two men of identical weight climb up through a staircase of definite height in 15 seconds and 20 seconds respectively. The ratio of their power is ______________.

3: Two springs of spring constant k and 3k are stretched by applying same force. The ratio of potential energy stored in them respectively will be _________________.

4: Solve the following:

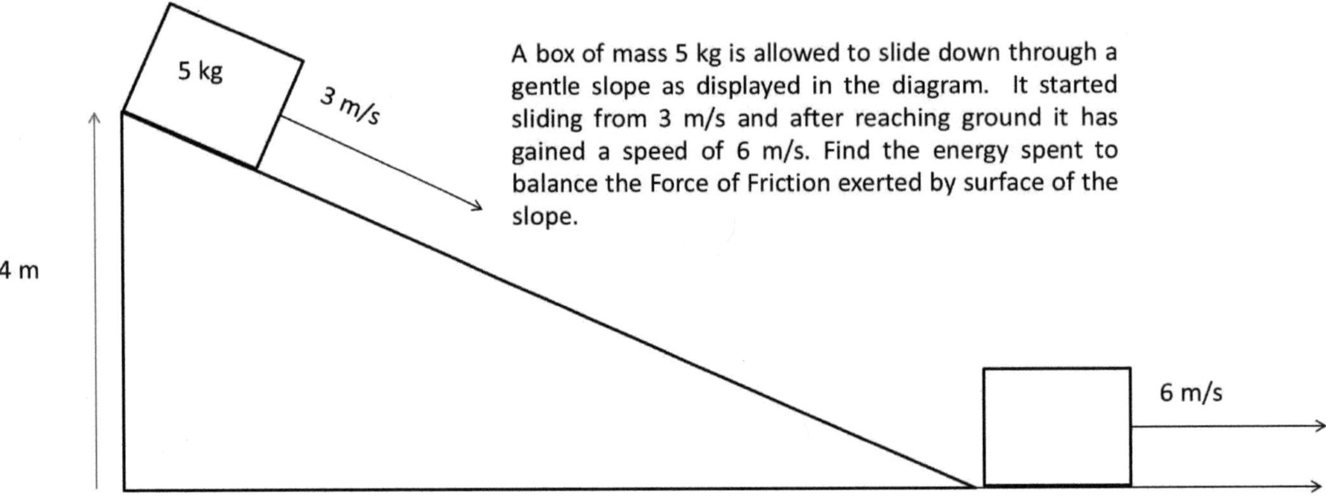

A box of mass 5 kg is allowed to slide down through a gentle slope as displayed in the diagram. It started sliding from 3 m/s and after reaching ground it has gained a speed of 6 m/s. Find the energy spent to balance the Force of Friction exerted by surface of the slope.

---

[1] Energy: Energy of a body is defined as the capacity or ability of a body to do work. The SI unit of energy is joule (J) (unit of energy and work is same). There are various forms of energy in the nature, few of them are mechanical energy (potential energy + kinetic energy) heat energy, chemical energy and light energy. Mechanical energy includes kinetic energy and potential energy. The energy possessed by a body by the virtue of its motion is called kinetic energy. Kinetic energy possessed by a body can be calculated by

$E_K=(1/2)mv^2$; [m = mass of body; V = velocity of body.]

A force of constant magnitude F is acting on the body. Here initial velocity of the body is u and final velocity is v. As there is no dissipative forces, work done on the body will be stored in the form of changes (in status of kinetic energy).

W=Fs; The energy possessed by a body due to its position or configuration is called potential energy.

Power stands for rate of doing work, or work done per second.

5: A mass of 10 kg is moving in a straight line with a constant speed of 10m /s. It is exposed to a retarding force of -0.1 Joule/ meter during its travel in the same direction from 20 m to 30 m. Calculate its final kinetic energy.

6: A Force –Displacement Graph is displayed below.

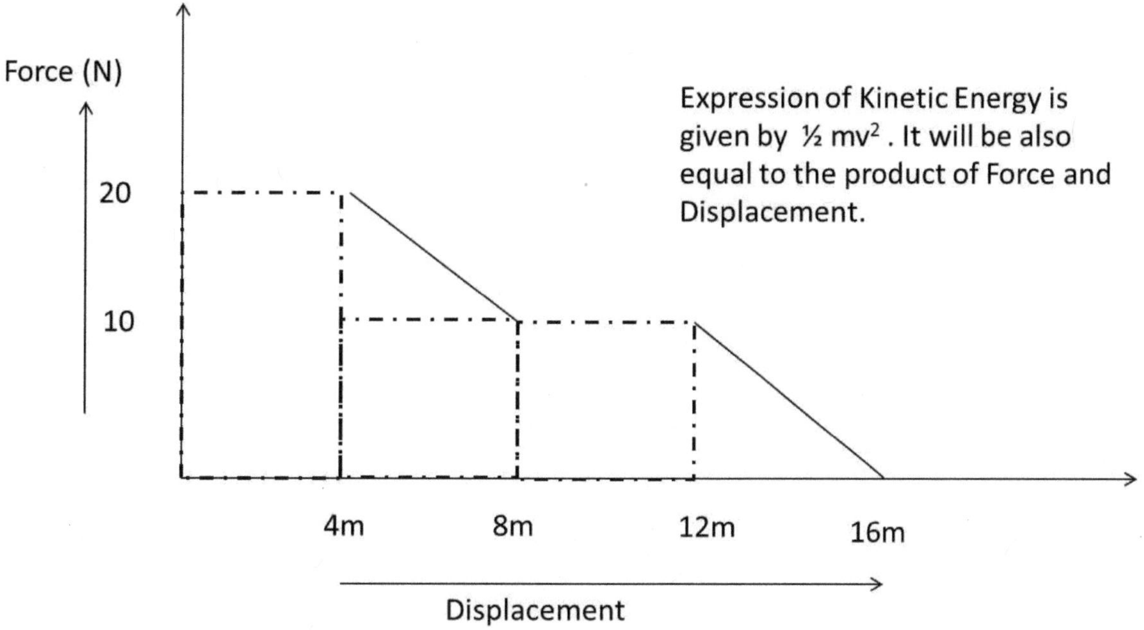

Calculate the total Kinetic Energy of the object when it was 16 m distant from the place from which it has started moving.

7: We calculate work done by any force on the basis of displacement achieved by the object under influence of force applied on it.

Three different forces used to lift three different objects of identical mass to a height of 20 m.

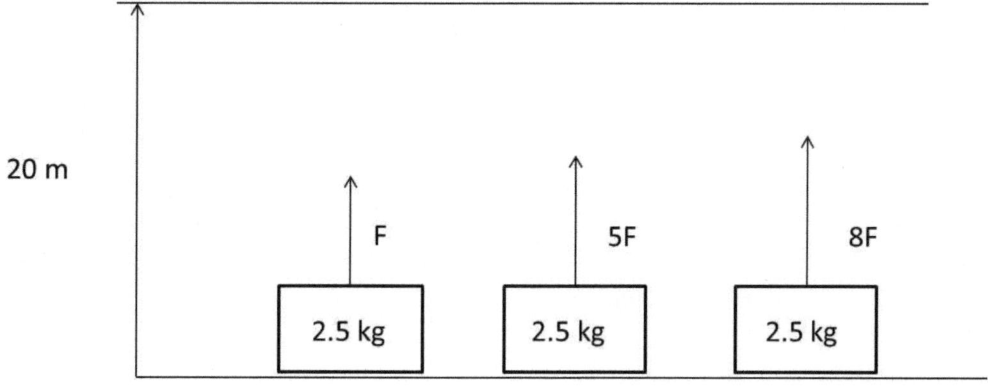

A: Calculate work done by each forces on respective objects.
B: Calculate work done by each forces against force of gravity.

8: Force works on any object through horizontal and vertical components. There are three instances in which three different forces worked on the object of identical mass.

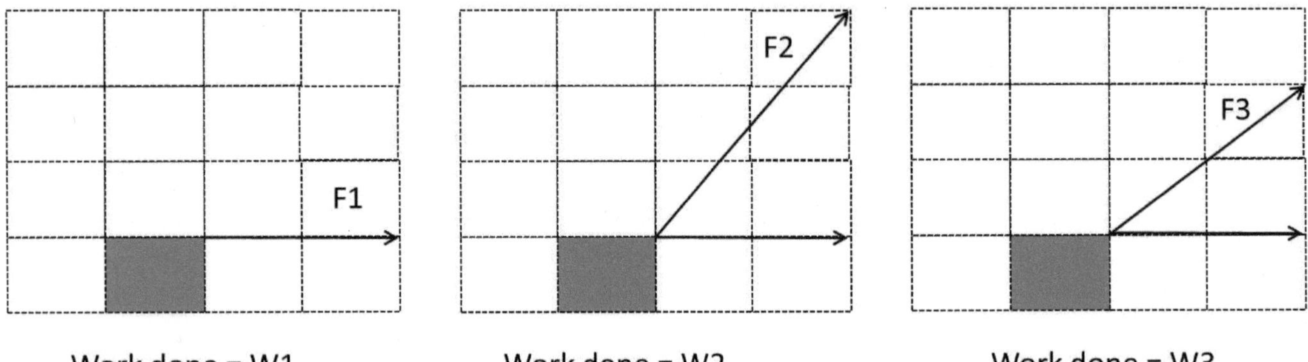

Given that horizontal components of all the three forces are equal to each other. All the three objects are also equal. Compare the work done by all these three forces on respective objects.

9: Solve the following:

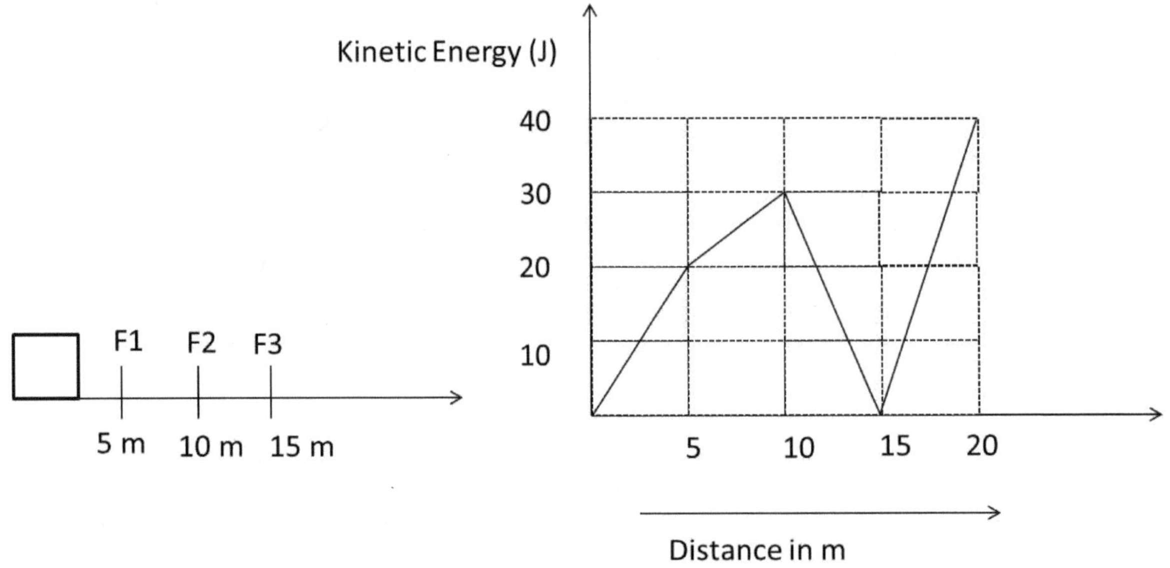

Three different forces (F1, F2 and F3) are applied on same object at different intervals as shown in the figure. The Kinetic Energy gained by the object at different such instances are plotted in the form of an energy – displacement graph.

Slope of the graph indicates ________________________________.

Establish relationship between F1, F2 and F3.

10: Gravitational Potential gained by an object of mass 10 kg if it is raised from a height of 20 m to that of 50 m. [Acceleration due to gravity = 9.8 ms^{-2} ;]

11 Given in Fig. are examples of some potential energy functions in one dimension. The total energy of the particle is indicated by a cross on the ordinate axis. In each case, specify the regions, if any, in which the particle cannot be found for the given energy. Also, indicate the minimum total energy the particle must have in each case.

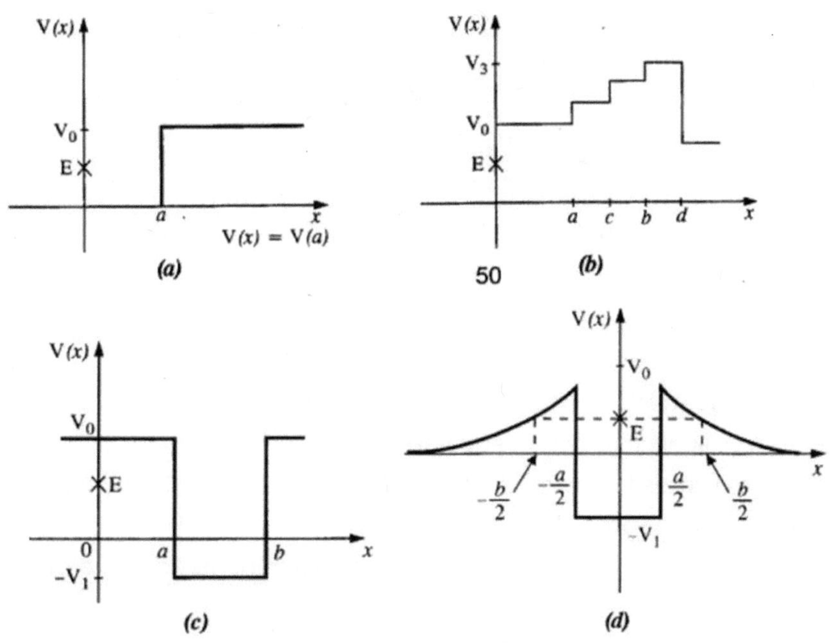

12: Select the correct alternative:---

(a) When a conservative force does positive work on a body, the potential energy of the body increases/decreases/ remains unaltered.

(b) Work done by a body against friction always results in a loss of its kinetic/potential energy.

The rate of change of total momentum of many-particle system is proportional to the external force/sum of the internal forces on the system.

(c) In an inelastic collision of two bodies, the quantities which do not change after the collision are the total kinetic energy total linear momentum/total energy of the system of two bodies.

13 True False --

In an elastic collision of two bodies, the momentum and energy of each body are conserved.

The total energy of a system is always conserved, no matter what internal and external forces on the body are present.

Work done in the motion of a body over a closed loop is zero for every force in nature.

In an inelastic collision, the final kinetic energy is always less than the initial kinetic energy of the system.

Solution:

1: Work is not done in cases where force applied is not bringing displacement. Work is not done in conditions such b, d and f. 2: 4:3; 3: Ratio is 3:1;

4: Difference of total Kinetic Energy and Potential Energy at the top – Kinetic Energy at the bottom = Energy consumed to balance the force of friction.

5: Hints/ Solution ---

KE_i = ½ mv^2 = 500 J;

F_1 at x = 20 is 0.1 X 20 N = 2 N;

F2 = 3 N;

Average Retarding Force= 2.5 N;

Work Done (W) = 2.5 X (30-20) = 25 J;

Final KE = KE_i - W = (500- 25) J = 475 J

Work done by retarding force is to be subtracted from the Kinetic Energy that the particle had at the beginning.

6: Area of the graph is equal to total Kinetic Energy of the object.

7: Work done = Force X Displacement; W1 = F X 20 ; W2 = 100 F and W3 = 160 F;

Work done by all the three forces against gravity is equal to each other;

8: W1 = W2 = W3; In all the three cases force acted and displacement attained are equal;

9: Slope of the graph indicates Applied Force; F3>F1>F2;

10: mgh = 10 X (50-20) X 9.8 N = ____________. [It is also termed as Gravitational Potential Energy]

11: (a) We know that Total energy E = KE + PE, kinetic energy can never be negative. In the region between x = 0 & x = a.

Potential energy is '0'. So, kinetic energy y is positive. In region x > a the potential energy has a value greater than 'E'. So kinetic energy will be negative in this region. Hence the particle cannot be present in the region x > a.

(b) Here PE > E, the total energy of the object and as such the kinetic energy of the object would be negative. Thus object cannot be present in any region on the graph.

(c) Here x = 0 to x = a & x > b, the P E is more then E so, K E is negative. The particle cannot be present in these portions.

(d) Object cannot exist in this region as PE>KE.

12: (a) Work done by conservative force is equal to the negative of potential energy. When work done is positive, potential energy decreases.

(b) Kinetic energy, because friction does work against motion of the body.

(c) External force, because in many-particle systems, the internal forces in the system cancel each other and hence cannot change the net momentum of the system.

(d) In inelastic collision, total energy and linear momentum are conserved. However, kinetic energy decreases.

13: False, the momentum and energy of each body are conserved.

False, the external force on the system may increase or decrease the total energy of the system.

False, for the non-conservative forces (friction) the work done in closed-loop is not zero.

True, usually in an inelastic collision the final kinetic energy is always less than the initial kinetic energy of the system.

Assignment I

1: Avinash can run with a speed of 8 m s^{-1} against the frictional force of 10 N, and Kapil can move with a speed of 3 ms^{-1} against the frictional force of 25 N. Who is more powerful and why?

2: Can any object have mechanical energy even if its momentum is zero? Explain with reason.

3: Can any object have momentum even if its mechanical energy is zero? Give reasons.

4: The power of a motor pump is 2.5 kW. How much water per minute the pump can raise to a height of 10 m? (Acceleration due to Gravity g = 10m s^{-2})

5: The weight of a person on a planet P is about half of that on the earth. He can jump upto 0.4 m height on the surface of the earth. How high he can successfully jump on the planet P?

6: The velocity of a body moving in a straight line is increased by applying a constant force F on it, for some distance in the direction of the motion. Prove that the increase in the kinetic energy of the body is equal to the work done by the force on the body.

7: A rubber ball is dropped from a height of 10 m and allowed it to fall freely under the influence of gravity. If the energy of the ball reduces by 40% after striking the ground, how much high can the ball bounce back? (g = 10 m s^{-2})

8: A bullet fired on a tree trunk loses $1/4^{th}$ of its kinetic energy. It will travel ___ cm more inside the trunk. [Assume that a constant rate of retardation is applied on the moving bullet by the tree trunk.] [Ans : 15 cm]

9: A vehicle of mass 1000 kg moving with a velocity of 15 ms^{-1} is brought to rest by applying brakes. If the sliding friction working between road and the tyres is 6000 N then calculate the distance travelled by that vehicle before coming to rest. [Ans: 18.5 m]

10: Consider the following:

A ball moves towards a wall with an initial speed of u by making a definite angle θ with the wall.

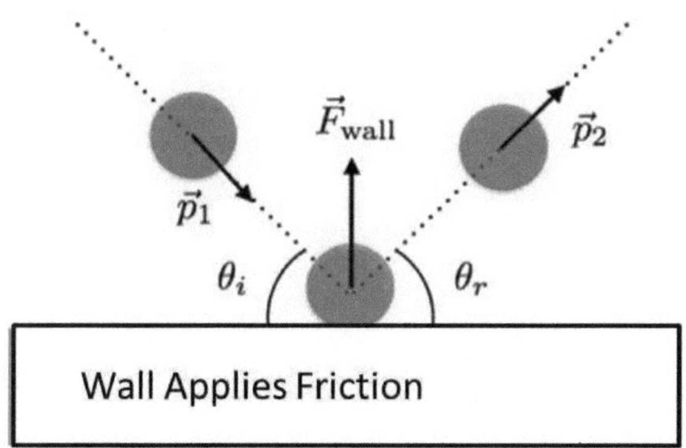

As the ball hits the wall at an angle and rebounds, there is a change in the momentum only along the direction perpendicular to the wall. The change along the wall is zero.

The change in momentum of the ball during collation is ________________.

[Ans: 2mu sinθ; away from the wall;]

11:

Assignment II

1: If an electric iron of 1500 W is used for 50 minutes everyday, Find electric energy consumed in the month of April.

2: A body projected vertically from the earth reaches a height equal to earth's radius before returning to the earth. The power exerted by the gravitational force is greatest

(a) at the highest position of the body. (b) at the instant just before the body hits the earth.

(c) it remains constant all through. (d) at the instant just after the body is projected.

3: A metal ball of mass 2 kg moving with speed of 36 km/h has a head on collision with a stationary ball of mass 3 kg. If after collision, both the balls move as a single mass, then the loss in K.E. due to collision is

(a) 100 J (b) 140 J (c) 40 J (d) 60 J.

4: A cyclist comes to a skidding stop in 10 m. During this process, the force working on the cycle due to the road is 200 N and is directly opposed to the motion. (a) How much work does the road do on the cycle ? (b) How much work does the cycle do on the road ?

[Work done by road = – 2000 J; work done by cycle on the road is zero as there is no displacement.]

5: Consider the following situation:

A: A weightlifter holding a 150 kg mass steadily on his shoulder for 30 s does no work on the load during this time.

B: A block moving on a smooth horizontal table is not acted upon by a horizontal force (since there is no friction), but may undergo a large displacement.

C: For the block moving on a smooth horizontal table, the gravitational force mg does no work since it acts at right angles to the displacement.

D: The moon's instantaneous displacement is tangential while the earth's force is radially inwards and $\theta = \pi/2$.

E: In many examples the frictional force opposes displacement and $\theta = 180^{\circ}$.

Select the situation during which work is done.

[Ans: E; it is negative as $\cos 180^{\circ} = -1$]

6: In a ballistics demonstration a police officer fires a bullet of mass 50.0 g with speed 200 m s^{-1} on soft plywood of thickness 2.00 cm. The bullet emerges with only 10% of its initial kinetic energy. What is the emergent speed of the bullet ? [Ans: 63.2 m s^{-1}]

Worksheet 10 [Unsolved]

1: Two different components of a force work differently to keep an object moving.

A body moves a distance of 10 m along a straight line under the action of a 5 N force. If the work done is 25 J, then angle between the force and direction of motion of the body is

(a) 60° (b) 75°
(c) 30° (d) 45°.

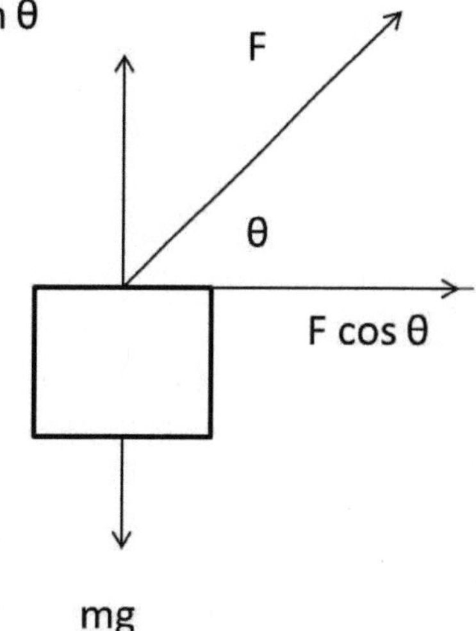

Aid Box: Force working towards the direction of movement is equal to F cos θ ; Another component F sin θ is working to balance thrust applied by the object on ground.

2: A mass of 1 kg is thrown up with a velocity of 100 m/s. After 5 seconds, it explodes into two parts. One part of mass 400 g comes down with a velocity 25 m/s. The velocity of other part is (Take g = 10 ms^{-2})

(a) 40 m/s (b) 80 m/s (c) 100 m/s (d) 60 m/s

3: Two equal masses m1 and m2 moving along the same straight line with velocities + 3 m/s and –5 m/s respectively collide elastically. Their velocities after the collision will be respectively

(a) – 4 m/s and +4 m/s (b) +4 m/s for both

(c) – 3 m/s and +5 m/s (d) – 5 m/s and + 3 m/s.

4: Two bodies with kinetic energies in the ratio of 4 : 1 are moving with equal linear momentum. The ratio of their masses is

(a) 4 : 1 (b) 1 : 1 (c) 1 : 2 (d) 1 : 4.

5: A shell, in flight, explodes into four unequal parts. Which of the following is conserved?

(a) Potential energy (b) Momentum (c) Kinetic energy (d) Both (a) and (c).

6: The kinetic energy acquired by a mass m in travelling distance d, starting from rest, under the action of a constant force is directly proportional to

(a) m (b) m^0 (c) $m^{½}$ (d) $(1/m)^{-½}$.

7: How much water a pump of 2 kW can raise in one minute to a height of 10 m ? (take g = 10 m/s^2)

(a) 1000 litres (b) 1200 litres (c) 100 litres (d) 2000 litres

8: A bullet of mass 10 g leaves a rifle at an initial velocity of 1000 m/s and strikes the earth at the same level with a velocity of 500 m/s. The work done in joule overcoming the resistance of air will be

(a) 375 **(b)** 3750 (c) 5000 (d) 500

9: The coefficient of restitution e for a perfectly elastic collision is

(a) 1 (b) 0 (c) ⍰ (d) –1

10: When a mass falls on a spring from a height h the work done by the loss of gravitational potential energy of the mass is stored as the potential energy of the spring.

10: Answer the following ---

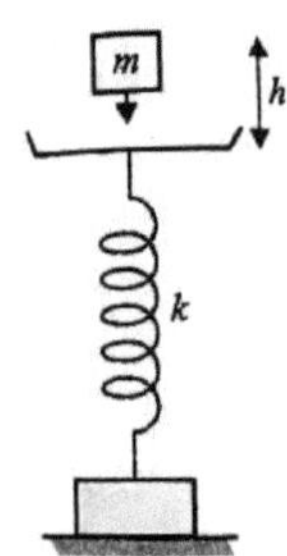

A body of mass m fell from a height h onto the pan of a spring balance. The masses of the pan and the spring are negligible, the stiffness of the latter is x. Having stuck to the pan, the body starts performing harmonic oscillations in the vertical direction. Find the amplitude and the energy of these oscillations.

11: If kinetic energy of a body is increased by 300% then percentage change in momentum will be

(a) 100% (b) 150% (c) 265% (d) 73.2%.

12: Force of friction is a type of ______________________ force.

13: When we allow any object to fall freely under the influence of gravity then sum total of __________ and ______________ energy at all the place of movement is constant.

14: Solve the following ;

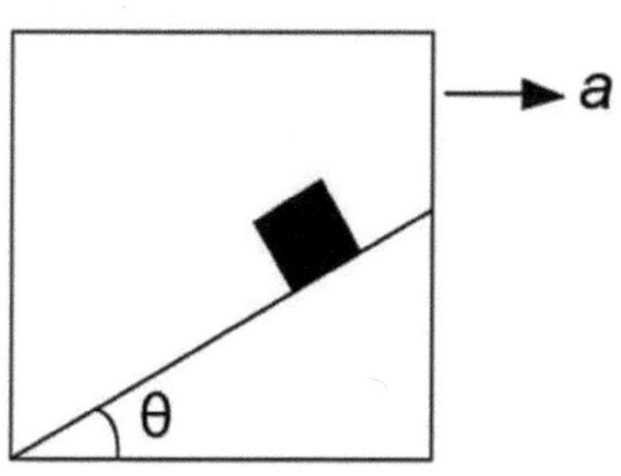

A block is sliding along inclined plane as shown in figure. If the acceleration of chamber is a, as shown in the figure. The time required to cover a distance L along incline is:

Aid Box

Applying pseudo force ma along left direction of the block. The net acceleration along the incline will be $a_{effective}$= acosθ + gsinθ

The time required will be L=0×t+ ½ $a_{effective}t^2$

Answer: $L = \sqrt{\frac{2L}{(a\cos\theta + g\sin\theta)}}$

15: A child is sitting on a swing. Its minimum and maximum heights from the ground 0.75 m and 2 m respectively, its maximum speed will be

(a) 10 m/s (b) 5 m/s (c) 8 m/s (d) 15 m/s.

16: Observe the diagram below and calculate total work done by the force.

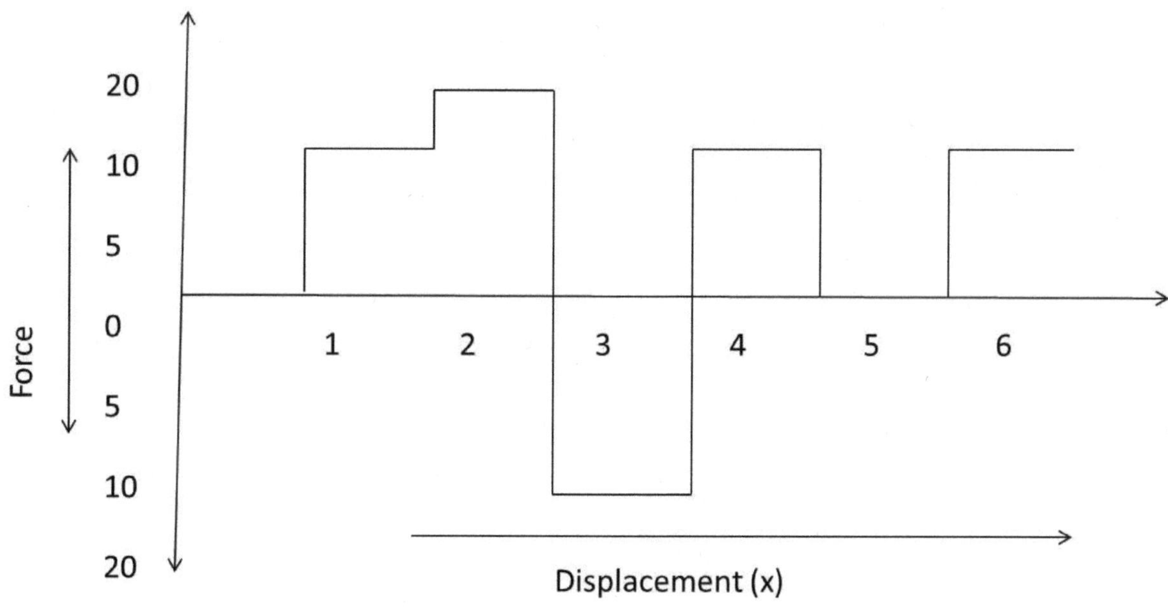

Suggested solution to Q 10:

As the pan is of negligible mass, there is no loss of kinetic energy even though the collision is inelastic. the mechanical energy of the body m in the field generated by the joint action of both the gravity force and the elastic force is conserved i.e. ΔE = 0. During the motion of the body m from the initial to the final (position of maximum compression of the spring) position ΔT = 0, and therefore ΔU = ΔUgr + ΔUsp = 0

$$\text{or} \quad -mg(h+x)+\frac{1}{2}\kappa x^2 = 0$$

On solving the quadratic equation :

$$x = \frac{mg}{\kappa} \pm \sqrt{\frac{m^2g^2}{\kappa^2}+\frac{2mgh}{\kappa}}$$

As minus sign is not acceptable

$$x = \frac{mg}{\kappa} + \sqrt{\frac{m^2g^2}{\kappa^2}+\frac{2mgh}{\kappa}}$$

If the body m were at rest on the spring, the corresponding position of m will be its equilibrium position and at this Δx (say) due to the body m will be given position the resultant force on the body m will be zero. therefore the equilibrium compression by

$$\kappa \Delta x = mg \quad \text{or} \quad \Delta x = mg/\kappa$$

Therefore seperation between the equilibrium position and one of the extreme position i.e. the sought amplitude

$$a = x - \Delta x = \sqrt{\frac{m^2g^2}{\kappa^2}+\frac{2mgh}{\kappa}}$$

The mechanical energy of oscillation which is conserved equals E = $U_{extreme}$, because at the extreme position kinetic energy becomes zero. Although the weight of body m is a conservation force, it is not restoring in this problem, hence Uextreme is only concerned with the spring force. Therefore

$$E = U_{extreme} = \frac{1}{2}\kappa a^2 = mgh + \frac{m^2g^2}{2\kappa}$$

2. Physics of Sound

Sound is also a kind of energy[2]. It is produced due to vibrations of particles present in the material medium. Because of that reason sound propagates through material medium. Without material medium sound cannot propagate. .

Propagation of sound[3] is also depending upon nature of the material medium. It can be faster in denser medium than compared to its propagation throough any rarer medium.

Human beings can recognise sound within the range of 20 Hz to 20,000 Hz. Sound waves are transverse waves of mechanical type. The type of diagram used to explain property of sound waves are of specific type. We can even represent loudness of sound through graph.

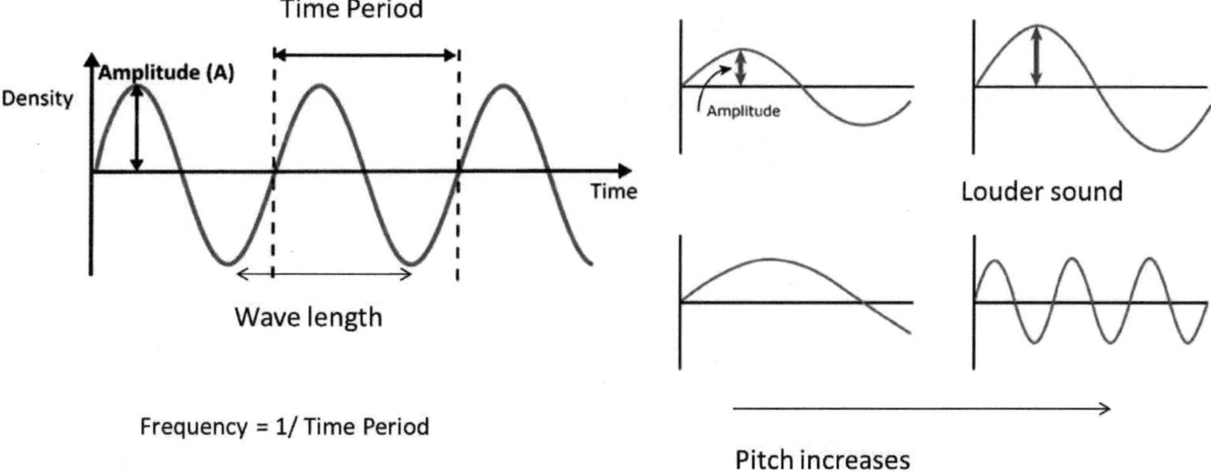

Particles of wave oscillate parallel to the directions of wave motion. That is why this type of wave is called a transverse wave. Frequency stands for the number of oscillations (a complete wave) per second. Time Period stands for time taken by a unit wave to propagate. Speed of sound can be calculated by working out the product of frequency and Time Period. [Velocity of sound (v) = frequency (f) x wavelength (λ)]

Amplitude is the maximum vertical shift of the vibrating particles on the either side of the wave. Sound also follows same rules as those of light. Only difference is that sound waves require a wider reflector for ensuring proper reflection of the sound wave directed towards it. Another factor is that we have a limitation of recognising sound as per the rule of our perception of listening. We may not be able to recognise any reflection

---

[2] Sound is a form of energy which produces a sensation of hearing in our ears. The sound of human voice is produced due to vibration in the vocal chord. Sound propagates in the form of longitudinal waves and these waves require material medium to propagate. Hence sound waves are mechanical waves. A wave in which the particles of the medium oscillate to and fro in the same direction in which the wave is moving is called longitudinal wave. A wave motion is said to transverse if the particles of the medium through which the wave propagates vibrate in the direction perpendicular to the direction of propagation of the wave. The frequency of wave is defined as the number of waves produced per second. The frequency of a sound wave is defined as the number of complete oscillations made by the particle of medium in one second. It is denoted by greek letter u (nu). Its SI unit is hertz (Hz). The distance between two consecutive compressions or two consecutive rarefactions is called wavelength.

of sound if it is forwarded to our auditory nerve before an interval of one tenth of a second. That time is called Perception of Hearing.

Try to recognise different parts displayed in the following diagram.

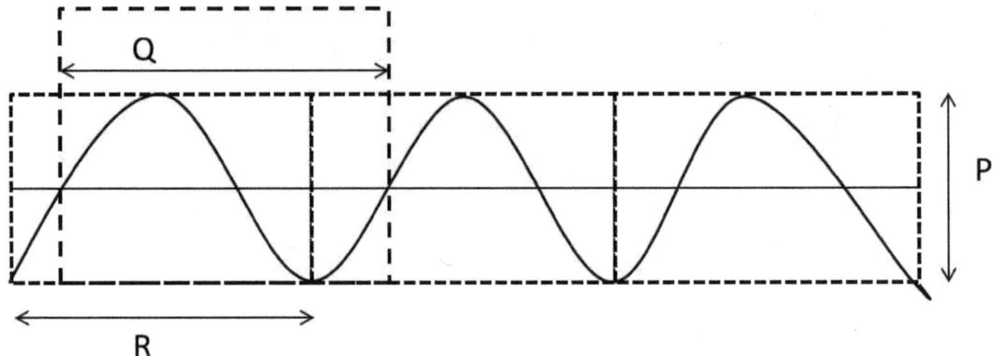

Wavelength = ________; Amplitude = ________;
Frequency = ______________; Time Period = _______;

Two different types of sound waves are represented in the form of diagram. Identify them and write their respective features. Which one of them will provide shrill voice?

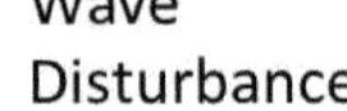

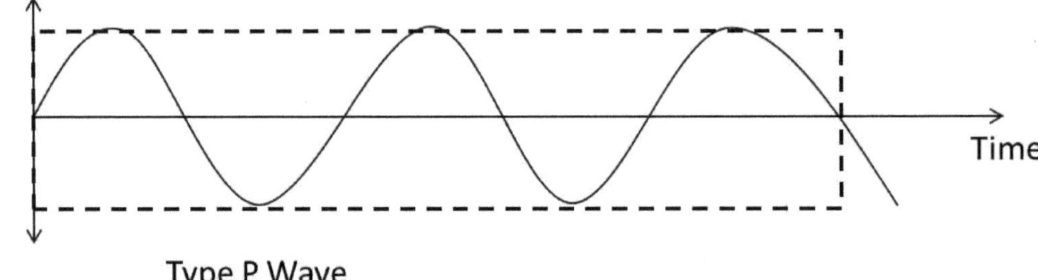

Type P Wave

Wave
Disturbance

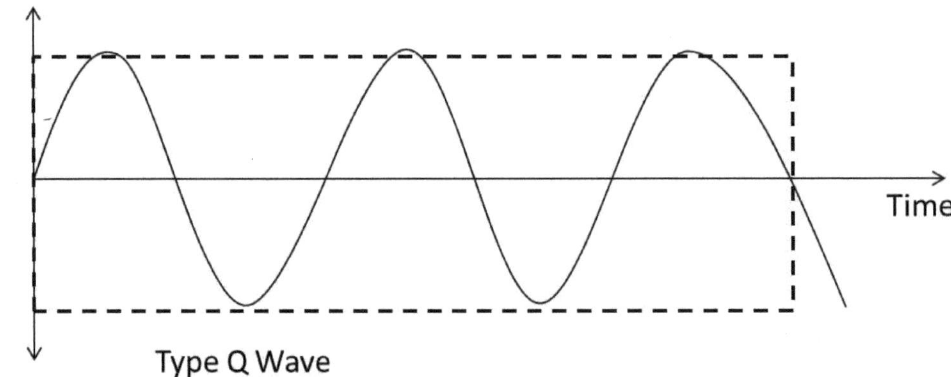

Type Q Wave

Type P = ____________________; Type Q = ______________________________;

Worksheet 1

A:Calculate the wavelength of a sound wave whose frequency is 220 Hz and speed is 440 m s^{-1} in a given medium.

[Hints: speed of sound = Frequency x Wavelength]

B: A person is listening to a tone of 1000 Hz sitting at a distance of 450 m from the source of the sound. What is the time interval between successive compressions from the source ?

C: A person has a hearing range from 20 Hz to 20 kHz. What are the typical wavelengths of sound waves in air corresponding to these two frequencies? Take the speed of sound in air as 344 ms^{-1}.

D: Anamika and Nikhil are at opposite ends of an aluminium rod. One strikes the end of the rod with a stone. Find the ratio of times taken by the sound wave in air and in aluminium to reach the second child.

[Speed of sound in air = 346 m/s and in aluminium = 6420 m/s;]

E: Operating frequency of an ultrasonographic scanner is 4.2 MHz. It is used in hospitals for scanning development of tumor in human body. Speed of sound in tissue system is estimated as 1.7 km/s. Find wavelength of the sound in tissue system.

F: The magnitude of the maximum disturbance in the medium on either side of the mean value is called _______________of wave.

G: Frequency and Time Period of Sound are ____________ related.

[Ans A: Wavelength[4] = 2 m; B = Interval = 0.001 second; C = 17.2 m and 0.0172 m; D = 18.55; E = 4.05×10^{-4} m; F = amplitude; inversely]

---

[4] Relation between time period (T) and frequency (u) T=1/v

Relation between speed of wave (υ), wavelength (λ) time period (T) and frequency (υ) υ = υλ.

The time taken by two consecutive compressions or rarefactions to cross a fixed point is called time period of wave. In other words, time taken by particle of medium to complete one oscillation is known as time period. It is represented by the symbol T. Its SI unit is second (s).

Worksheet 2

1: Two types of sound waves are represented as type P and Type Q. Use them to identify other sound tyeps.

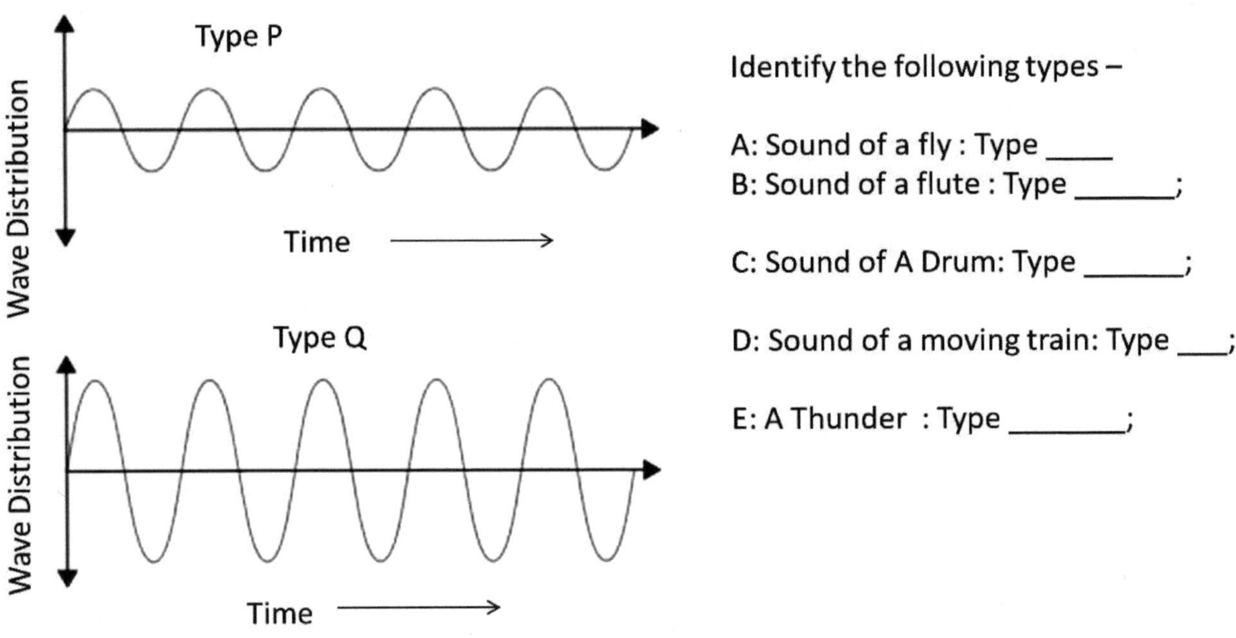

Identify the following types –

A: Sound of a fly : Type ____
B: Sound of a flute : Type ______;

C: Sound of A Drum: Type ______;

D: Sound of a moving train: Type ___;

E: A Thunder : Type _______;

2: How the brain interprets the frequency of an emitted sound is called its __________. The faster the vibration of the source, the higher is the frequency and the higher is the ____________.

3: The loudness or softness of a sound is determined by its _______________. Greater the ______________ of vibration of source, greater is the loudness of sound.

4: ____________sound can travel a larger distance as it is associated with high energy.

5: It is that characteristics which enables us to distinguish one sound from another having same loudness and pitch.

6: A sound of single frequency is called a________. The sound which is produced due to a mixture of several frequencies is called a note and is pleasant to listen to.

7: ___________ is unpleasant to hear. ___________ is pleasant to hear and is of rich quantity.

8: The landing and taking off of the air-planes causes lot of noise pollution which may lead to _____________, ____________________________.

Ans 1: A and B = Type P; C, D and E = Type Q; 2: pitch[5]; 3: amplitude[6]; 4: Loud; 5: The quality or timber of sound; 6: tone; 7: Noise; Music; 8: deafness, high blood pressure and other health problems.

---

[5] *The pitch of sound produced by an object of low frequency is low and the source described as flat sound.*
The pitch of sound produced by an object vibrating with high frequency is high and the sound is described as shrill sound.

[6] *A sound wave moves away from the source, its amplitude as well as its loudness decreases.*

Worksheet 3

1: Statement regarding Echo and its uses are displayed below.

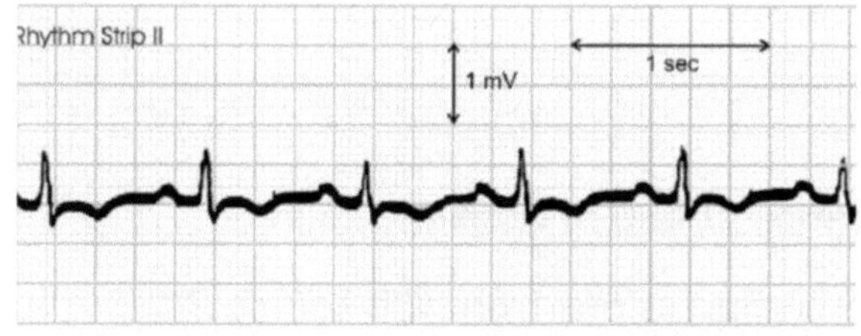

Normal ECG Report of a 22 Year old Patient.

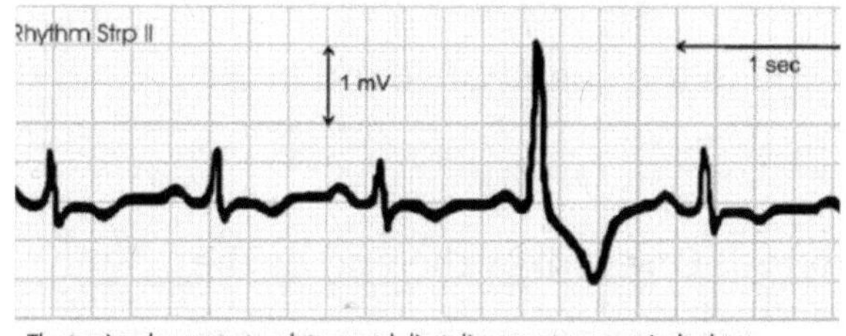

The tracing demonstrate a late or end-diastolic premature ventricular beat.

Some basic conditions required for the formation of Echo are as follows ---

a) An echo is the phenomenon of repetition of sound by reflection from an obstacle.

b) The sensation of sound lasts in brain for (1/10) of a second. This property is called persistence of hearing. To hear a distinct echo the time interval between the original sound and the reflected one must be at least 0. 1 second.

c) For hearing a distinct echo, the minimum distance of the obstacle from the source of sound should be 17.2 m.

d) This property of sound is used in Medical Science for diagnosing different fatal diseases.

e) Echo cannot be used to locate any kind of disease or ulcer present inside the brain box of human beings or any other vertebrates.

f) It is also used to measure depth of ocean bed by producing echo from a moving ship.

Find out the statement which is not correct.

2: The three characteristics of a musical sound are: __________, __________ and ________________.

3: ___________________ : The number of compressions or rarefactions taken together passing through a point in one second is called frequency.

4: ___________________ : It is the time taken by two consecutive compressions or rarefactions to cross a point.

5: ___________________ : It is the magnitude of maximum displacement of a vibrating particle about its mean position.

6: A sound created in a big hall will persist by repeated reflection from the walls until it is reduced to a value where it is no longer audible. The repeated reflection that results in the persistence of sound is called________.

7: It is the fundamental frequency that determines the __________of a sound.

8: It is observed that when a wire mounted on a sound board is plucked, the surface area of vibrating air increases and sends greater amount of energy. So the ____________of vibration is large and louder is the sound heard.

9:

Solution:

1: e; 2: Loudness, Pitch and Quality; 3: Frequency; 4: Time Period; 5: Amplitude; 6: reverberation; 7: pitch;

8: amplitude;

Worksheet 4

A:Calculate the wavelength of a sound wave whose frequency is 220 Hz and speed is 440 m s^{-1} in a given medium.

[Hints: speed of sound = Frequency x Wavelength]

B: A person is listening to a tone of 1000 Hz sitting at a distance of 450 m from the source of the sound. What is the time interval between successive compressions from the source ?

C: A person has a hearing range from 20 Hz to 20 kHz. What are the typical wavelengths of sound waves in air corresponding to these two frequencies? Take the speed of sound in air as 344 ms^{-1}.

D: Anamika and Nikhil are at opposite ends of an aluminium rod. One strikes the end of the rod with a stone. Find the ratio of times taken by the sound wave in air and in aluminium to reach the second child.

[Speed of sound in air = 346 m/s and in aluminium = 6420 m/s;]

E : Some distinct factors regulate loudness of sound. Select such factors.

The various factors on which loudness of sound heard by a listener depends are:

A. Amplitude of wave, ☐

B. Distance of source of sound, ☐

C. Surface area of vibrating body, ☐

D. Speed of sound wave, ☐

E. Sensitivity of listener and ☐

F. Intensity of sound. ☐

Select the factors on which loudness of sound depends. Put Y for yes and N for no.

F: To reduce_____________, the roof and walls of the auditorium are generally covered with sound absorbent materials like compressed fibre board, rough plaster or draperies. The seat materials are also selected on the basis of their sound absorbing properties.

G: _______________is a medical instrument used for listening to sounds produced within the body, chiefly in the heart or lungs.

Ans : A: Wavelength = 2 m; B = Interval = 0.001 second; C = 17.2 m and 0.0172 m; D = 18.55; E: all factors excluding D; reverberation; F: Stethoscope

Worksheet 5

1: Sound travels at 1540 m/s everywhere in body

average speed of sound in soft tissue

Sound travels in straight lines in direction transmitted

Sound attenuated equally by everything in body

(0.5 dB/cm/MHz, soft tissue average)

2: Let the time interval between transmission and reception of ultrasound signal be t and speed of sound through sea water be υ. The total distance, 2d, travelled by the ultrasound.

Rhinoceroses communicate using infra sound of frequency as low as 5 Hz.

Whales and elephants produce sound in infrasonic wave.

Children under five and some animals, such as dogs can hear infrasonic sound.

Earthquake produces infrasonic waves.

Ultrasound is produced by dolphins, bats and porpoises. R

Moths of certain families can hear high frequency waves.

3: Ultrasonography: The technique of obtaining of images of internal organs of the body by using ultrasonic waves is called ultrasonography. An ultrasound scanner is a medical instrument which is used by doctors to detect abnormalities such as stones in gall bladder and kidney or tumours in different organs. In this technique, the ultrasound scanner produces ultrasounds which travel through the tissues of the body, and if there are stones in the gall bladder or kidney or there is tumour in any internal organ, then the ultrasound waves get reflected from these regions due to the change in tissue density. These reflected ultrasound waves are converted into electrical signals and fed to the computer generating a three dimension images of the organ on the monitor of the computer.

4: We cannot recognise ultrasonic sound as the wave is of ________________________ type.

5: Two application of ultra-sound in medical science are: ______________________ and ________________.

6: Elephants can produce and listen _______________________ sound which we may not be able to recognise.

7: Bats are capable of producing and catching ________________sound which is beyond the range of our audible sound range.

8: Cholera, TB and Malaria are _______________ diseases.

.

Worksheet 6

1: A ____________ is a form of disturbance that transmits energy from one place to another without the actual flow of matter as a whole.

2: Water waves or sound waves are called ______________ as they require a material medium for their propagation.

3: ________________ waves don't require any material medium for their propagation.

4: Point out at least three differences in between the following types of waves.

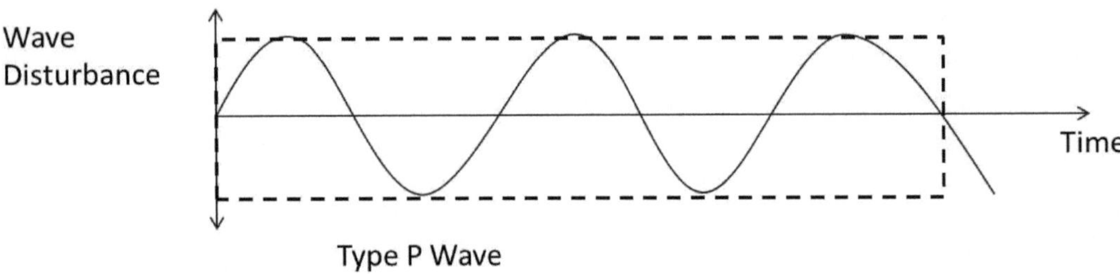

Type P Wave

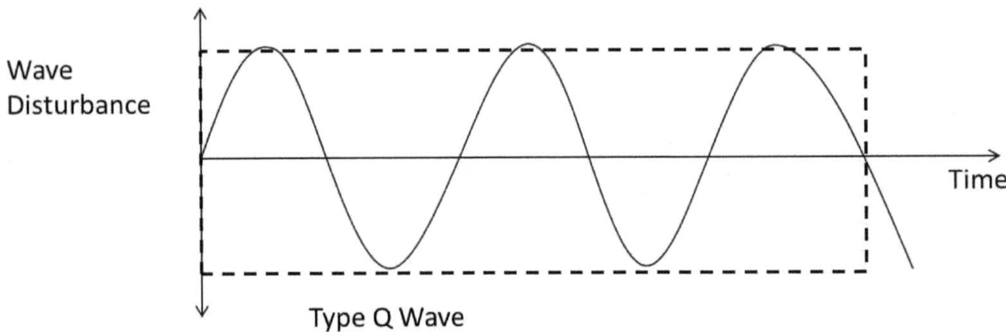

Type Q Wave

Type P = __________________; Type Q = __________________________;

5: A person while standing in front of a cliff has made a louder sound and recognised the echo after an interval of 1.5 second. Find the distance of that cliff from the person if speed of sound in air is estimated as 340 ms $^{-1}$.

6: ________________ waves are associated with moving electrons, protons, neutrons and other fundamental particles and even atoms and molecules as a whole.

7: Which of the following statement related to SONAR is not correct?

a) Sonar is a device that uses ultrasonic waves to measure the distance, direction, and speed of objects located under water.

b) In a megaphone, a tube followed by a conical opening reflects sound successively for the purpose of guiding most of the sound waves from the source in the forward direction towards the audience.

c) Ultrasonics are also used to certain extent to detect earthquakes.

d) Like property of light, sound waves also obey laws of reflection.

8: Observe the vibrations created by Tuning Forks.

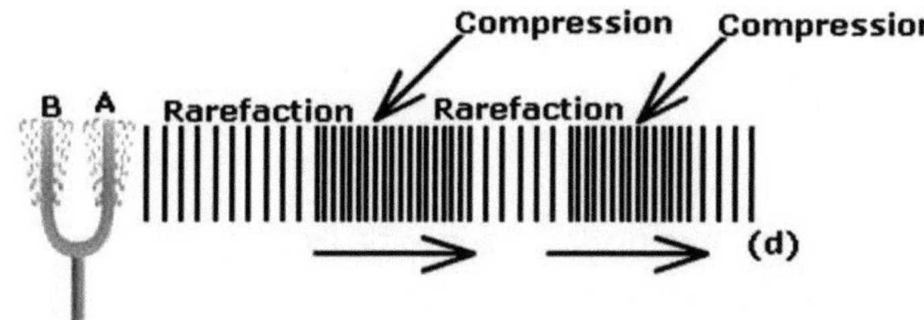

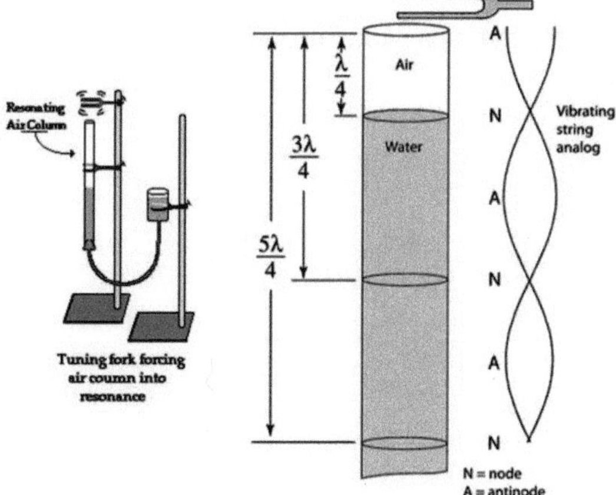

When the tuning fork is hit with a rubber hammer, the tines begin to vibrate. The back and forth vibration of the tines produce disturbances of surrounding air molecules. Since the vibration of air molecules is solely due to vibration of nearby tine of tuning fork.

_________________ of tines of tuning fork and vibrating air column are similar.

9: Solve the following:

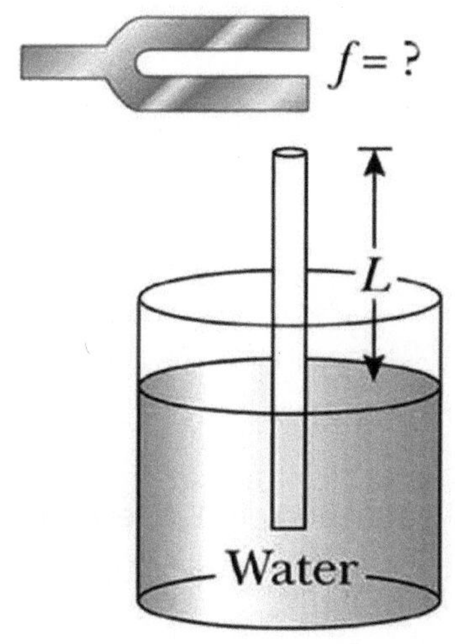

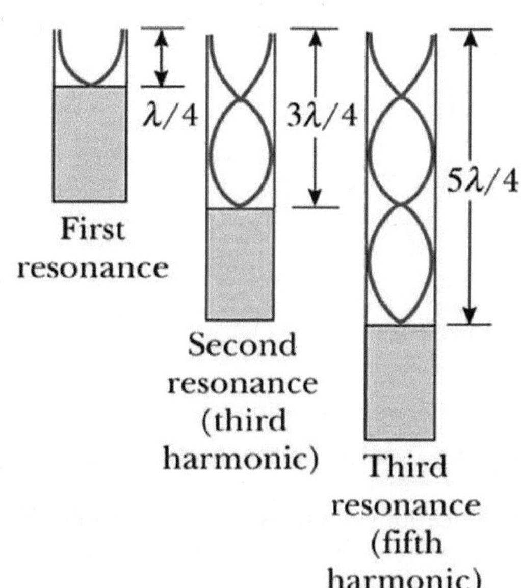

All the harmonics obtained due to vibrations of Tuning Fork and air column above water are in the pattern of [nλ + λ/4]; here n stands for any natural number;

Value f this wave during 7th harmonic will be ___________;

Solution :

1: wave; 2: mechanical; 3: Light or electromagnetic; 6: Matter/ Mechanical; 7: c; 8: Frequency; 9: n = 3;

Worksheet 7

1: Verify the pattern of harmonics ...

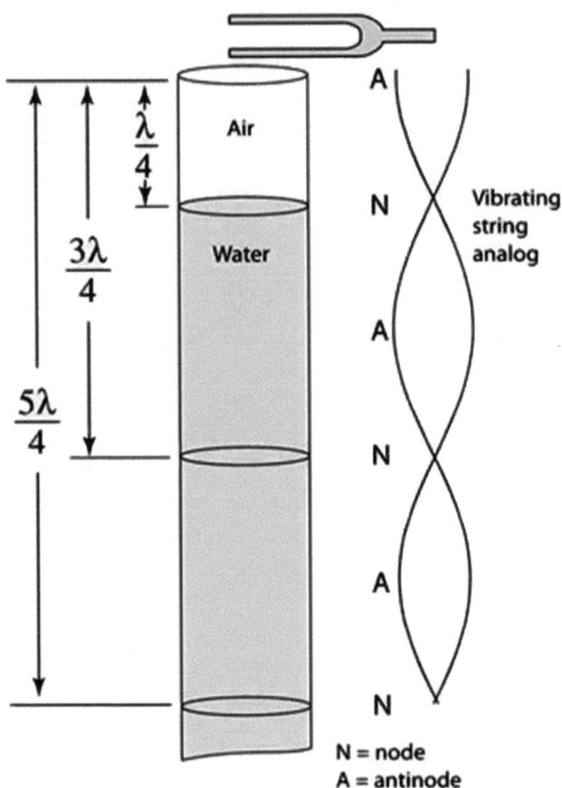

Nodes and Antinodes are created when air column above the water present in a test tube vibrates.
Antinodes are created in the pattern of 1, 2, 3, ,,,,,,, as per the sequence of first, second, third ,, harmonics.
The number of Antinodes created if the fifth harmonic is produced due to vibration of tuning fork will be _____.

2: It is observed that the interval between sending and receiving signal of wave in water body is 1.4 second. If speed of sound in water is 1428 ms^{-1}, calculate the depth of sea at that position. [Ans: 510 m]

3: We are aware of different applications of ultrasound in our daily life.

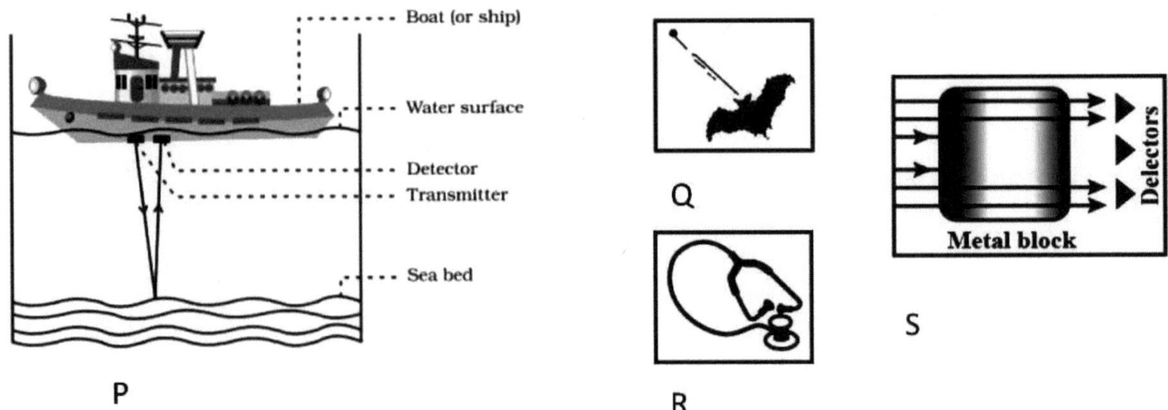

Any one of the above mentioned activity is not an activity of ultrasound. Identify that activity.

Worksheet 8

I: Sound is a kind of energy and requires a material medium to propagate. Go through the factors responsible for regulating intensity of sound:

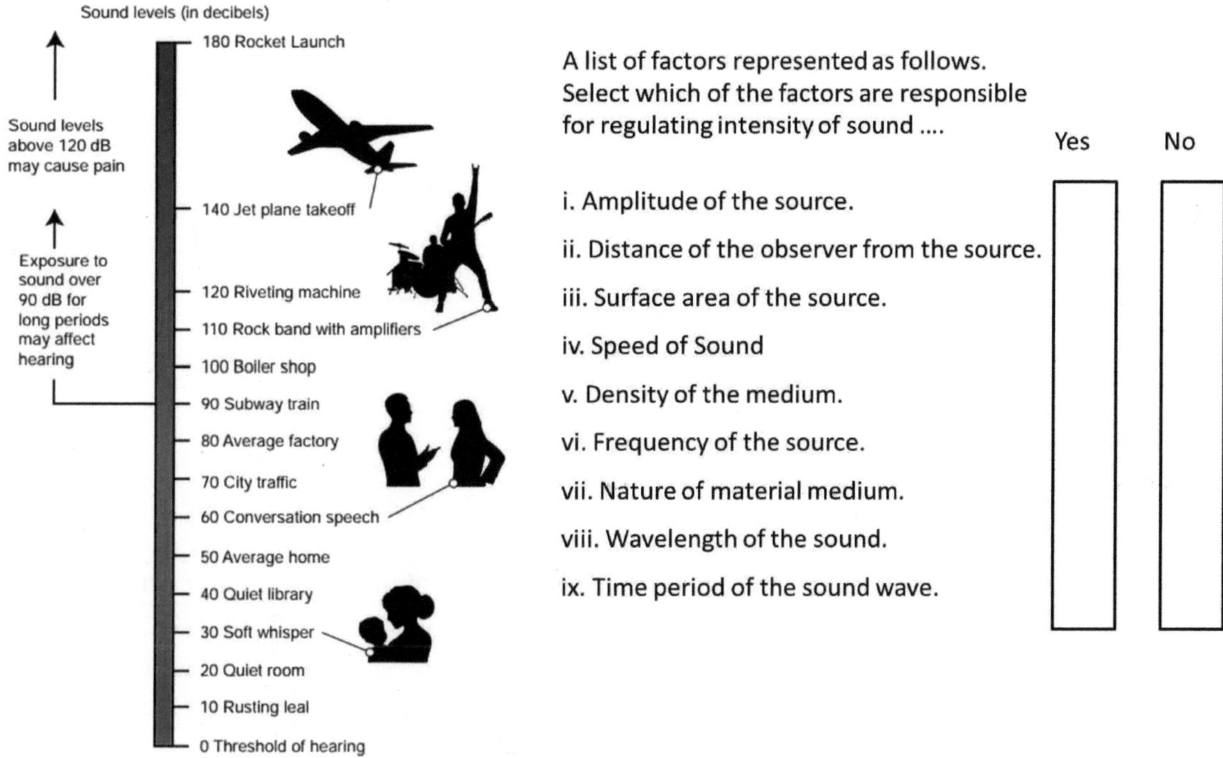

A list of factors represented as follows. Select which of the factors are responsible for regulating intensity of sound ....

Yes No

i. Amplitude of the source.

ii. Distance of the observer from the source.

iii. Surface area of the source.

iv. Speed of Sound

v. Density of the medium.

vi. Frequency of the source.

vii. Nature of material medium.

viii. Wavelength of the sound.

ix. Time period of the sound wave.

II:

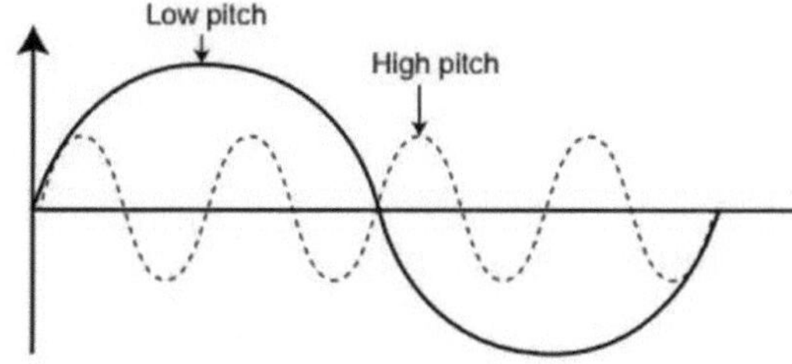

Pitch is the characteristics of sound by which we can distinguish whether a sound is shrill or base.

Statements:

A: High pitch sound is shrill and low pitch sound is flat.

B: Two music sounds produced by the same instrument with same amplitude, will differ when their vibrations are of different frequencies.

C: It characterises shrillness of sound as hoigh pitched sound is shrill.

D: Pitch is not depending upon speed of sound or nature of material medium.

E: Frequency varies inversely with Pitch of sound.

III: A hiker produced sound towards a 465 m distant cliff. wavelength of that sound is 0.750 m. The echo is heard after 2.75 s. What is the time period of that sound wave?

[Frequency = Speed of Sound/ Wavelength; Time Period = 1/ Frequency;]

IV: Identify following waves as Longitudinal and Transverse Waves.

	Longitudinal	Transverse
1: Radio Waves		
2: Ultrasonics		
3: Surface Water waves		
4: Sound of a drum		
5: Rock music		

V: Factors influencing speed of sound in a material medium are of definite types. Select right types of such factors ---

Factors regulating Speed of Sound	in air	in solid
1: Pressure of medium		
2: Temperature of medium		
3: Density of medium		
4: Nature of medium		
5: Elastic Property of medium		

VI: The ____________ of sound in wood is much larger as compared to that in metals.

VII: The voice of ladies and children is of higher ________ than that of men.

VIII: The sound is reflected and refracted according to the same laws as the ___________ does.

IX: The wavelength for ________ is very small, therefore they are not diffracted by the ordinary objects or holes etc.

Solution: I: Yes: other options ; No: iv, vi, viii, ix; II: Option E is not correct; III: III = 2.22 X 10 -3 s ; IV: Longitudinal Wave= Ultrasonics[7]; V: damping; VI: pitch; VII: light; VIII: ultrasonics;

[7] *Ultrasonic waves are longitudinal waves of frequency greater than 20,000 Hz. This implies that a human being cannot hear beyond 20,000 Hz, i.e. the maximum frequency of audible sound is 20,000 Hz.*

Worksheet 9

A: Aman pronounces a, b , c, d and e and heard the echoes of last four syllables pronounced by him . Time taken by him to produce and listen one syllable is 1/5th of a second. Sped of sound in air is 340 ms^{-1}. Calculate the distance of reflecting surface from Aman.

Aid Box:
The man cannot hear the syllable a as at the instant when echo of syllable a is about to reach to the man, he pronounces e. Thus the time taken by man to pronounce all syllables is equal to the time taken by the sound to reach back to the man.

B: Waves produced on the surface is 20 cm. Velocity of wave is 24 ms^{-1}. Calculate the time in which ten successive waves are produced.

C: Key of a mechanical piano struck gently during first time and then struck again but much harder during second time. During the second case ....

(a) sound will be louder but pitch will not be differ.

(b) sound will be louder and pitch will also be higher;

(c) sound will be louder but pitch will be lower;

(d) both loudness and pitch will remain unaffected;

(e) Loudness and pitch cannot be compared in this regard.

D: Select the desired condition depending upon which sound travels in air. Sound travel in air if,

(a) particles of medium travel from one place to another independently.

(b) there is no moisture in the atmosphere.

(c) disturbance of particles resent in air column moves.

(d) both particles as well as disturbance travel from one place to another.

E: A sound wave has a frequency of 2 kHz and wavelength of 15 cm. How much time will it take to travel 1.5 km?

F: What is the wavelength of a sound wave in air at 20° C with a frequency of 22 MHz? [Speed of sound in air at 20^{0}C is 344 ms^{-1}; 1 MHz = 10^{6} Hz;]

A = 136 m; B = 83.3×10^{-3} seconds; C = a; D = c; E = 5 s; F: $\lambda = 15.64 \times 10-6$ m or 15.64 μm.

Worksheet 10

1: A stone dropped from the top of a tower of height 300 m high splashes into the water of a pond near the base of the tower. When is the splash heard at the top given that the speed of sound in air is 340 ms-1? (g = 9.8 ms-2)

2: A steel wire has a length of 12.0 m and a mass of 2.10 kg. What should be the tension in the wire so that speed of a transverse wave on the wire equals the speed of sound in dry air at 2 0°C = 340 ms^{-1}.

3: A bat emits ultrasonic sound of frequency 1000 kHz in air. If this sound meets a water surface, what is the wavelength of (a) the reflected sound, (b) the transmitted sound? Speed of sound in air = 340 ms^{-1} and in water = 1486 ms^{-1}.

4: A hospital uses an ultrasonic scanner to locate tumours in a tissue. What is the wavelength of sound in a tissue in which the speed of sound is 1.7 km s^{-1}? The operating frequency of the scanner is 4.2 MHz.

5: Two sitar strings A and B playing the note (number of beats become 3) are slightly out of tune and produce beats of frequency 6Hz. The tension in the string A is slightly reduced and the beat frequency is found to reduce to 3Hz. If the original frequency of A is 324 Hz, what is the frequency of B?

6: Explain with reason –

(a) In a sound wave, a displacement node is a pressure antinode and vice versa.

(b) Bats can ascertain distances, directions, nature and sizes of the obstacles without any “eyes”.

(c) A violin note and sitar note may have the same frequency, yet we can distinguish between the two notes.

(d) Solids can support both longitudinal and transverse waves, but only longitudinal waves can propagate in gases, and

(e) The shape of a pulse gets distorted during propagation in a dispersive medium.

7: A train, standing at the outer signal of a railway station blows a whistle of frequency 400 Hz in still air. (i) What is the frequency of the whistle for a platform observer when the train (a) approaches the platform with a speed of 10 ms^{-1}? (b) Recedes from the platform with a speed of 10 ms^{-1} (ii) what is the speed of sound in each case? The speed of sound in still air can be taken as 340 ms^{-1} .

8: A train, standing in a station-yard, blows a whistle of frequency 400 Hz in still air. The wind starts blowing in the direction from the yard to the station with a speed of 10 ms-1. What are the frequency, wavelength, and speed of sound for an observer standing on the station’s platform? Is the situation exactly identical to the case when the air is still and the observer runs towards the yard at a speed of 10 ms^{-1}? The speed of sound in still air can be taken as 340 ms^{-1}?

Ans:

1: 8.7 second; 2: 10^4 N; 3: a= 3.4×10^{-4} m; b = 1.486×10^{-3} m; 4: 4.1×10^{-4} m; 5: 318 Hz;

Explanation: Let υ1 and υ2 be the frequencies of strings A and B respectively.

Then, υ1 = 324 Hz, υ2 =? Number of beats, b = 6

υ2 = υ1 ± b = 324 ± 6! e., υ2 = 330 Hz or 318 Hz

Since the frequency is directly proportional to square root of tension, on decreasing the tension in the string A, its frequency υ1 will be reduced i.e., number of beats will increase if υ2 = 330 Hz. This is not so because number of beats become 3.

Therefore, frequency υ2 = 318 Hz. because on reducing the tension in the string A, its frequency may be reduced to 321 Hz, thereby giving 3 beats with υ2 = 318 Hz.

6: (a) In a sound wave, a decrease in displacement i.e., displacement node causes an increase in the pressure there i.e., a pressure antinode is formed. Also, an increase in displacement is observed due to the corresponding decrease in pressure.

(b) Bats emit ultrasonic waves of high frequency from their mouths. These waves after being reflected back from the obstacles on their path are observed by the bats. These waves give them an idea of distance, direction, nature and size of the obstacles.

(c) The quality of a violin note is different from the quality of sitar. Therefore, they emit different harmonics which can be observed by human ear and used to differentiate between the two notes.

(d) This is due to the fact that gases have only the bulk modulus of elasticity whereas solids have both, the shear modulus as well as the bulk modulus of elasticity.

(e) A pulse of sound consists of a combination of waves of different wavelength. In a dispersive medium, these waves travel with different velocities giving rise to the distortion in the wave.

7: 412 Hz; 389 Hz;

[Hints: (a) Frequency = [340/ (340-10)] X400 Hz = 412 Hz; (b) [340/ (340+10)] X400 Hz = 389 Hz;]

8: Frequency = 400 Hz; Wavelength = 0.875 m;

Worksheet 11

1: Information sheet related to ECG is represented below:

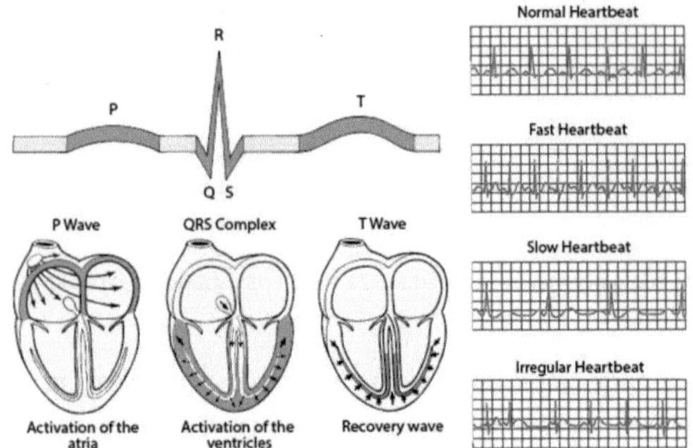

An electrocardiogram (ECG) represents the electrical current moving through the heart during a heartbeat. The current's movement is divided into parts, and each part is given an alphabetic designation in the ECG.

Many kinds of abnormalities can often be seen on an ECG. They include a previous heart attack (myocardial infarction), an abnormal heart rhythm (arrhythmia), an inadequate supply of blood and oxygen to the heart (ischemia), and excessive thickening (hypertrophy) of the heart's muscular walls.

Each heartbeat begins with an impulse from the heart's pacemaker (sinus or sinoatrial node). This impulse activates the upper chambers of the heart (atria). The P wave represents activation of the atria.

Next, the electrical current flows down to the lower chambers of the heart (ventricles). The QRS complex represents activation of the ventricles.

The electrical current then spreads back over the ventricles in the opposite direction. This activity is called the recovery wave, which is represented by the T wave.

Which of the following statement related to ECG is not correct?

I. Many kinds of abnormalities can often be seen on an ECG. They include a previous heart attack (myocardial infarction), an abnormal heart rhythm (arrhythmia), an inadequate supply of blood and oxygen to the heart (ischemia), and excessive thickening (hypertrophy) of the heart's muscular walls.

II. Certain abnormalities seen on an ECG can also suggest bulges (aneurysms) that develop in weak areas of the heart's walls.

III. Aneurysms may result from a heart attack.

IV. If the rhythm is abnormal (too fast, too slow, or irregular), the ECG may also indicate where in the heart the abnormal rhythm starts.

V. Abnormal report related to ECG and other related information helps doctors to determine the cause of a disease and to find out the most appropriate treatment.

Which of the above mentioned statement is not correct?

A: Only I; B: I, II, III and V; C: Only V; D: All are correct;

2: We know that ________________ waves require vibration of particles in direction of wave motion. These waves can be produced on a spring. Now, if the string is elastic, such waves can be produced as particles can vibrate along the length of the string.

3: Loudness of sound is regulated by its __________________.

4: Which of the following statement is not correct?

a) Sonar[8] is a device that uses ultrasonic waves to measure the distance, direction, and speed of underwater objects.

b) In a megaphone, a tube followed by a conical opening reflects sound successively to guide most of the sound waves from the source in the forward direction towards the audience.

c) Ultrasonic sound is not used to detect earthquakes.

d) Like light, sound waves also obey laws of reflection. System of reflection in both the case is different as sound wave is not an electromagnetic wave as like that of light wave.

5: Answer the following:

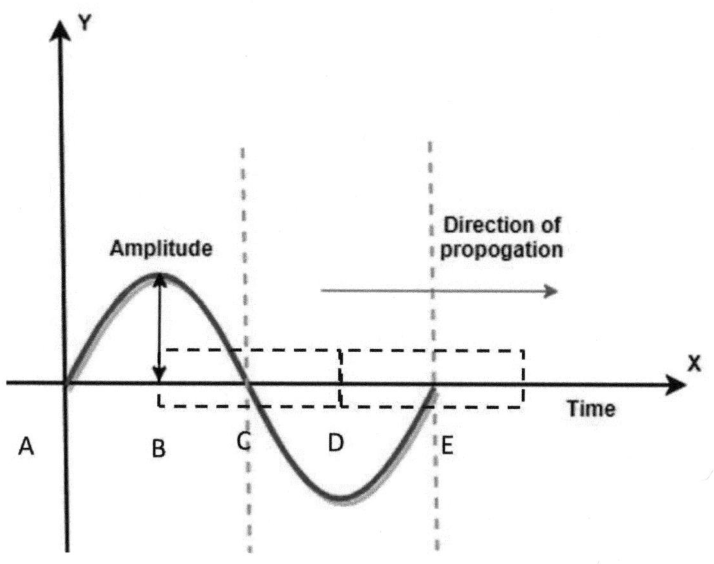

Half of the wavelength in the given sound wave is :

I: AB
II: BC
III: BD
IV: DE
V: BD
VI: CD

Select the correct option.

Solution: 1: D; 2: longitudinal; 3: Amplitude[9]; 4: d; 5: Option V;

---

[8] *Infrasound, sometimes referred to as low status or inaudible sound, describes sound waves having frequency below the lower limit of human audibility. Hearing becomes gradually less sensitive as frequency of sound wave decreases. So for humans to perceive infrasound, the sound pressure must be recognisable and sufficiently high.*
Ultrasound is sound waves with frequencies higher than the upper audible limit specified for of human hearing. Ultrasound is not different from "normal" (audible) sound in its physical properties, except that humans cannot hear it. This limit varies from person to person and is approximately 20 kilohertz in healthy young.
During the 1930s American engineers developed their own underwater sound-detection technology, and important discoveries were made, such as the existence of thermoclines and their effects on sound waves.
Americans began to use the term SONAR for their systems, coined by Frederick Hunt to be the equivalent of RADAR.
[Howeth: Chapter XXXIX. Washington. 1963
"AIP Oral History: Frederick Vinton Hunt, Part II". 23 February 2015.]

[9] *The loudness or softness of a sound is determined basically by its amplitude. A sound wave spreads out from its source. As it moves away from the source its amplitude as well as its loudness decreases.*
The loudness of sound decreases with an:
(1) Increase in the distance between the ear and the source
(2) Decrease in the amplitude of the vibrating body.

3. Ecology and Environment

The place where organisms live makes a habitat. Collection of such habitats, along with the interaction of organisms, forms an ecosystem. Whatever we see around us makes our environment. .

Worksheet 1

1: Statements related to Tropospheric Pollution are as follows:

a) Tropospheric pollution is caused by both inorganic and organic gases. Gases like oxides of nitrogen, oxides of sulphure, oxides of carbon, H_2S, HCN, HCl etc. constitute inorganic pollutants.

b) Organic pollutants include mercaptants, hydrocarbons, formaldehyde, alcohol, certain organic acids chlorinated hydrocarbon etc.

c) Some of these are released as such in the atmosphere and are known as primary pollutants. Some others are formed in the atmosphere as a result of chemical reactions.

d) CFC is not a primary pollutant.

e) Tropospheric Pollution may result in the depletion of the ozone layer in a long run and become the direct reason of global warming.

f) These are called secondary pollutants. A few examples are : Ozone, chlorofluorocarbons (CFCs), formaldehyde, acrolein, methyl isocyanate etc. Let us briefly study some of the tropospheric pollutants.

Identify if any statement in the given list is wrong.

2: Which of the following statement related to formation of wind is not true?

I. Winds are caused due to unequal heating of atmospheric air.
II. The air above the land gets heated faster and starts rising.
III. As this air rises, a region of low pressure is created and air over the sea moves into this area of low pressure.
IV. The movement of air from one region to the other Creates winds.
V. During the day, the direction of the wind would be from the sea to the land.
VI. During night time, the direction of the wind would be from the hills to the plains.
VII. Land breeze and see breeze are results of difference in the heat of the atmosphere.

3: Different vibrating bodies produce three different types of sound. Sound P is used to detect cracks present in a metal block. Sound Q is used to measure depth of sea bed and sound R is used to measure any disease or lump present in human body. ________________ is a device which can produce these types of sound.

4:

Solution:

1: No; 2: VI; 3: SONAR .

Worksheet 2 [Unsolved]

1: Why do organisms need water?

2: How do clouds is formed?

3: What is the major source of freshwater in the city/town/village where majority of population live?

4: DO you know any activity which may be polluting potable water sources? Make a list of five such sources.

5: Some factors responsible for soil formation are as follows:

(i) The Sun: It causes uneven heating of rocks which causes cracking and ultimately breaking up rock particles into smaller pieces. [Weathering Process]

(ii) Water: It breaks rocks both by freezing and under the influence rapid flow. [Weathering and Transport]

(iii) Wind: It causes erosion of rocks by making them divided into smaller particles. It also carries sand from one place to the other under the influence of violent wind. [Denudation and transportation]

(iv) Living organisms: Organisms like Lichens and moss plants grow on the rock surface and cause rock surface to break down into fine particles and form a thin layer of soil. The roots of big woody trees sometimes go on developing into cracks in the rocks. As the roots grow bigger, the crack is forced to enlarge enabling formation of cracks and furrow of varying types.

Statements:

A: All the factors mentioned above act differently upon the top layer of earth and in this way they take part differently in the formation of soil.

B: Soil formation process mechanism never depends entirely on sun, wind or water. There are some chemical changes which often make the process accomplishable.

C: Soil formation is not a chemical process. It is entirely a physical process and caused by physical agents such as heat, water and wind.

D: Soil formation is also accomplished under the influence of microorganisms and other living beings.

Which of the statement regarding the process of soil formation is not acceptable?

6: The removal of humus rich and fertile topsoil by flowing water or wind is known as soil erosion. If this process continues for a prolonged time period then all soil may get washed away and the rocks underneath may get exposed to other weathering agents. It may lead to the loss of all valuable resources. Crop fields may lose productivity. It may also disturb the normal confluence of the natural drainage system (such as river system). Prevention of soil erosion is also important for retention of soil fertility and other related activities.

Suggest at least three ways to prevent soil erosion.

7: What are the different states in which water is found during the entire process of water cycle?

8: ____________ and ____________ are two biologically important compounds that contain both oxygen and nitrogen.

Worksheet 3 [Unsolved]

1. List any three human activities which would lead to an increase in the carbon dioxide content of air.
2. What are the two different forms of oxygen found in the atmosphere?
3. Why is the atmosphere essential for continuation of life on the earth?
4. Statement related to role of water in our daily life :

   (i) All cellular and bio molecular processes take place in water medium.

   (ii) All the reactions that take place within our body and within the cells occur between substances that are soluble or remain as suspended particle in water.

   (iii) Substances are also transported from one part of the body to the other in a dissolved form or in a micro level particulate form (oil droplets).

   (iv) Water makes up about maximum amount (nearly 70%) of body-weight of living organisms.

   (v) It helps in the digestion of food and absorption of nutrients in body fluid. Hence, organisms need to maintain the level of water within their bodies in order to stay active as well as alive.

   (vi) It helps in maintaining body temperature of the organism [thermoregulation].

   (vii) Virus particles also contain water and make the virus particle differently active.

   Find out the statement which is not relevant.
5. Living organisms depend totally or entirely on soil. Some statements related to dependency of organisms on soil are mentioned below:

   (i) Soil provides a natural habitat for various different organisms (such as bacteria, fungi, algae) which help in improving the quality of the soil. Thus, they maintain the fertility of the soil.

   (it) Number of insects, animals like rats, rabbits, etc., build their home in the soil.

   (iii) Earthworms perform all their activities in the soil. They maintain fertility also as their excreta is rich in nitrogen.

   (iv) Soil provides anchorage to roots and provides strength to the shoot and nutrients to the plants for their growth and development.
6. Soaps containing sodium salts are formed by heating fat with aqueous sodium hydroxide solution. This process is called ______________________.
7. Tincture of Iodine is a powerful _________________.
8. Chlorine in the concentration of 0.2 to 0.4 p.p.m. in aqueous solution can be considered as ________.
9. Boric acid in dilute aqueous solution is a weak antiseptic for _______________.
10. _________________ acts as a sink for CO.

Worksheet 4

1. Diagram of water cycle is represented below along with some supporting sentences. Find out the wrong statements.

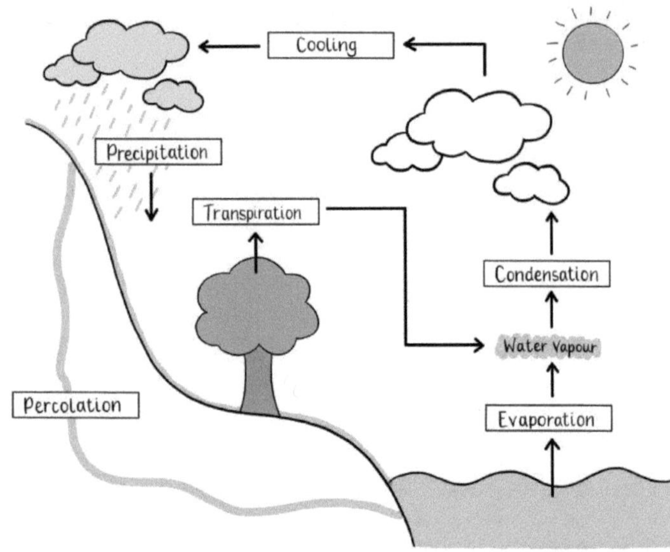

Statement:

A: This diagram is representing a Water Cycle.

B: Metabolism of Sugar and Fat is concerned with this cycle.

C: Protein metabolism is not the concern of Carbon Cycle.

D: Condensation and evaporation are two physical processes just opposite to each other.

E: Transpiration is also a process which can be included in this process of water cycle.

2. Statements related to Carbon Cycle are as follows.

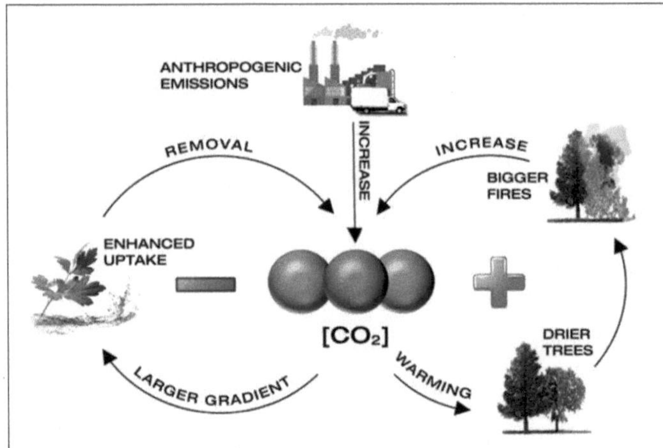

a) Carbon Cycle is centrally regulated by CO_2.
b) Major contribution of CO_2 in atmosphere is made by human activities, like large factories, deforestation and open fumigation of fire wood.
c) Deforestation implies an indirect stress upon the environment by curtailing the share of oxygen to atmosphere by plants which were previously alive.
d) Development fully functional large canopy is a time taking process. That is why recharging of oxygen to atmosphere by the process of afforestation will also take time.
e) Global warming is also a negative factor which hampers the balance of O_2 and CO_2 in atmosphere.
f) We cannot curtail use of fossil fuel as most of the human activities depend upon that source and renewable sources are still under-explored.

Find out points which you feel unfit in terms of the process of carbon cycle.

3. "Carbon cycle and oxygen cycle in atmosphere are inter-related. One cycle influences the other." If this statement is wrong then make needful corrections and write the correct statement.

4. A stone is dropped in a pond from a tower of height h. If the speed of sound in air is v then calculate the total time after which the sound of splash can be heard at the top of tower.

5. An underwater SONAR device operating at 68 KHz produced a beam of ultrasonic directed upwards. Speed of sound in air is 330 ms^{-1}. Find the frequency and wavelength of that sound produced by SONAR. [Frequency = 68 KHz; Wavelength = 5 mm]

Worksheet 5

1. Which one of the following statements is not true?

    a. Clean water would have a BOD value of 5 ppm.

    b. Fluoride deficiency in drinking water is harmful. Soluble fluoride is often used to bring its concentration upto 1 ppm.

    c. When the pH of rain water is higher than 6.5, it is called acid rain.

    d. Dissolved Oxygen (DO) in cold water can reach a concentration upto 10 ppm.

2. Which of the following statement related to green chemistry is not true?

    a. Green chemistry is the design, development, and implementation of chemical products.

    b. It concerned with processes to reduce or eliminate the use and generation of substances hazardous to human health and the environment.

    c. It refers to the redesign of chemical products and processes with the goal of reducing or eliminating any negative environmental or health effects.

    d. It is also concerned with the types of reactions which are related to the depletion of ozone layer.

3. About 20 km above the earth, there is an ozone layer. Which one of the following statements about ozone and ozone layer is true?

    a. It is beneficial to us as it stops U.V. radiation.

    b. Conversion of O3 to O2 is an endothermic reaction.

    c. Ozone is a triatomic linear molecule.

    d. It is harmful as it stops useful radiation.

4. Among the following, the one that is not a greenhouse gas is

    (a) sulphur dioxide (b) nitrous oxide (c) methane (d) ozone.

5. Which of the following are depleting ozone layer?

    (a) CFC (b) Oxides of Carbon (c) Hydrofluorocarbon (d) Both a and c.

6. "Anaerobic decomposition of organic material in flooded rice fields produces _______________. Paddy fields account for around 20% of human-related emissions of this pollutant which escapes into the atmosphere and contributes to the family of potent greenhouse gas." Complete the statement.

7. ____________water is commonly used across manufacturing and within industry when the highest quality of water is required.

8. ____________ water is water free from impurities through _______________ process. This process involves boiling the water and then condensing the steam into a clean container.

9. "The presence of coliform bacteria, such as _________, in surface water, is a common indicator of faecal contamination. The number of coliform bacteria in water samples can be determined by the "most probable number method". It is a type of test which assumes cultivable bacteria meet certain growth and biochemical criteria depending upon which their population increases. If tests suggest that coliform bacteria are present in numbers in excess of the Coliform Index, then faecal contamination is suspected." Complete this statement and give example of some of such bacteria.

10. The reason which ensures the dark colour of top layer water of any aquatic medium is due any one or all of the following reasons:

    a. It is due to the presence of huge amount of organic matter.

    b. Organic matter is composed of roots, dead leaves, insects, small organisms and animals which eventually get degraded to form humus [a dark coloured organic matter].

    c. It is due to contamination of water with unused fossil fuel and other organic pollutants.

    d. Humus is black in colour due to presence of large quantity of carbon in it.

11. About 20 km above the earth, there is an ozone layer. Which one of the following statements about ozone and ozone layer is true?

    (a) It is beneficial to us as it stops U.V. radiation.

    (b) Conversion of O_3 to O_2 is an endothermic reaction.

    (c) Ozone is a triatomic linear molecule.

    (d) It is harmful as it stops useful radiation.

12. Which of the following is not correct about carbon monoxide?

    (a) It forms carboxyhaemoglobin.

    (b) It reduces oxygen carrying ability of blood.

    (c) The carboxyhaemoglobin (haemoglobin bound to CO) is less stable than oxyhaemoglobin.

    (d) It is produced due to incomplete combustion.

13: Select correct alternative ---

Assertion: To hear distinct beats, the difference in frequencies of sound producing devices should be 10 Hz.

Reason: Persistence of hearing of human beings is 0.1 second. So sound produced having frequencies more than 10 Hz cannot be recognised by the human brain.

Option:

A: Both Assertion and Reason are correct and Reason is the correct explanation of Assertion.

B: Assertion is correct but reason is wrong.

C: Assertion is wrong but reason is correct.

D: Both Assertion and Reason are correct but Reason is not the correct explanation of Assertion.

4. Health and Medication

This section deals with common diseases people face and related measures one should take for getting rid of from such anomalies. As per the structure of the NEET Syllabus we can cover up some more relevant points.

The disease may be acute type or it may be of chronic type.[10]

Activity 1

On the basis of the description and other features displayed about acute and chronic disease find the acute and chronic diseases from the list duly provided.

Acute diseases	Chronic diseases
Acute diseases are diseases that last for a short span of time.	Chronic diseases are those that last for a long period of time.
Acute disease does not cause a major effect on general health. Example: cough, dysentery, etc.	Chronic diseases cause a major effect on general health. Example: elephantiasis, tuberculosis, etc.

	Acute Disease	Chronic Disease
Malaria	☐	☐
Tuberculosis	☐	☐
Filaria	☐	☐
Plague	☐	☐

2: __________ depends on three parameters - physical, mental, and social well-being.

According to WHO, it is a state of complete physical, mental, and social well-being and not merely the absence of disease or infirmity"

[10] Acute disease last for a short period of time. Common cold, viral fever and malaria are of such type.
Chronic diseases last for long time period. Tuberculosis, Cancer, Filaria are of such types of diesases. Treatment of chronic diseases last for a long time period. These diseases even put patrients in extreme type of health problem.

Activity 2

A. Many microbial agents can commonly move from an affected person to someone else in a variety of ways. Such disease-causing microbes can spread through the air.

B. This occurs through the little droplets thrown out by an infected person who sneezes or coughs. Someone standing close by can breathe in these droplets, and the microbes get a chance to start a new infection.

C. Examples of some diseases spread through the air are the common cold, pneumonia and tuberculosis.

D. The more crowded our living conditions are, the more likely it is that such airborne diseases will spread.

E. T.B. can be considered as communicable disease as it sreads from person to person by air.

F. Cancer is non-communicable, AIDS spreads via body fluids, and cholera spreads through infected water.

1. Trace out if the above mentioned chard is containing any wrong statement.
2. Make a list of three water borne diseases.
3. High blood pressure, genetic abnormalities and blood cancer all are _______________ disorder, so this disease cannot be transmitted from one person to another.
4. The diagram given below is popularly known as ________________________ Triangle. This diagram reflects inter-relationship of host, agent and environment.

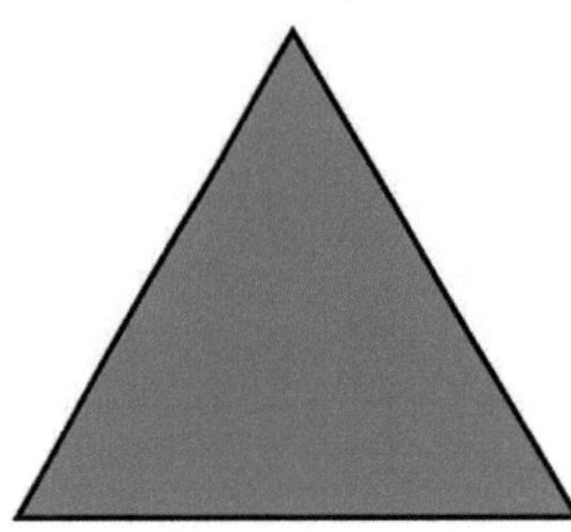

5. Public health surveillance involves which of the following activities?

   A. Serving as a late warning system for public health concerns

   B. Documentation of the impact of an intervention

   C. Marketing efforts to highlight progress toward specific goals

   D. Monitoring and clarifying the pathogenicity of health problems

Activity 3

1: Complete the following ---

Modes of transmission of some category of diseases are as per the following. Complete this table by providing some examples of such categoriesed diseases.

Mode of Transmission	Example
1. Airborne transmission	
2. Fecal-oral transmission	
3. Direct contact transmission	
4. Sexual contact transmission (this is a special instance of direct contact transmission)	
5. Direct inoculation transmission • Blood transfusion of contaminated blood • Use or accidental puncture by contaminated needles • Splash of contaminated body fluids on mucous membrane or a break in the skin	
6. Transplacental (vertical) Mother to fetus	
7. Animal or insect bite transmission	

2: The constant presence of a disease or infectious agent within a given geographic area or population group is referred to as:

A. Epidemic B. Pandemic C. Endemic D. Contagion

3: Which statement below best describes passive surveillance?

A. Passive surveillance is the action of receiving and collecting health data undertaken by public health authorities.

B. Passive surveillance is health departments receiving information regarding legally reportable conditions.

C. Passive surveillance is public health department outreach activities to assimilate health data.

D. Passive surveillance involves field deployment to clinics, hospitals, and clinical laboratories.

4: Which of the following are public health actions and interventions that could be obtained from public health surveillance?

A. Prophylaxis B. Education C. Early identification cation of problems

D. Prevention and control E. Health care cost containment

5: Observe the table given below and answer the questions as follows ---

Mineral	Major Deficiency Disorders
Iodine	Goiter, hypothyroidism, iodine deficiency disorders, increased risk of stillbirth, birth defects infant mortality, cognitive impairment
Calcium	Decreased bone mineralization, Rickets, Osteoporosis
Iron	Iron deficiency anemia, reduced learning and work capacity, maternal and infant mortality, Low birth weight
Zinc	Poor pregnancy outcome, impaired growth (stunting), genetic disorders, decreased resistance to infectious diseases
Fluoride	Increased dental decay, affects bone health
Selenium	Cardiomyopathy, increased cancer and cardiovascular risk

All the deficiency disorders mentioned above cannot be considered as _____________ disease.

6: To determine if an outbreak exists, which of the following factors must be considered?

a) Increased number of cases for a given time, place, and population as reported.

b) More severe disease presentation

c) Usual exposure routes to pathogens

d) Presenting disease is common for a given area (disease that is unusual for a given area)

e) Outbreaks with zoonotic and human component present in it

f) Typical strains or variants of organisms (unusual strains or variants of organisms)

3: The best protection against contracting cholera is: [provide answer in yes or no]

A. Vaccination for cholera— .

B. Avoiding people infected—

C. Avoiding contaminated food and water—

D. Avoiding undercooked food—

4: Cases of Goitre are more common in hilly areas than in coastal areas.

The reason is ____.

Worksheet 4

1: Identify which of the following criteria is a contraindication for administering the diphtheria, tetanus, pertussis (DTaP) vaccine?

A: Temperature of 104°F following previous administration of the DTP or DTaP vaccine

B: Family history of seizures or any other surgical operations.

C: Encephalopathy of unknown etiology within 7 days following previous administration of the DTP or DTaP vaccine

D: Family history of sudden infant death syndrome because of any unknown reason.

E: Family history of an adverse event after DTP or DTaP administration if reported.

F: Immunodeficient family member if any or reports household contact.

2: Which of the following activities/strategies, in accord to your opinion, can be utilized to prevent or minimize widespread influenza infection?

A. Conduct community outreach program

B. Offer flu shot clinics

C. Teach regarding proper hand washing

D. Take antiviral medications as prescribed by the physician

E. All of the above

F. A, B, and C

3: Which of the following criteria must be met for a patient with suspected/confirmed TB to be on home isolation? [More than one options]

❑ Patient can care for himself or herself and not require hospitalization for other medical conditions.

❑ Patient does not live with immunocompromised persons of any type at home.

❑ Patient has someone at home who can take care of him or her with better understanding.

❑ Patient does not live with TST-negative children at any instance.

❑ Environmental assessment finds the home compatible with effective isolation.

❑ Patient concerned does not live in a congregate setting such as shelter, nursing home, or single-room-occupancy hotel.

4: The standard treatment for latent TB infection is to:

A. Give isoniazid daily for 9 months.

B. Give rifampin and isoniazid daily for 18 months.

C. Closely monitor the patient's health status and then give isoniazid only if TB disease develops up to a considerable level.

D. Treat the patient with a regimen of four drugs for 6 months.

E. Treat the patient with a regimen of three drugs for 12 months.

5: Which of the following factors contributed to the spread of the flu in 1918?

a. The lack of a flu vaccine during that time.

b. Failure to close public places and public meetings during the spread of pandemic.

c. Misconceptions about the transmission of the flu as were in practice.

d. Only a and c.

e. All the three factors a, b and c.

6: Symptoms of active TB pulmonary disease are:

A. Cough, fever, night sweats, chest pain—

B. Pain and scheduled mucus secretion from both the lungs. —

C. Orthostatic hypertension, cardiomegaly—

D. Weight loss, dependent edema, coughing—

7: When screening for Tuberculosis (TB), there are several tests commonly utilized. However, a definative diagnosis of TB can only be confirmed by any one of the following:

A. TB blood test

B. Mantoux tuberculin skin test (TST)

C. Chest x-ray

D. AFB Sputum smear

E. Sputum culture

F. A thorough medical history

.8: In accord to your opinion which of the following statements about TB is true?

A. TB is caused by a virus—NO, TB is caused by a bacterium.

B. TB only affects the lungs—NO, TB can affect other parts of the body including the brain, kidneys, or spine .

C. TB can be fatal—YES, if untreated, TB can be fatal.

D. TB is highly contagious—NO, while TB is contagious, it is not easy to catch. It is more likely that you would be infected by TB by being exposed to the bacterium from someone you live with or work closely with.

9. ________________ is the pathogen which causes Cholera.

10: ____________________ diseases like Down 's syndrome are non-curable.

11: Infection caused by any pathogen other than ____________________ cannot be treated successfully by administering antibiotics.

5. Revision Works

Combined questions for practice are included in this section.[11]

Test Paper 1

1: Who among the following are vulnerable to disease?

A: Men working outdoors doing building construction. B: Infants and small children in the community

C: Senior citizens in a high-rise apartment building. D: Recent immigrants living in congregate housing

E: Hospital workers in a community hospital.

2: A particle of mass 2 kg is projected up a rough plane inclined at an angle of 45° to the horizontal. The coefficient of friction between the particle and the plane is 0.15. If the particle travels 5 m up the plane before coming to rest, find the speed with which the particle was projected. [8.32 ms^{-1}]

3: There are three different components of forces identified in a moving block. Force of friction working against the movement is not represented. Which of the components of force is working to bring displacement of the object?

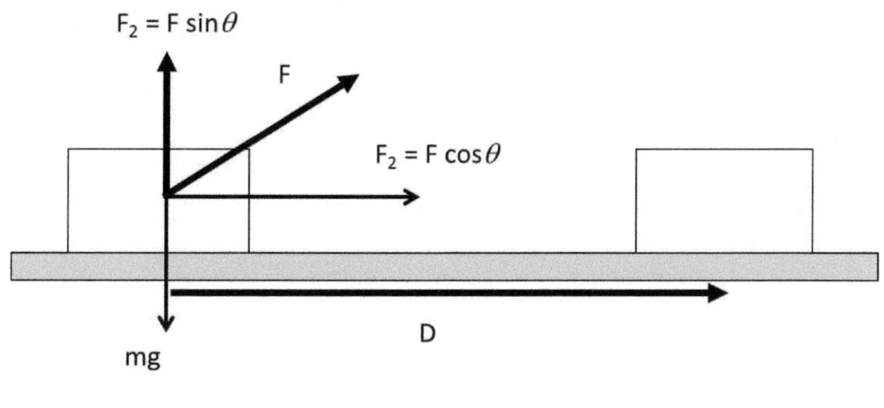

W = D * ___________

4: A mass M dropped from height H. What is speed just before hitting the ground? (Neglect friction of air)

5: Write three applications of Ultra sound in medical science.

6: A person standing in front of a cliff produced a louder sound and heard the echo after an interval of 1.6 seconds. Find the distance of that cliff from the person if speed of sound is 340 ms^{-1}.

7: " __________waves are electromagnetic waves. Such waves are transverse in nature and do not require a medium to travel, hence they can travel in vacuum. __________ waves are longitudinal waves and require a medium to travel. They do not travel in vacuum." Complete this statement.

---

[11] Answer sheets of this obtain can be obtained from the source. Write to us at senjisc@gmail.com for obtaining the same.

Test Paper 2

1: Children more susceptible to lead poisoning because young children:

A. Put things in their mouths

B. Often have diets high in calcium

C. Do not have mature digestive systems

D. Crawl and play on the floors

E. Absorb the lead more easily

F. A, B, D, and E

G. A, D, and E

H. A and E.

2: A particle of mass 5 kg slides down a smooth slope inclined at an angle of 30° to the horizontal. Given that the particle starts from rest, find the distance travelled along the slope when the particle has reached a speed of 4.9 ms^{-1}. [Ans : 2.45 m.]

3: A particle of mass 3 kg is pulled 6 m by a horizontal force of 10 N across a smooth horizontal surface. If the particle started from rest, find its speed when it has travelled 6 m. [Ans: 6.32 ms^{-1}]

4: Complete the following:

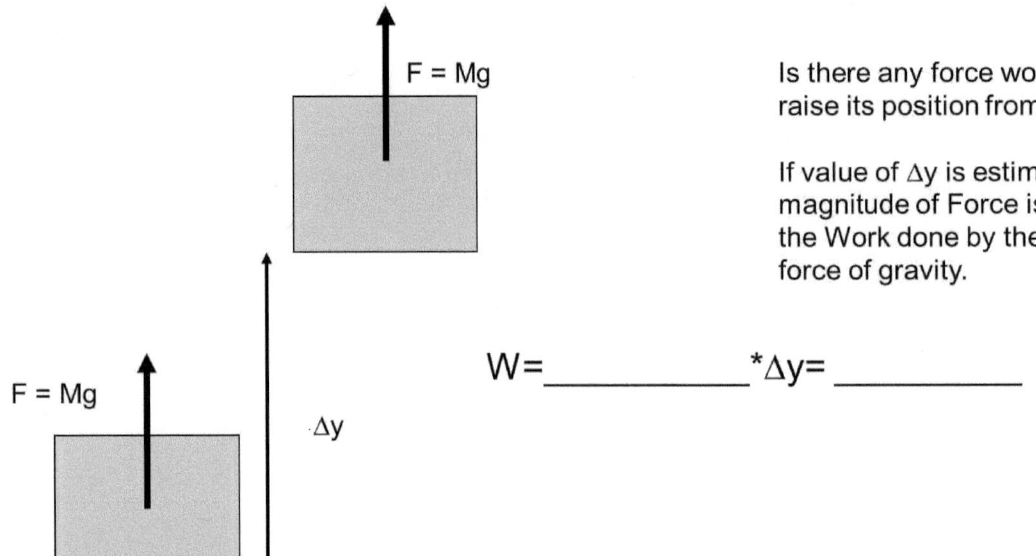

Is there any force working on the object to raise its position from its ground state?

If value of Δy is estimated as 10 m and magnitude of Force is 980 N then calculate the Work done by the force against the force of gravity.

5: A person lifted a load of 40 kg on his head and moved forward a linear distance of 125 m and then unloaded it down. Total amount of work done by that parson against the force of gravity is _________ .

6. Work done by a force:

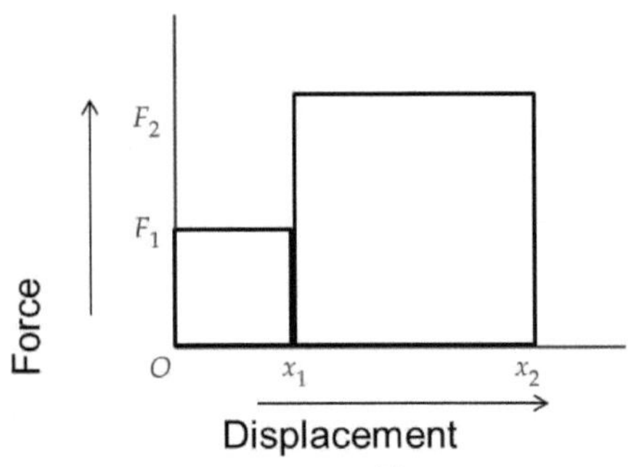

Find out the total work done by combination of forces (F1 and F2) if no other forces are working in this case for bringing changes in position of the moving particle.

7: What types of sound are inaudible? Write ranges of frequency of such inaudible sound waves.

8: A particle of mass 3 kg is moving down a rough slope inclined at an angle of 30° to the horizontal. The particle passes a point *A* at 3 ms^{-1} and a point *B* 2 m down the slope at 4 ms^{-1}. Calculate the work done against friction.

9: Engine of a car exerts a driving force of 1500 N. If the car is travelling at a constant speed of 35 ms^{-1}, calculate the power of the engine.

10: The engine of a car is generating power of 18 kW. Find the driving force produced when the car is travelling at a speed of:

a) 12 ms^{-1} b) 20 ms^{-1} c) 30 ms^{-1} [Hints: Force = Power/ Speed]

11: Solve the following:

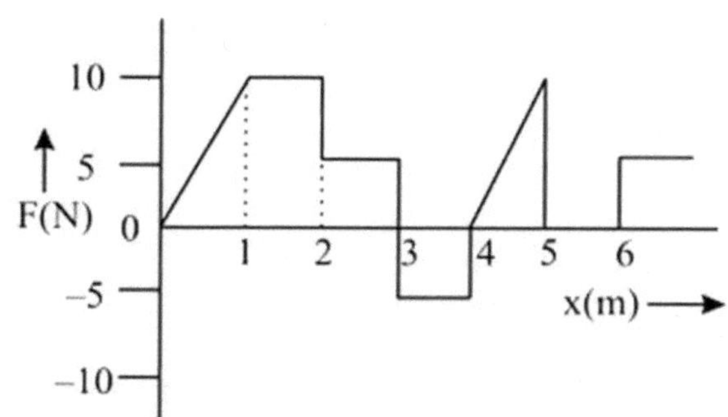

Applied force can bring displacement. It is also observed that work done by a definite force can be calculated as per the displacement acquired by the object. Calculate the total work done by all the forces acting on the object as displayed in the given graph.

12: Compare:

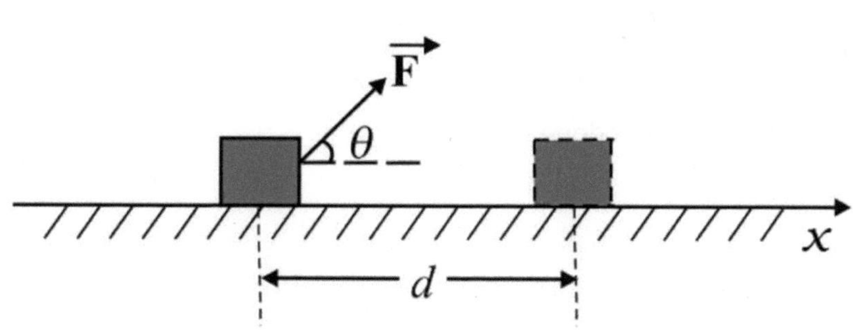

Compare the magnitude of force which will work on the moving block if the intermediate angle with which the force is working varies as follows:

I: 30^0
II: 45^0
III: 60^0
IV: 90^0

13: What determines quality of sound?

14: Write two basic differences between sound and noise.

15: Because of what reason one may not be able to recognise the propagation of ultra sound?

16: Write names of pathogen organisms for the following:

Malaria, Filarial, Cholera, Typhoid, Kala Azar

17: __________ is a type of microscopic pathogen which cannot be cured by administering antibiotics.

18: What will be reading of a spring balance for an object placed on it if a lift starts coming down under the influence of the force of gravity?

Test Paper 3

1: Chronic exposure of a person to benzene can lead to:

A. Cardiac disease and other anomalies related to circulatory system—

B. Chronic obstructive pulmonary disease or problem of trachea—

C. Development and growth of Cancer—

D. Kidney failure—

2: If we throw a ball vertically up then at top most position ______________ energy it will be at its maximum and ___________ energy will become zero.

3: CFC and Methane are considered as _________________ gases as they are also responsible for depletion of ozone layer.

4: Time Period = 1/ __________________.

5: Find the horizontal force that causes a particle of mass 2.5 kg to gain a speed from 2 ms^{-1} to 5 ms^{-1} over a distance of 10 m while moving on a smooth horizontal surface. [Ans: 2.625 N]

6: A __________________ force is a force which causes a particle to lose energy. Applying brake to a moving car is one such example.

7: Observe the force displacement graph and answer the questions.

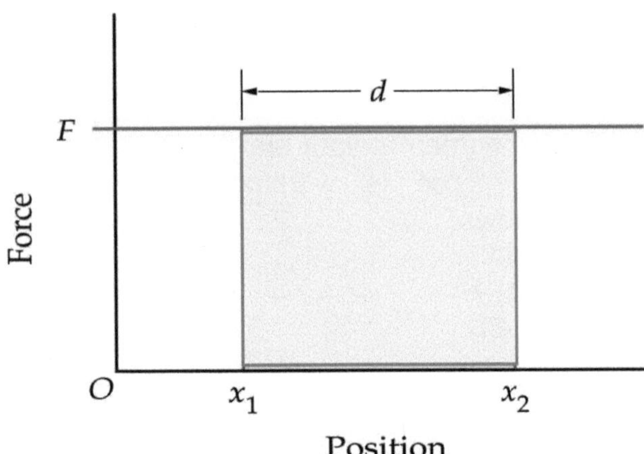

A Force position graph of a moving object is given below.
Work done by the force within the interval of position x1 and x2 can be calculated as

Work done = ________ X ____________;

5: Write the main cause of following diseases:

Scurvy, Beri Beri, Goitre, Fragile bones, Night Blindness

6: Deficiency of this may cause loss of memory and even become responsible for malfunction of nervous system. Identify it.

7: Acromegaly is a kind of ___________________ disease.

8: Almost all genetic disorders are non-curable.

Test Paper 4

1: Answer the following:

Identify if work done by force in the following cases are positive, negative or zero.

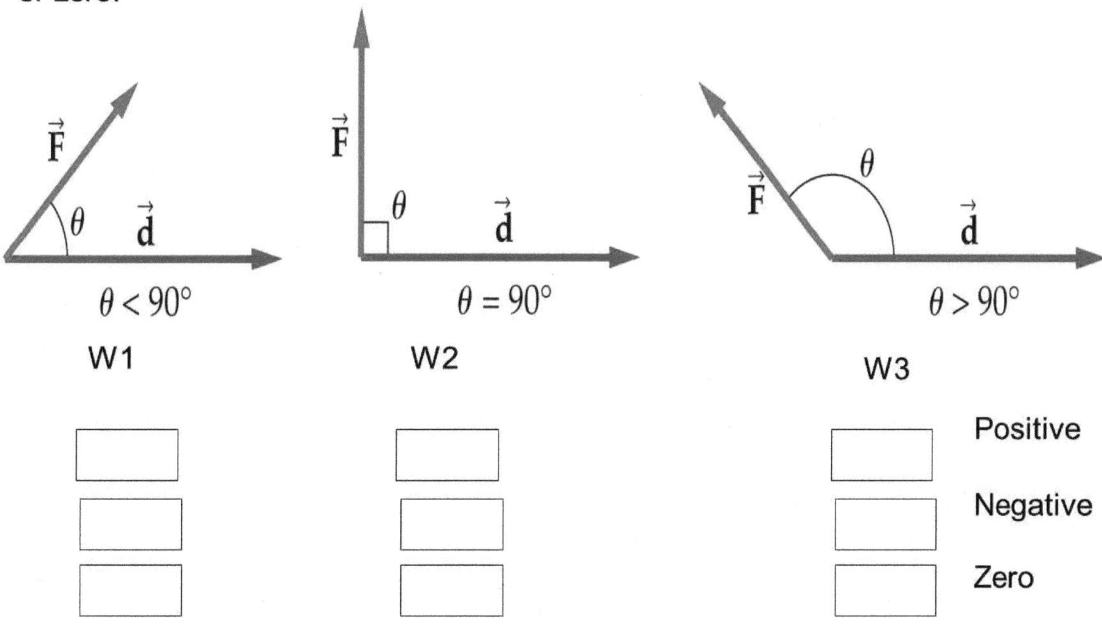

2: Compare ...

An object is thrown with an initial velocity V from point P. It reaches point R and instantly turns back to point P and ultimately stops. Find the relation between the kinetic energy that the object has at point P and energy lost on the way due to friction.

3: Why sound cannot propagate through space having no atmosphere?

4: What will happen to frequency of a sound wave if its time table is doubled?

5: Which force works against the moving car which moves on roads?

6: Cholera, Typhoid, Malaria and Plague are ____________ types of diseases.

7: Force of Friction is a kind of ________________ Force which cannot be retained back.

Test Paper 5

1: Compare:

Three different rectangular plates are hanged as shown in the figure given below from equally labeled horizontal plane. If the masses of these plates are equal, then find the relation between the potential energies of these three plates marked as P, Q and R.

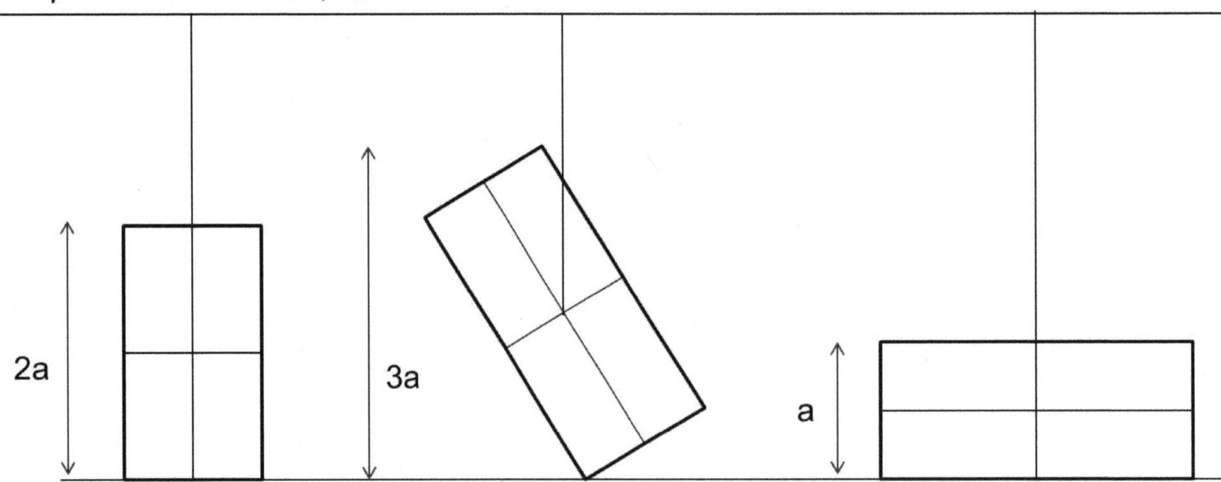

2: A Force – Displacement Graph is displayed as follows. On the basis of this diagram calculate the work done by forces on the object in between instances of x= 0 m to x = 13 m.

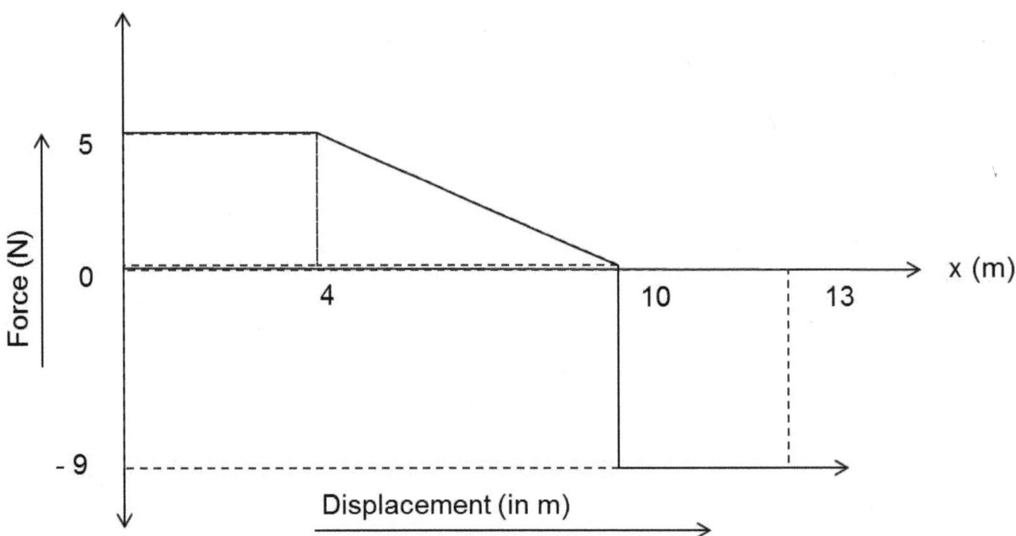

3: A bus and a car are moving with same velocity along a straight road. Which one of them is moving with greater momentum? Which of them will be stopped easily?

4: A bullet moving with an average speed of 1500 m/s hits a piece of wooden block and comes to stop after penetrating 12 cm inside the block. Find the uniform retardation implied by the wooden block on the moving bullet.

5: A radio signal is moving with a frequency of 500 MHz. Write the wave length of this signal.

6. Evaluation

Combined evaluation is from the topics covered u in this workbook. Supporting answers are incorporated wherever considered necessary. All the answers can be obtained from the source.[12]

Test Paper A

1: Any one of the following situation might develop if we apply a force on any object.

Since work done is given by W=Fs cosθ

A. So for parallel case $\theta=0^0$; and W=Fs

B. For opposite case $\theta=180^0$. and W=−Fs

C. For any angle other than 90^0, [$0^0 < \theta > 180^0$,] W=Fs cos θ

D. For $\theta = 90^0$; W=Fs cos 90^0.

So in some of the above cases, we can say that work has been done. Select such cases.

2: If the mass of the Sun were reduced to ten times smaller and the universal gravitational constant were ten times larger in magnitude, which of the following is not correct?

(a) Raindrops will fall faster. (b) Walking on the ground would become more difficult.
(c) Time period of a simple pendulum on the Earth would decrease. (d) g on the Earth will not change.

3: There are 5 tube lights each of 40 W installed in a house. All these lights are used on an average for 6 hours a day. An immersion heater consumes 1500 W a day. Find the units of electricity consumed in the month of April.

4: The kinetic energy of an object of mass, m moving with a velocity of 20 ms^{-1} is 100 J. What will be its kinetic energy when its velocity increases up to a multiple of three? What will be its kinetic energy when its velocity is increased five times?

5: What types of waves produce any audible sound?

6: Write names of three smaller bones present in our inner ear which are responsible for transmitting audio signals to the corresponding nerves.

7: What are the three components resent in epidemiological triangle?

8: Find instances during which we can say that the work is done.

(a) Nikhil is swimming in a river. (b) A truck is carrying a heavy load.
(c) A wind mill is involved in lifting water from a dug well.
(d) A green plant is carrying out photosynthesis. (e) An electrically operated engine is pulling a goods train.
(f) Food grains are getting dried when it is exposed in the sun. (g) A sailboat is moving due to wind energy.

---

[12] For obtaining all the answers one can drop a mail at senjisc@gmail.com. Some more study materials are available at the source. One can even obtain previous year Distant Learning Packages of Organisations of well repute.

Test Paper B

1: Point out at least three differences between two different types of waves as displayed in the following diagram.

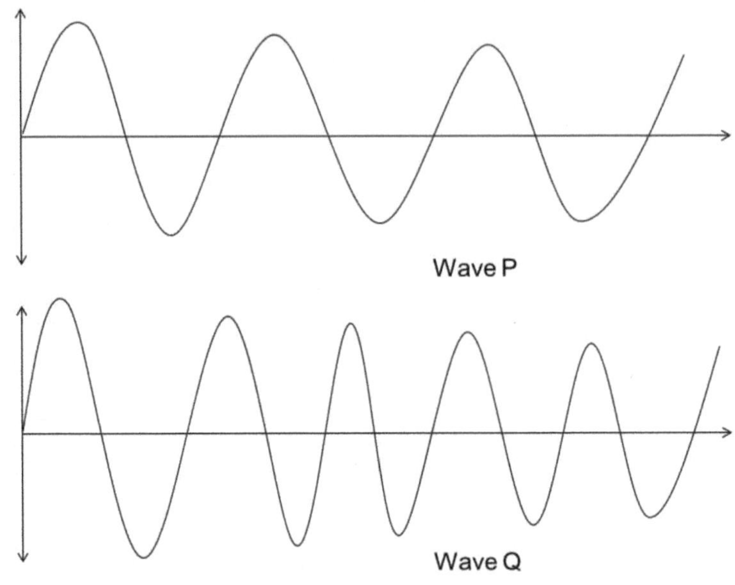

2: An object thrown at a certain angle to vertically upwards moves in a curved path and falls back again to the ground. The initial and the final points of the path of the object lie on the same horizontal plane. Find out the work done by the force of gravity on that object.

3: Definite force acting on a 30 kg mass changes its velocity from 5 m s^{-1} to 20 m s^{-1}. Calculate the work done by the force.

4: A particle of mass 10 kg initially at rest moves under the action of an applied horizontal force of 12 N on a table having coefficient of kinetic friction = 0.1. Find out the following ---

(a) Work done by the applied force in 10 s,

(b) Work done by friction in 10 s,

(c) Work done by the net force on the body 10 s,

(d) Change in kinetic energy of the body in 10 s.

5: A stone of mass 0.5 kg is sliding down a rough plane inclined at an angle of 15° to the horizontal.

The stone passes a point A with a speed of 10 ms^{-1} and a point B with a speed of 6 ms^{-1}.

a) Find the loss of mechanical energy of the stone as it moves from point A to point B.

b) Calculate the coefficient of friction between the stone and the plane.

6: It is observed that when a conservative force does positive work on a body, the potential energy of the body increases/decreases/remains unaltered. [Select the correct alternative.]

7: In an ____________ collision, the final kinetic energy is always less than the initial kinetic energy of the system because in this collision some kinetic energy usually changes into some other form of energy such as heat, sound etc. [Complete the statement.]

Test Paper C

1: An engine pumps water continuously through a hose. Water leaves the hose with a velocity v and m is the mass per unit length of the water jet. What is the rate at which kinetic energy is imparted to water?

2: An engine pumps water through a hose pipe fitted to its delivery outlet. Water passes through the pipe and leaves it with a velocity of 2 m/s. The mass per unit length of water moving through the pipe is 100 kg/m. What is the power of the engine?

3: An electron and a proton are detected in a cosmic ray experiment. The proton was there with kinetic energy 10 keV, and the electron was maintaining kinetic energy equal to 100 keV. Which is moving faster, the electron or the proton? Obtain the ratio of their speeds, (mass of an electron = 9.11×10^{-31} kg, mass of a proton = 1.67×10^{-27} kg, 1 eV = 1.60×10^{-19} J.)

4: A pump on the ground floor of a building can pump up water to fill a tank of volume 30 m^3 in 15 min. If the tank is 40 m above the ground, and the efficiency of the pump is 30%, how much electric power is consumed by the pump. [Ans: power = 43.567 kW]

[Aid box: power of the pump = mgh/t; The pump is working with 40% efficiency. Power of pump will be calculated on that basis.]

5: A trolley of mass 325 kg carrying a sandbag of 25 kg is moving uniformly with a speed of 36 km/h on a frictionless track. After a while, sand starts leaking out of a hole which is developed on the floor of the trolley at the rate of 0.05 kg s^{-1}. What is the speed of the trolley after the entire sand is dropped down through the hole?

6: Sound wave is represented in the form of a diagram:

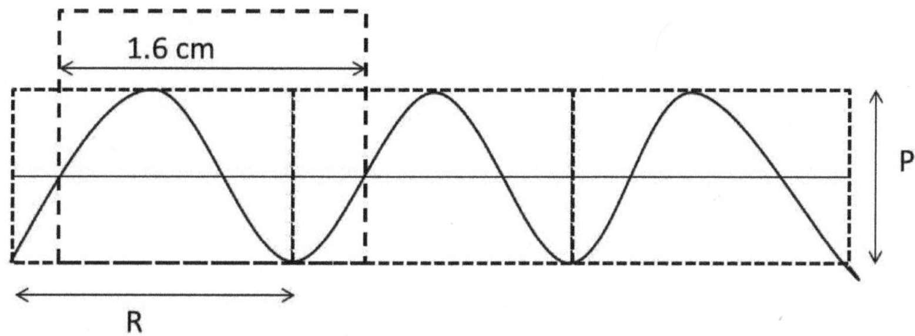

Wavelength = _______; Amplitude = _______;

Frequency = ____________; Time Period = _______;

Speed of sound in atmosphere is estimated as 340 ms^{-1}. Find the frequency of sound wave which is represented in the given diagram.

7: A parcel of mass 30 kg is hauled up a slope inclined at an angle of 30° to the horizontal. The parcel is hauled by means of a constant force of 300 N at an angle of 45° to the line of greatest slope of the plane. The acceleration of the parcel up the plane is 0.1 ms^{-2} and the total resistance to motion is *R*N.

a) Find the work done by the force in hauling the parcel, from rest, 10 m up the slope.

b) By considering work and energy, find the value of *R*.

8: A family regularly uses 10 kW of power.

(a) It is estimated that direct solar energy is incident on the horizontal surface at an average rate of 200 W per square meter. If 30% of this intake of energy can be converted to useful electrical energy, how large an area is needed to supply 10 kW?

9: A particle of mass 2 kg is projected up through a rough plane inclined at an angle of 45° to the horizontal plane. The coefficient of friction which is working between the particle and the plane is 0.15. If the particle travels 6 m up the plane before coming to rest, then find the speed with which the particle was initially projected.

10: Compare: [Put four different options in four places provided.]

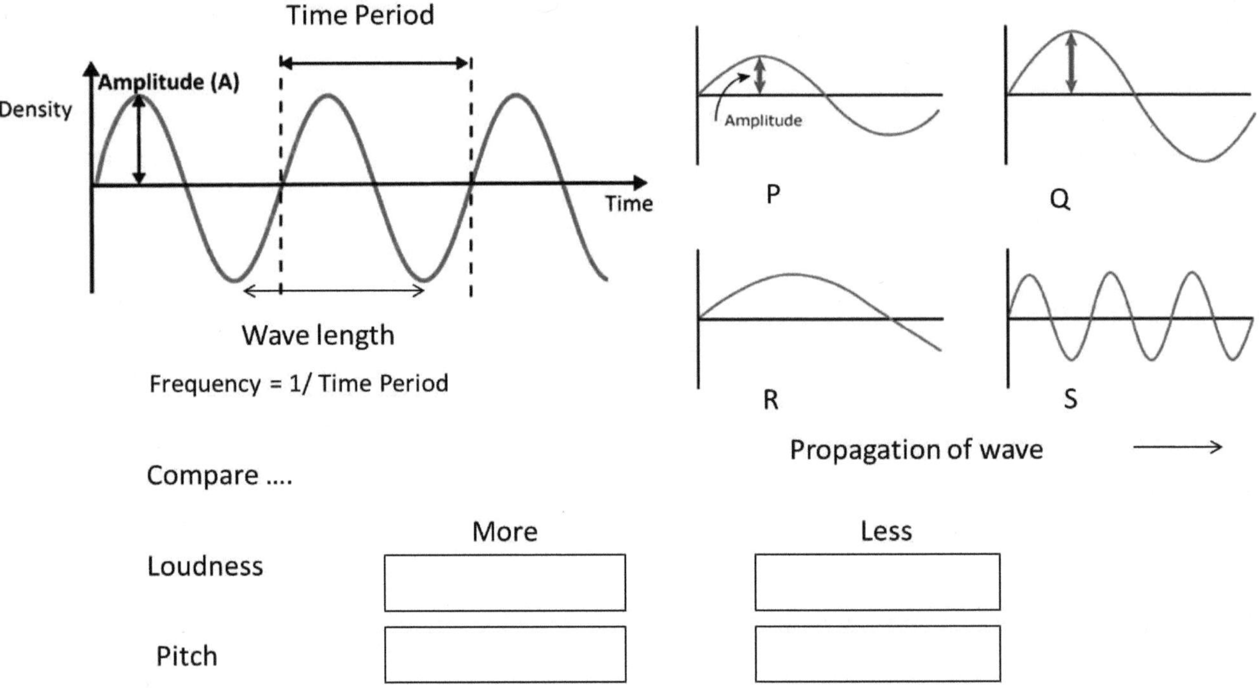

11: A 220 V, 100 W bulb is connected to a 110 W supply line. Calculate the power consumed by that bulb in 4 hours. [Ans 25 W]

12: A girl (35 kg) sits on a trolley (5 kg). That trolley is given an initial velocity of 4 ms^{-1} by applying a force. It travels a distance of 16 m before coming to rest. Calculate the work done by that force on trolley.

[Ans: 320 J]

13: What causes Night blindness?

14: What types of vision problems develop if a patient is suffering from Presbiopia?

15: ________________ and ________________ are called body protecting nutrient as they help us to fight different types of infections and diseases.

16: Down's syndrome is a kind of ________________________ disease.

7. Selected Worksheets

Most of the Worksheets are topic based. Some of the following worksheets are activity based.

Worksheet 1

1: Complete the following --

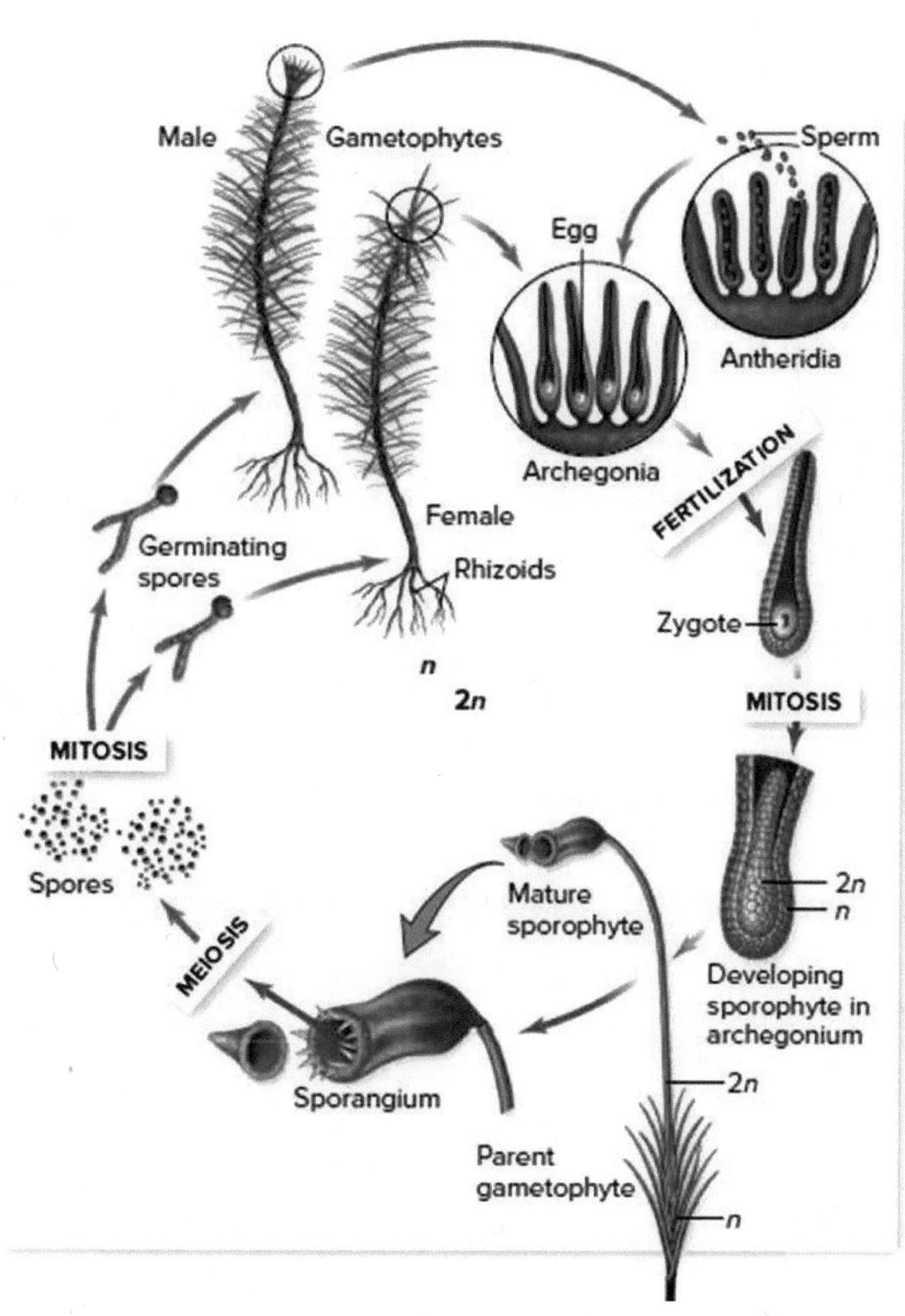

Life cycle of moss represents alternation of generation in which ____________________ and ______________ generations follow each other. Archegonia produces ______ and antheridia produces _______________.

2: A collection of different types of cells having similar function is called __________.

3: Inner linings of the trachea of human respiratory system possesses ____________ ______________ epithelium.

4: Complete the following:

The ____________ _____________model explains sugar movement.

I: plants actively transport sugar from the source
II: sugar flows to the sink due to pressure differences

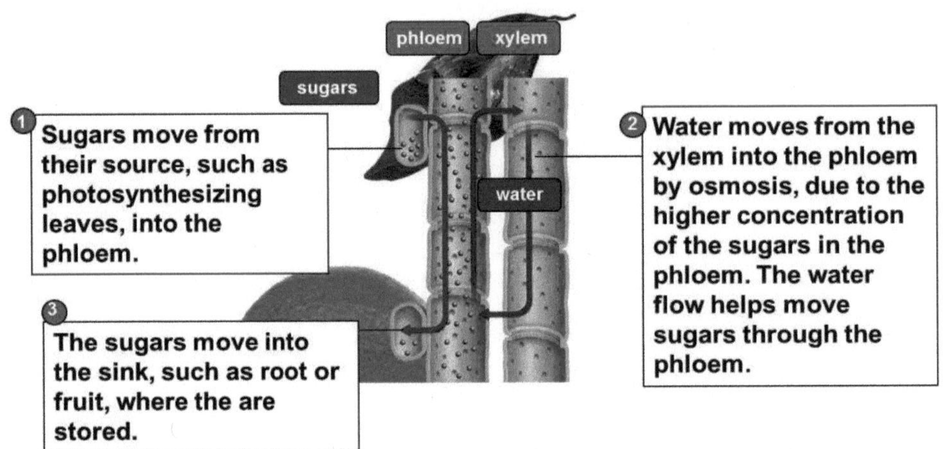

5: Answer the following:

Water travels from roots to the top of trees.

- absorption occurs at roots
- cohesion and adhesion in xylem vessel.
- transpiration which is taking place at leaves.

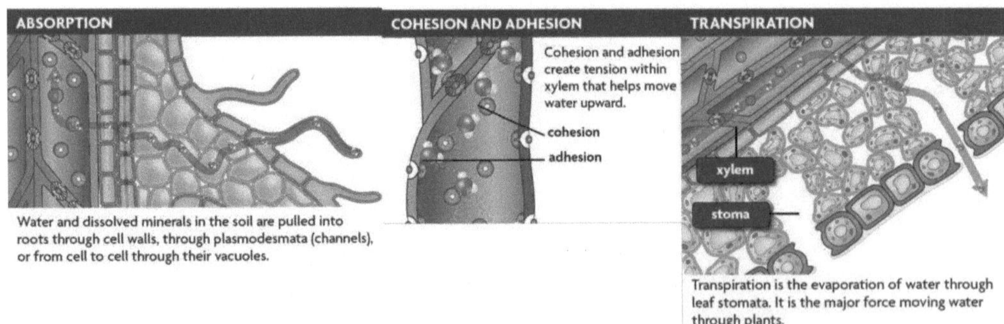

Water and dissolved minerals in the soil are pulled into roots through cell walls, through plasmodesmata (channels), or from cell to cell through their vacuoles.

Transpiration is the evaporation of water through leaf stomata. It is the major force moving water through plants.

All the three factors responsible for Ascent of Sap through Xylem Vessel is displayed above. What will happen if a plant of fresh water is placed in saline water?

6: Complete the following:

Statements regarding functioning of Phloem:

I. Phloem carries sugars from site of photosynthesis to rest of the other parts of the plant.
II. This tissue contains specialized cells.
III. sieve tube elements have holes at the terminal portion where it joins the another collection of tissue.
IV. The medium of circulation through phloem is water. No other chemicals get contaminated with it.
V. companion cells help sieve tube elements
VI. unlike xylem, cells of phloem tissue remain alive.

Option: Statement ___ is not exclusive for this vascular tissue.

7: Select the correct option:

Which of the following statement (s) regarding Xylem is/are not true?

I. Water and dissolved minerals move through xylem.
II. Xylem vessels have a continuous channel starting from roots up to leaves in the form of elongated cell.
III. Xylem contains specialized cells.
IV. vessel elements are short and wide
V. tracheid cells are long and narrow
VI. cells of this vasculat tissue die at maturity.

A: Only I is wrong. B: Only II is Wrong
C: All are wrong D: All are correct

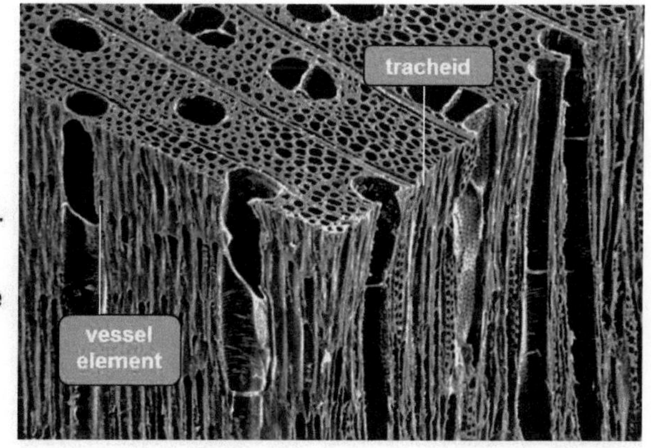

8: _____________ and ______________ are two different types of vascular tissues present in flowering plants.

9: Statement regarding function of roots is as follows:

I: Roots anchor plants and absorb mineral nutrients from soil.
II: Provides support to the shoot of plant.
III: Roots absorb, transport, and store nutrients.
IV: Root hairs help absorption of water from water.
V: All roots modify differently to store food and to promote vegetative propagation whenever needed.

Option: Statement ____ is not exclusive for all types of roots.

10: Complete the following:

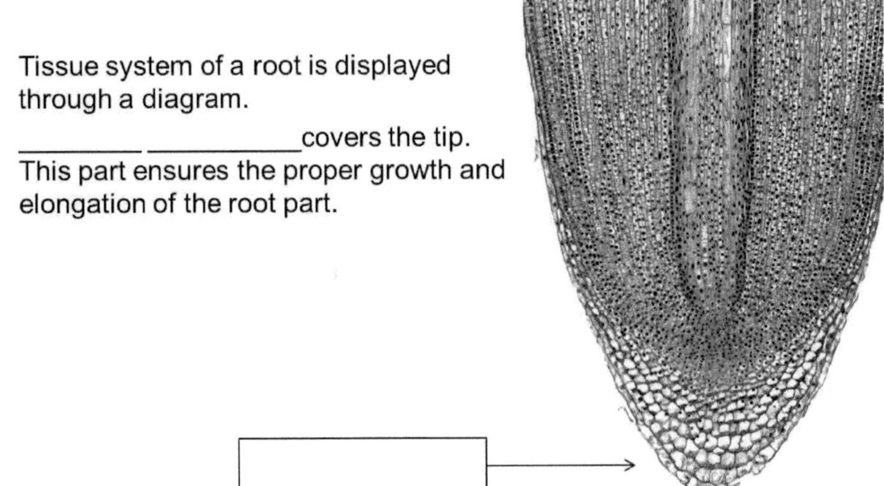

11: Sample of two types of seeds are displayed below. Identify them -- ---

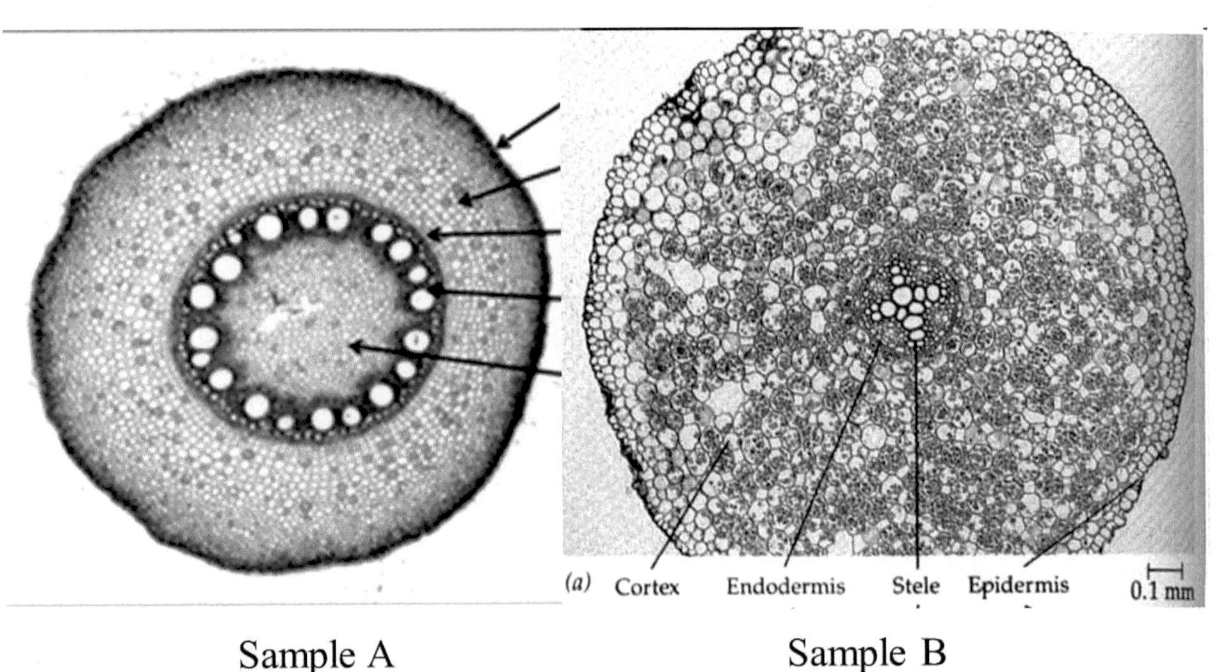

Sample A   Sample B

12: Which tissue forms the woody and fibrous parts of a flowering plant?

13: Answer the following:

_________________ _________________ part of this root system will grow faster and this part will be filled with Parenchyma only.

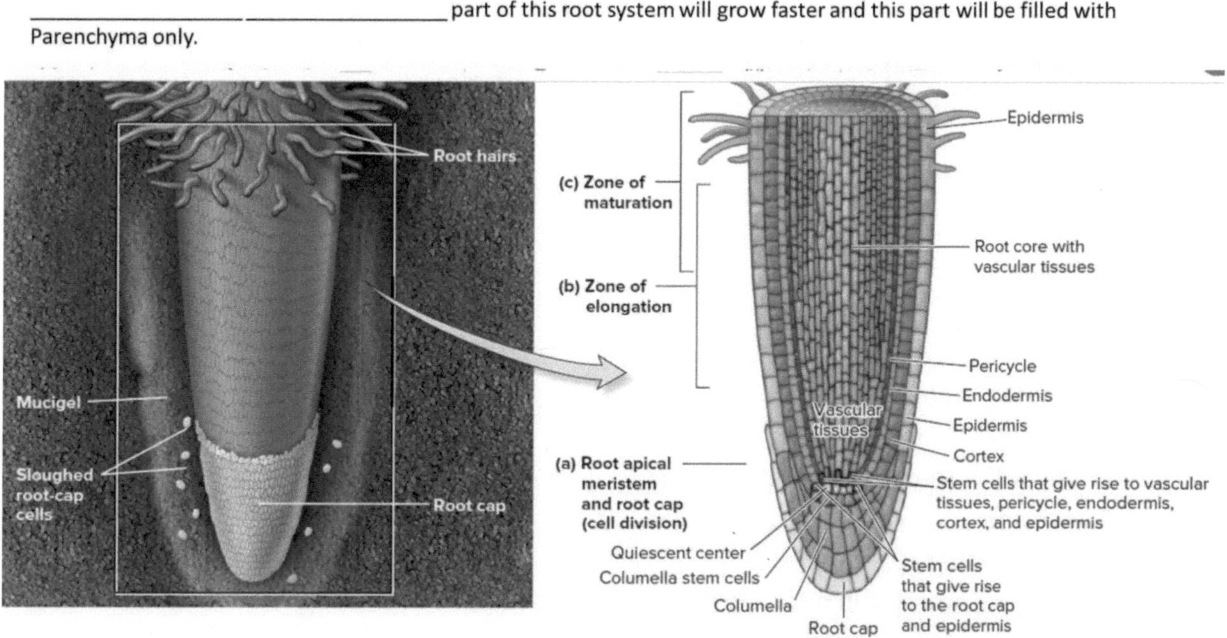

14: Select the correct option:

- Vascular tissue transports water, minerals and organic compounds.

I. two networks of hollow tubes
II. xylem transports water and minerals
III. phloem transports photosynthetic products
IV. Stems have phloem and leaves have xylem.

Options:

A: IV is not correct.

B: II and III are wrong.

I is wrong.

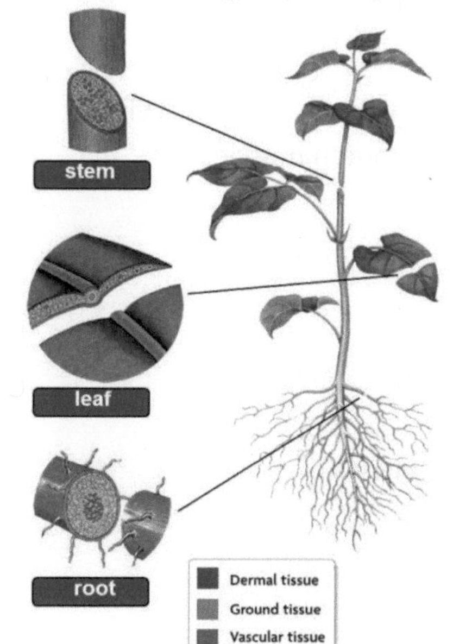

Answers: --- 1: Sporophytic and Gametophytic; ova and sperm; 2: tissue; 3: Pseudostratified columnar;

4: Pressure-flow; 5: Ascent of Sap will be halted; 6: IV ; 7: B; 8: xylem and phloem; 9: V; 10: root cap;

11: Sample A = Monocot; Sample B = Dicot; 12: Sclerenchyma; 13: Apical Meristem; 14: IV;

Worksheet 2

1. What is a ligament?
2. Name the tissue which forms the inner lining of blood vessels
3. Name the functional unit of a muscle.
4. Name any two granulocytes
5. What are cell junctions?
6. Name the tissue that lines the intestinal wall.
7. State the function of neuroglial cells.
8. Name few epidermal structures.
9. Define organ.
10. What is the function of the ligament?
11. Give an example of a heterochrony gland.
12. Name the cells from which thrombocytes are produced.
13. Where are W.B.C. formed?
14. What are the endocrine glands?
15. What is the function of antithrombin in our blood?
16. In which type of nerve fibre, the nerve impulse will move faster?
17. State the role of ligaments in the human body.
18. Name the protein found in the white fibres,
19. What do ESR and EDTA stand for?
20. What are myoepithelial cells?
21. What do fibroblasts synthesise? j
22. How is coagulation prevented in an uninjured blood vessel?
23. Name the two fundamental types of smooth muscles.
24. What is double circulation?
25. What is the trachea?
26. What is clitellum?
27. What is worm casting?
28. What is the scientific name of an earthworm?
29. Why is cockroach called Urecotelic?
30. What is the function of Malpighian tubules?
31. What is the trachea?
32. What are nephridia?
33. Define the term—hermaphrodite.
34. Name the mouthparts of earthworm.
35. Does the rat possess tonsils?
36. What is the functional unit of the cockroach eye?
37. What is coelom?
38. State the difference between male and female frog.
39. What are Pilitactiles?
40. Name the larval stage in the life history of the frog.

Solutions:

1. It is a connective tissue that joins one bone to another bone.
2. Squamous epithelium
3. Sarcomere.
4. Eosinophils and basophils.
5. Cell junctions are the structures that hold the adjacent cells of tissue together when they are not separated widely by extracellular material.
6. Columnar epithelium.
7. Serves as packing and supporting material between the nerve cells.
8. Answer:
9. Hair, nails, claws and scales.
10. Organ: A number of tissues together form an organ that works as a unit for the benefit of an organism.
11. The ligament is a dense fibrous connective tissue that connects bones at the joints.
12. Pancreas.
13. Megakaryocytic cells.
14. In the bone marrow, lymph nodes and spleen.
15. They are ductless glands that secrete hormones directly into the bloodstream.
16. It acts as an anticoagulant that prevents the clotting of blood in our blood vessels.
17. Myelinated nerve fibre.
18. It joins bones at the joints
19. Collagen.
20. Erythrocytes Sedimentation Rate, Ethylene Diamine Tetra Acetic Acid.
21. Cells showing the peculiar characteristics of both muscles and epithelial tissues.
22. The fibroblast in areolar tissue synthesizes collagen and elastin proteins.
23. It is due to the secretion of heparin by most cells.
24. Single unit smooth muscle. Multi-unit smooth muscle.
25. The blood passes twice through the heart to move through the body.
26. It is a tube that is a part of the breathing apparatus of air-breathing animals.
27. It is a prominent circular band of glandular tissue which surrounds the 14th to 16th segments in the earthworm body.
28. It is the insoluble and undigested food that is given out along with soil through the anus.
29. Pheretima Posthuma.
30. It is called Urecotelic because it excretes in the form of uric acid.
31. It helps in excretion.
32. It is a tube that is a part of the breathing apparatus of air-breathing animals.
33. Excretory organs of earthworm.
34. It is the condition in which both testes and ovaries are produced by the same individual
35. Mandibles, maxillae, labium, labrum and hypopharynx.
36. No, the rat does not possess tonsils.
37. Ommatidium.
38. It is the true body cavity, space between the body wall and the alimentary canal.
39. The male frog bears copulatory pads and well developed local sacs whereas they are absent in the female. They are bristles found on both the sides of nostrils in the rat.
40. Tadpole.

Worksheet 3

1: Various functions of Epithelial Tissues are given below—

a) Protection: It protects the underlying or overlying soft tissues from threats like heat, injury, chemicals, virus and bacteria etc.
b) Absorption: It absorbs the digestive food especially with columnar epithelial cells present in the inner linings of the intestine.
c) Secretion: The glandular epithelial cells lining the inner cavities secrete various substances like mucous, enzymes and hormones which are necessary for various metabolic activities.
d) Excretion: The epithelial cells of kidney tubules and sweat glands help in the excretion of wastes from the body.
e) A single organ can have different types of epithelial tissue based on the substances to which different surfaces are to be exposed. Protective tissue tends to be thicker, made of multiple layers of cells and often has inclusions such as keratin to provide mechanical strength and resistance.
f) Sensation: The nerve ending in the epithelial cells of the retina, olfactory organs and nasal chamber etc. receive the stimuli from the external atmosphere and transfer them to the brain for interpretation.
g) Other specific functions: The trachea contains the ciliated epithelium to facilitate the transport of mucous and other substances from one part of the structure to another. The pulmonary epithelium helps in the exchange of gases during respiration and the germinal epithelium of testes and ovaries are responsible for formation of sperms and ova respectively. The epithelium also forms the exoskeleton structure as scales, feathers, hairs, nails, claws, horns etc. in different organisms.

Statement:

A: All the functions are perfectly represented for displaying the function of epithelial tissues present in majority of vertebrates.

B: Other specific functions are not exclusive for all members of vertebrates. Derivatives of skin like scales, hairs, feathers etc. may be of dermal or epidermal origin.

C: Role of epithelium for receiving and passing on sensation is not properly represented in point f.

D: Most of mammals contain layers of thick keratinized dead epithelial cells protecting them against water loss and other external stresses or extremities.

Option: Find out the wrong statement (s)

I: Option B is wrong. II: Both C and D; III: Only C; IV: Only e;

2: Epithelial tissue rests on a structure called the___________ _____________. It consists of two parts – the basal lamina and the reticular connective tissue settled underneath. The basal lamina is secreted by the cells of the epithelial tissue itself and contains proteins, glycoproteins, and collagen IV, a type of structural protein that forms sheets of the tissue.

3: Epithelia can also be classified based on the shape of the cells, giving rise to three types:

P: ________________ epithelial tissue: consists of extremely thin cells that resemble the scales of a fish.

Q: ________________ epithelial tissue: contains cells that appear square shaped in cross-section but are marginally longer than they are wide

R: ________________ epithelial tissue: consists of elongated cell involved in absorption of materials.

4: Statement regarding stratified epithelial tissue is as follows ---

a) These epithelia consist of more than one layer of cells and only one layer remains in direct contact with the basement membrane. Similarly, only one layer of cells has the apical surface exposed to the lumen of the organ or to the external environment.
b) These tissues often have a protective role, and the extent of friction or abrasion often determines the number of layers of cells present in it.
c) This type of epithelia is found in skin, with having many dead and keratinized cells, providing protection against water and nutrient loss.
d) Stratified cuboidal epithelia are found surrounding the ducts of many glands, including mammary glands located in the breast and salivary glands located in the mouth.
e) Stratified columnar epithelia are rare, found predominantly in some organs of the reproductive system, and in the conjunctiva of the eye.
f) Transitional epithelia are a special subset of stratified epithelia that consist of ovoid cells that can stretch based on the pressure of liquids inside the organ.
g) They are exclusively found in the excretory system. None other tissues constitute this system.

Option: Statement _____ is not displaying the true fact related to Stratified Epithelial Tissue.

5: Provide key terms:

I: ___________– Part of the cell membrane of epithelial cells that faces the lumen. Differing in composition from the rest of the cell, it often contains cilia or microvilli and many specialized proteins.

II: ____________– Slender, cytoplasmic extrusions present in nearly every mammalian cell. Some are motile cilia that are involved in the movement of substances.

III: ____________– Inner space of tubular structures such as ducts or the respiratory and gastrointestinal passages.

IV: ____________ – Large number of minute projections seen from the plasma membrane of some cells, designed to increase the surface area of the cell for secretion or absorption.

6. Which of these epithelia can stretch to increase the volume of the organ based on internal water pressure?

A. Simple squamous epithelia
B. Simple columnar epithelia
C. Transitional epithelia
D. Stratified columnar epithelia

7. How is a pseudostratified epithelium different from a truly stratified tissue?

A. The nuclei are at the same level in pseudostratified epithelia.
B. The apical and basal surfaces are aligned.
C. There are multiple cell layers in pseudostratified epithelia.
D. All the cells in a pseudostratified epithelium interact with the basement membrane.

8. Which of these is an important function of epithelial cells?

A. Protection from chemical abrasion
B. Secretion of hormones and enzymes
C. Absorption of nutrients
D. All of the above

9: Statement related to Gap Junctions is as follows---

a) The two types of cell junctions in present in tissues of vertebrates are anchoring junctions and tight junctions.

b) Anchoring junctions link up cells through structure of proteins that are connected directly to the cell's cytoskeleton. Tight junctions are areas where cells are bound very closely together to form a barrier, and they are often found in epithelial cells. This type of tissue is found on the surface of the body covering and lining of organs.
c) Plant cells do not have gap junctions, but they do have plasmodesmata, which are channels that connect the cytoplasm of two adjacent plant cells of a tissue.
d) Plasmodesmata are structured differently than gap junctions due to plant cells having thick and rigid cell walls.

Select the Wrong statement --

A. Functionally Gap Junctions, Tight Junctions and Plasmodesmata are identical structures.
B. Gap junction is more stable than tight junction.
C. Function of Gap Junction, Tight Junction and Plasmodesmata is essentially the same.
D. Plant cells can regulate the passage of small molecules and communicate with each other only through their plasmodesmata.
E. Plasmodesmata are a rigid structure than compared to gap junction and tight junction.

Option ______ is wrong.

10: Provide Key Terms

I: – A type of cell junction in which cells is connected by a mass of proteins.
II: – A type of cell junction where cells are tightly bonded to form a barrier.
III: – Channels that connect the cytoplasm of adjacent plant cells.
IV: – A family of proteins that makes up gap junctions.

11. How many connexins are found in one gap junction channel?

A. 6 B. 4 C. 12 D. 2

12. What is the "bystander effect" in relation to gap junctions?

A. Molecules can enter neighboring cells without passing through extracellular fluid.
B. Cells next to a cell that is undergoing cell death can also die.
C. Cells can transmit therapeutic compounds to one another.
D. Gap junctions are only found in cells that are located next to other cells.

13. Which is NOT a function of gap junctions?

A. Forming a barrier
B. Allowing molecules to pass between cells
C. Electrically coupling cells
D. Ensuring correct embryonic development

14: write general characters of epithelial tissues.

Ans 1: III; 2: basement membrane; 3: P = Squamous; Q =Cuboidal ; R = Columnar; 4 : g;
5: I = Apical Surface ; II = Cilia; III = Lumen; IV = Microvilli ;

6: C is correct. Transitional epithelia present in the excretory system, lining the ureters, urethra and urinary bladder can stretch depending on the volume of urine. Simple squamous epithelia are present where there is absorption or movement of materials. Simple and stratified columnar epithelia usually have a secretory function.

7: D is correct. Since all the cells of a pseudostratified epithelium rest on the basement membrane, they are classified as a simple epithelial tissue, rather than as a stratified epithelium. Their nuclei are often at different levels, their apical surfaces are not aligned with each other and consist of a single layer of cells.

8 : D is correct. Epithelia have a number of functions, including protection, secretion and absorption. They demarcate different surfaces from each other, and resist friction, invasion by pathogens, loss of water and nutrients in addition to enhancing the functions of various organs.

9: B; 10: Anchoring junction; Tight junction; Plasmodesmata; Connexin;

11: C is correct. Six connexins form a unit called a connexon, which is half of a gap junction channel. Two connexons put together form a gap junction channel, so 12 total connexins make up one channel.

12: B is correct. All of these choices are true about gap junctions, but only choice B describes the bystander effect. When a diseased or injured cell dies, it sends out signals that reach adjacent cells, which can cause them to also die. This is called the bystander effect because the cells are like innocent bystanders that become victims at the scene of a crime.

13: A is correct. Gap junctions do not form a barrier; they have the opposite function. They connect adjacent cells together and have important roles in cell communication and embryonic development. Choice A describes tight junctions.

14: General characters of epithelial tissues:

a) It consists of closely packed cells of various sizes and shapes. This tissue forms the lining membrane of several organs.

b) The cells of the membrane are arranged in one or more layers resting upon the thin non-cellular basement and these cells are supported by intercellular cementing substance and close vascular connective tissues.

c) The basement membrane is formed of protein fibres differently interspersed in the matrix of polysaccharide. The matrix for this layer is generally secreted by underlying connective tissue.

d) The cementing substance between the cells is formed of mucoprotein containing hyaluronic and calcium salts.

Worksheet 4

1. Can a moving body have relative velocity zero with respect to another body? Give an example.

2. Can there be motion in two dimensions with acceleration in only one dimension?

3. Is it true that a body is always at rest in a frame that is fixed to the body itself?

4. Tell under what condition a body moving with uniform velocity can be in equilibrium?

5. What does the speedometer records: the average speed or the instantaneous speed?

6. Can an object be accelerated without speeding up or slowing down? Give examples,

7. Is it possible to have the rate of change of velocity constant while the velocity itself changes both in magnitude and direction? Give an example.

8. Which motion is exactly represented by $\Delta s = v\Delta t$?

9. In which frame of reference is the body always at rest?

10. What is common between the two graphs shown in figs, (a) and (b)?

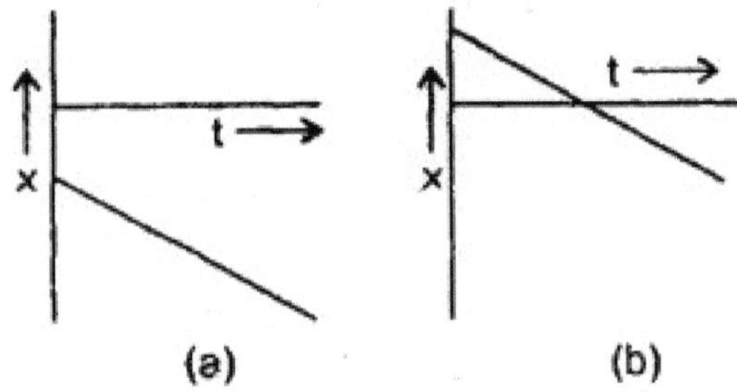

11. What is common between the two graphs shown in figs, (a) and (b)?

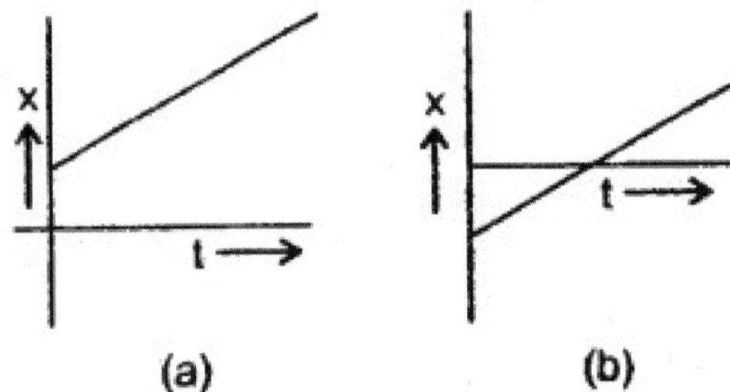

12. What is meant by a point object in Physics?

13. The displacement of a body is zero. Is the distance covered by it is necessarily zero?

14. Which of the velocity or speed is measured by the speedometer of a vehicle?

15. Can you think of a situation where a body falling under gravity has constant velocity?

16. Give an example of a motion which even though is accelerated motion yet it is called uniform motion.

17. How many-dimensional motion does the following have?

(a) Train moving fast on its track.

(b) A lizard moving on a wall in a room.

(c) Kite flying in the sky.

(d) Bee flying in a closed room.

18. When is the average velocity over an interval of time becomes equal to instantaneous velocity?

19. A coolie carries a bag of luggage from one side of a platform to another side on the same platform. How far vertically the load is shifted?

20. The displacement of a body is proportional to the square of time along a straight line. Is the body moving with constant velocity or constant acceleration?

21. When the train in which you are sitting starts moving by the side of another train without jerks, you find that the other train is moving but when you look to the platform you find that your train is moving. Name the phenomenon responsible for such a motion.

22. Under what condition the magnitude of the average velocity of a particle is equal to the average speed?

23. Two particles A and B are moving along the same straight line with B being ahead of A. Velocities remaining unchanged, what would be the effect on the magnitude of relative velocity if A is ahead of B? '

24. Define the speed of the object.

25. Why the speed of an object cannot be negative?

26. Can a body have zero velocity and still accelerating?

27. Can the direction of the velocity of a body change, when acceleration is constant?

28. Is the acceleration of a car is greater when the accelerator is pushed to the floor or when the brake pedal is pushed hard?

29. The displacement is given by x = 2 + 4t + $5t^2$. Find the value of instantaneous acceleration.

a = d2xdt2 = 10

30. A stone is thrown vertically upwards from the surface of Earth. What is the direction of (a) on its upward motion (b) on its downward motion?

31. Can Earth be regarded as a point object if only the orbital motion of Earth around the Sun is considered? Why?

32. The motion of two persons is shown by two straight lines on a displacement time graph intersecting each other at a certain point. What information do you get from the point of intersection?

33. Following two equations represents the x – t relation for the motion of an objects.

x (t) = x(0) + v(0)t + 12 at^2

and x(t) = v(0)t + 12 at^2

(a) What is the difference between them?

(b) the initial position of the object.

34. Can the speed of a body change if its velocity is constant? Why?

35. If the instantaneous velocity of a particle is zero, will its instantaneous acceleration be necessarily zero?

36. What is the shape of the displacement time graph of a particle having an average velocity equal to its instantaneous velocity?

37. Can there be a two-dimensional motion with acceleration in one dimension only? Give example.

38. Under what condition will the distance and displacement of a moving object will have the same magnitude?

39. Under what condition an object in motion cannot be considered a point object?

40. Define a point object.

41. Is the following graph possible for the motion of a particle moving along a straight line?

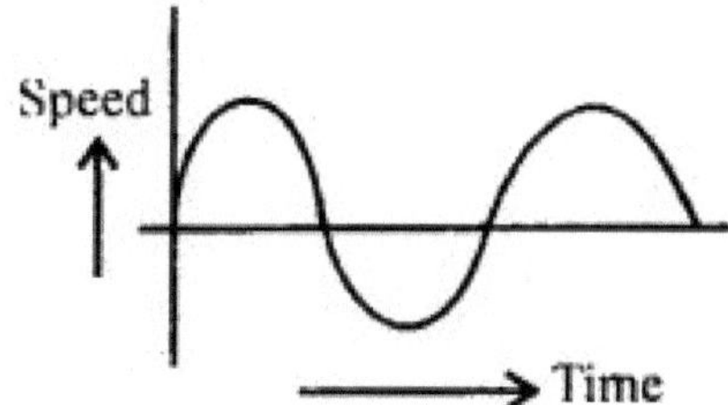

42. Explain why the graph in the above is not possible?

43. Why the following graph is not possible for the motion of a particle moving along a straight line?

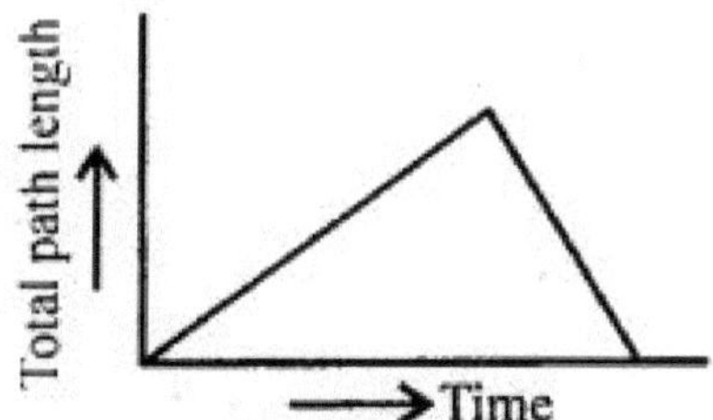

44. What happens to kinematic equations under time reversal?

45. What happens to the uniform motion of a body when it is given an acceleration at right angles to its motion?

46. To deal with physical phenomena, we consider objects even as big as Sun a point objects. Can you name physical phenomena in which Earth cannot be taken as a point object?

47. The average velocity of a body moving with uniform acceleration is given by 12 (u + v). Ii the acceleration changes from point to point can the average velocity be still given by this expression? Give reason.

48. Acceleration is defined as the rate of change of velocity. Suppose we call the rate of change of acceleration SLAP. Then

(i) What is the unit of SLAP.

(ii) How can you calculate instantaneous SLAP?

49. Why is the time stated twice in stating acceleration?

50. Separate the following in one, two and three-dimensional motion :

(a) a kite flying on a windy day.

(b) an insect crawling on a globe.

(c) a carom coin rebounding from the side of the board,

(d) a planet revolving around its star.

(e) the motion of a boat.

(f) the motion of a dropped body.

(g) the motion of a tennis ball.

(h) a charged particle moving under an electric field.

(i) movement of a saw while cutting wood.

(j) molecular motion.

(k) a charged particle moving under a magnetic field.

Solutions : ---

1. Yes, two trains running on two parallel tracks with the same velocity in the same direction.
2. Free Projectile Motion Calculator – calculate projectile motion step by step.
3. Yes, projectile motion.
4. Yes.
5. When the net force on the body is zero.
6. It records (or measures) the instantaneous speed.
7. Yes, circular motion.
8. Yes, in projectile motion.
9. It Represents motion with uniform velocity.
10. The body is always at rest in the frame attached to it i. e. inertial frame of reference.
11.

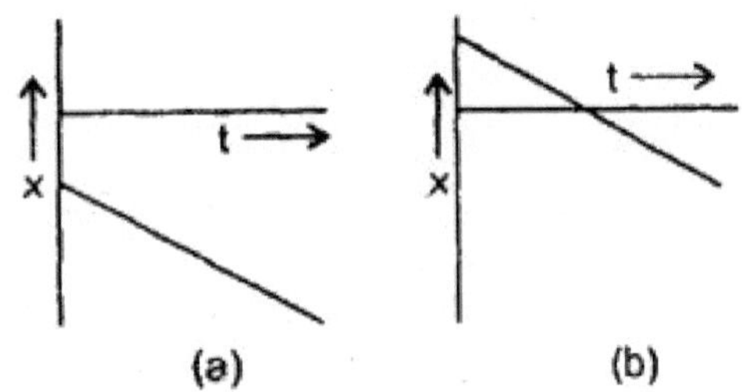

Both these graphs represent that the velocity is negative.

12. Answer:

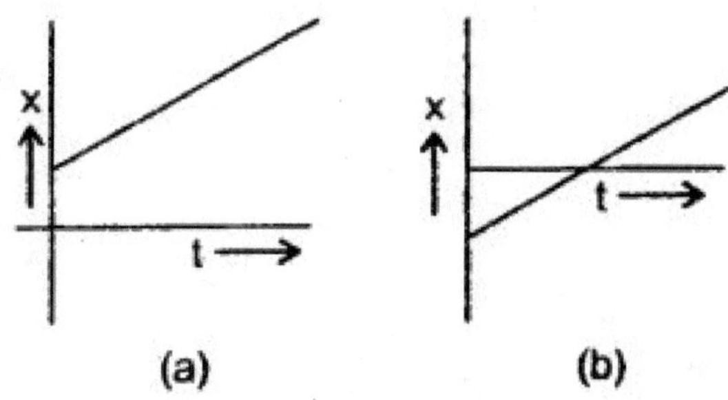

Both these graphs represent that velocity is positive.

13. An object is said to be a point object if its dimensions are very small as compared to the distance covered by it.
14. No.
15. Speed.
16. Yes, the terminal velocity of a body.
17. Answers:
    i. Uniform circular motion.
    ii. One dimensional motion.
    iii. Two-dimensional motion.
    iv. Three-dimensional motion.
18. When the velocity is constant.
19. Zero.
20. It is moving with constant acceleration.
21. Relative velocity is the phenomenon responsible for such a motion.
22. The magnitude of the average velocity of a particle is equal to the average speed if it moves with constant velocity.
23. The magnitude of the relative velocity will remain the same i.e. no effect on its magnitude.
24. The speed of an object is defined as the distance covered by it per unit of time.

25. The speed of an object cannot be negative because the distance can never be negative.
26. Yes.
27. Yes.
28. The acceleration of the car is greater when the brake pedal is pushed hard because the car comes to rest suddenly i. e. the rate of change of velocity of the car is large in this case, so the acceleration.
29. The velocity and acceleration of the stone?
30. Answers:

    (a) Velocity is vertically upward and acceleration is vertically downward.

    (b) Both velocity and acceleration are vertically downward.
31. Yes. This is because the size of Earth is very small as compared to the size of the orbit of the Earth around the Sun.
32. This means that the two persons cross each other at a certain place at a given instant of time.
33. Answers:

    (a) The first equation is a more general form of motion as it contains information regarding Answer:

    (b) No, the speed of a body cannot change if its velocity is constant which means that both the magnitude and direction of velocity do not change. The magnitude of velocity is speed, so speed cannot change.
34. No.
35. In this case, the velocity is uniform, so the x – t graph is a straight line.
36. Yes, a projectile motion which is two-dimensional one has acceleration only in one dimension i.e. vertically downward.
37. The distance and displacement of a moving object will have the same magnitude when it is moving with uniform velocity along a straight line.
38. A moving object cannot be considered as a point object if its size is not negligible as compared to the distance travelled by it.

39. It is defined as an object having dimensions (length, breadth, thickness etc.) very small as compared to the distance covered by it.
40. No.
41. This is because the speed for a given time is negative and speed is always positive.
42. This is because here the path length decreases with time while it must either increase or must remain constant.
43. The kinematic equations of motion don't change in the form under time reversal i.e. if t is replaced by -t.
44. The body will come in a circular motion when it is given acceleration at right angles to its motion.
45. The occurrence of solar or lunar eclipse does not allow Earth to be taken as a point objects otherwise the phenomena cannot be explained.
46. No, the average velocity cannot be given by 12 (u + v) in case the acceleration varies from point to point i.e. if it is not uniform. This is because the slope of the v-t graph does not remain the same at all points.
47. Answer: SLAP = Acceleration/time (By definition).

    ∴ Its unit will be = ms2 s = ms^{-3}.
48. Answer:

    Average SLAP = ΔaΔt $= \lim_{\Delta t \to 0} \frac{\Delta a}{\Delta t} = \frac{da}{dt}$

    ∴ Instantaneous SLA

    P = Limiting value of average SLAP

49. Answer:

    Since acceleration is the double rate of change of displacement

    i. e. a = d2xdt2, so time is stated twice in stating acceleration.
50. Answer:

    One dimensional motion : (e), (f), (i)

    Two dimensional motion : (b), (c), (d), (g), (h), (k).

    Three dimensional motion : (a), (j).

Worksheet 5

Question 1. Prove that the average velocity of a particle over an interval of time is either smaller than or equal to the average speed of the particle over the same interval.

Question 2. Two trains each of the length 109 m and 91 m are moving in opposite directions with velocities 34 km h^{-1} and 38 km h^{-1} respectively. At what time the two trains will completely cross each other?

Question 3. Ambala is at a distance of 200 km from Delhi. Ram sets out from Ambala at a speed of 60 km h^{-1} and Sham set out at the same time from Delhi at a speed of 40 km h^{-1}. When will they meet?

Question 4. A car travelling at a speed of 60 km h^{-1} on a straight road is ahead of a scooter travelling at a speed of 40 km h^{-1}. How would the relative velocity be altered if the scooter is ahead of the car?

Question 5. Draw the position-time graphs for two objects initially occupying different positions but having zero relative velocity.

Question 6. A ball is thrown vertically upward with a velocity of 20 ms^{-1}. It takes 4 seconds to return to its original position. Draw a velocity-time graph for the motion of the ball and answer the following questions:
At which point P, Q, R, the stone has :
(a) reached its maximum height.
(b) stopped moving?

Question 7. "It is the velocity and not the acceleration which decides the direction of motion of a body." Justify this statement with the help of a suitable example.

Question 8.
Two buses A and B starting from the same point move in a mutually perpendicular direction with speeds u_A km h^{-1} and u_B km h^{-1} respectively. Calculate the relative velocity of A w.r.t B.

Question 9. A draw velocity-time graph for a body which
(i) accelerates uniformly from rest,
(ii) then moves with a uniform velocity and
(iii) finally retarded uniformly.

Question 10. From a velocity-time graph, how do you calculate the average acceleration of a moving body?

Question 11. State whether the following two graphs in Fig. here represent the same type of motion or not. Name the motion of the particle.

Question 12. Draw the velocity-time graph for an object moving with uniform velocity. What does it show for $t < 0$?

Question 13. The displacement time graph of a body is shown in the figure below. What does the curve for $t < 0$ and $t > 0$ show?

Question 14. Distinguish between one, two and three-dimensional motion.

Question 15. A ball thrown upward reaches a height and comes bad downward. Out of the following statements, which one is true for displacement, velocity and acceleration.
(a) It varies continuously but never changes the sign.
(b) It varies continuously with the maximum, in the beginning, being zero at the top.
(c) It remains constant throughout the course of the journey.
(d) It only changes the sign when the ball is at the top.

Question 16. Derive the expression for the time taken by a body dropped from a height h to reach at Earth.

Question 17. In which of the following cases, the body may be considered a point object:
(a) A railway carriage moving without jerks between two stations.
(b) A monkey sitting on the shoulder of a cyclist moving smoothly in a circular track.
1 A beaker tumbling down the edge of a table, A spinning cricket ball that turns sharply on

hitting the ground.

Question 18. What do you understand by positive and negative time?

Question 19. If the displacement time graph of a particle is parallel to the displacement axis (b) the time axis, what will be the velocity particle? Why?

Question 20. An object is in uniform motion along a straight line. What will be its position-time graph if

(a) x_0 = +ve, v = +ve,

(b) x_0 = +ve, v = – ve,

(c) x_0 = – ve, v = +ve,

(d) x_0 = – ve, v = – ve.

The letters x_0 and v represent the position of the object at time t = 0 and the uniform velocity of the object respectively.

Question 21. Define displacement. What are its characteristics?

Question 23. What are the important points about the uniform motion?

Question 24. A car is being driven at a uniform velocity u. The driver suddenly puts his foot on the accelerator and the speed increases to v. Unfortunately after that his brakes failed. Show his velocity-time graph.

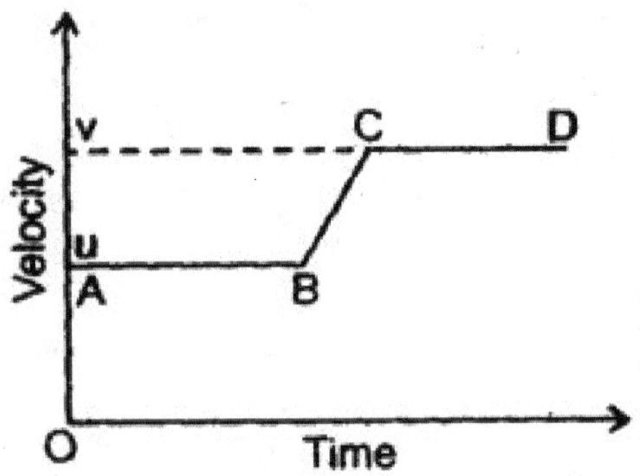

Question 25. Draw position-time graphs of two objects moving along a straight line when their relative velocity is (a) zero and (b) non-zero.

Question 26. In a circus, a motorcyclist takes 4 rounds on the same track in the globe of radius r with a velocity 5r.

Find (i) total displacement; (ii) total distance covered; (iii) total time is taken by him.

Question 27. Is it possible that the velocity of an object be in a direction other than the direction of acceleration? When?

Question 28. Is the rate of change of acceleration with the time important to describe the motion of a body? Why?

Question 29. Explaining with an example, why does a person sitting in a train think that the other train is at rest when both are moving on parallel tracks with the same speed and in the same direction?

Question 30. Can a body be said to be at rest as well as in motion? Explain.

Solutions: ---

Answer 1: Average velocity is defined as the ratio of the total displacement to the total time. Average speed is defined as the ratio of the total distance to the total time. Since displacement is less than or equal to the distance, therefore the average velocity is less than or equal to the average speed.

Answer 2: Total distance to be covered by the two trains in crossing each other= 200 m

The time taken in crossing = 10s

Answer 3: Time after which they meet = 2h.

Answer 4:
Similarly vsc = relative velocity of scooter w.r.t. car = – 20 kmh^{-1}

Thus we conclude that the magnitude of the relative velocity is the same in both cases but the direction of relative velocity is reversed if the scooter is ahead of the car.

Answer 5: The positive T time graphs for two objects initially occupying different positions but ty are parallel to each other as shown in Fig.

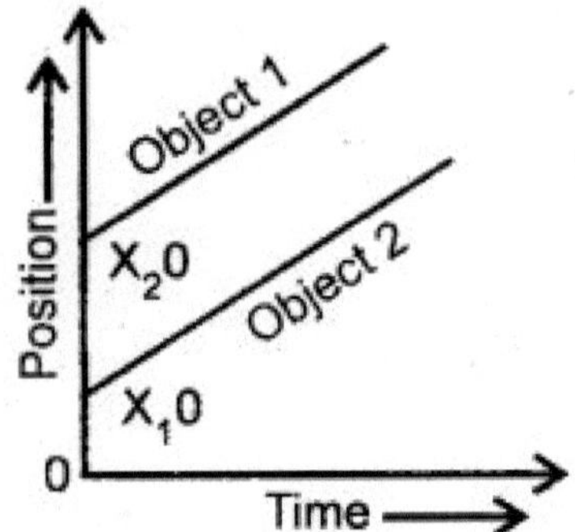

Answer 6: Let P represent the initial position at the time when the ball is thrown vertically upward.
Q represents the highest point reached by the ball.
R represents the original position of the ball after 4 seconds.

Thus the velocity-time graph for the motion of the ball is as shown in Fig.

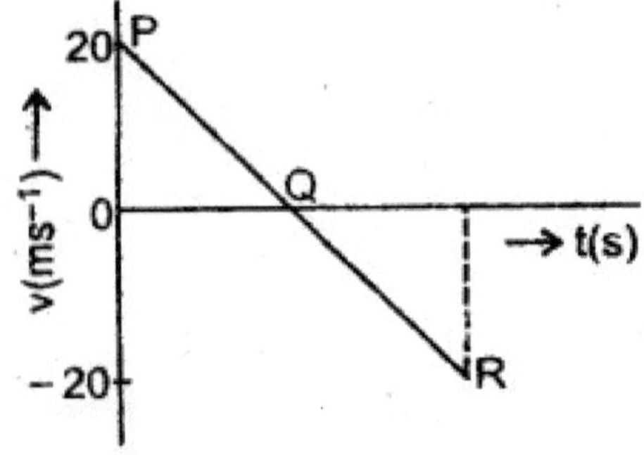

(a) We know that at the highest point, the velocity of the object is zero. So stone will reach its maximum height corresponding to point Q.

(b) The stone has stopped moving at point Q because at Q, v = 0.

Answer 7: The direction of velocity is always in the direction of motion of the body whereas the direction of acceleration may or may not be in the direction of motion of the body. Thus we conclude that it is the velocity that decides the direction of motion of the body.

Example: When a ball is thrown vertically upwards, the direction of motion of the ball and velocity is the same i.e. vertically upwards. On the other hand, the acceleration due to gravity on the ball acts vertically downwards i.e. opposite to the direction of motion of the ball.

Answer 8:

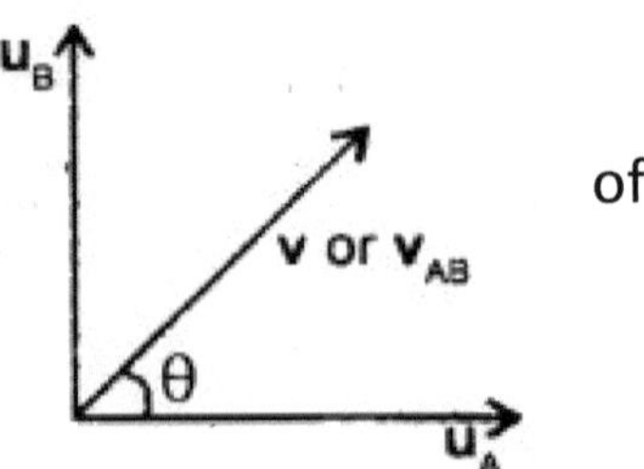

Thus, equations (1) and (2) give the magnitude and direction of relative velocity of A w.r.t. B.

Answer 9: The required velocity-time graph is shown in Fig. here

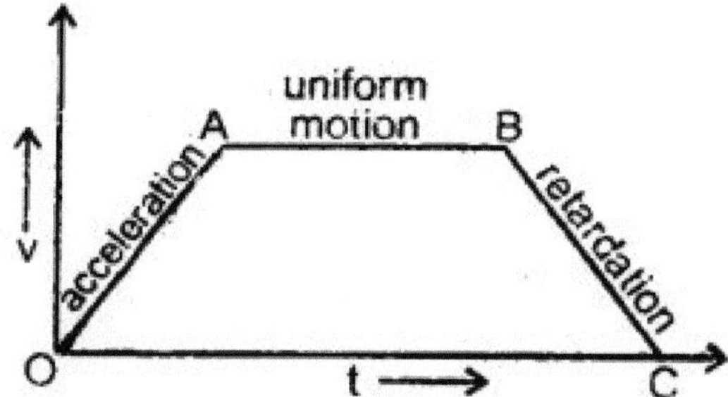

OA part of the graph represents the uniformly accelerated motion of the body.

Answer 9 -ii: AB part of the graph represents motion with uniform velocity.

Answer 9-iii: BC part of the graph represents motion with uniform retardation of the body.

Answer 10: The slope of the velocity-time curve gives the acceleration of the body. For this purpose, we take a small interval of time Δt and a corresponding change in velocity Δv such that $\Delta t = t_2 - t_1$ and $\Delta v = v_2 - v_1$. Over a very small interval of time Δt, arc AB may be considered as a chord AB, then.

$$a = \underset{\Delta t \to 0}{Lt} \frac{\Delta v}{\Delta t} = \frac{dv}{dt} = \frac{BC}{AC}.$$

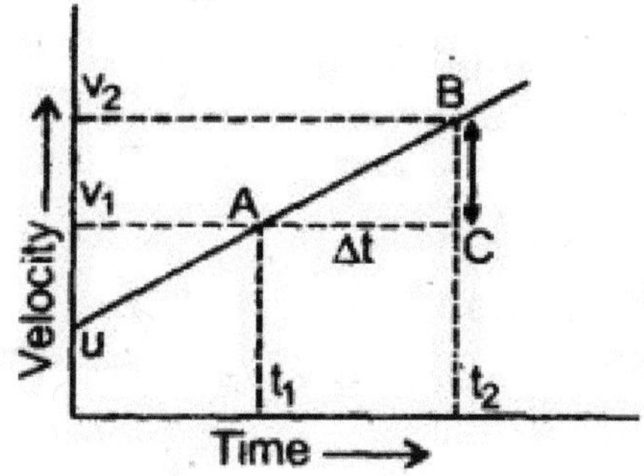

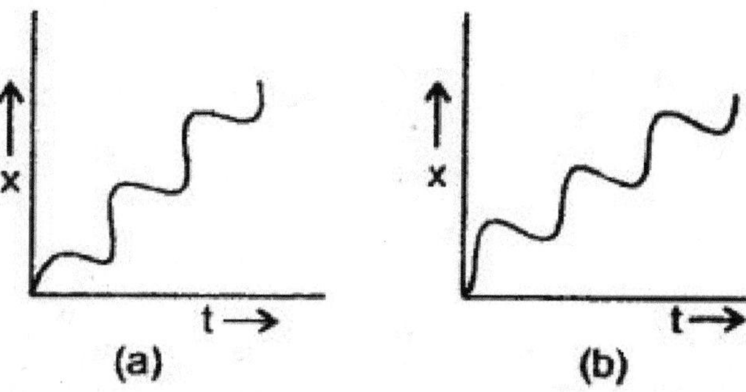

Answer 11: Yes. Both of these graphs represent the same type of motion. The motion of the particle represented by these graphs is non-uniform motion i.e. the particle is moving with variable velocity.

Answer 12: As the object moves with uniform velocity, the magnitude and direction of its velocity remain the same at all points of its path. Thus v – t graph' is a straight line parallel to the time axis as shown in Fig. here.

For t < 0, the v – t graph shows that the object is at rest till t = 0.

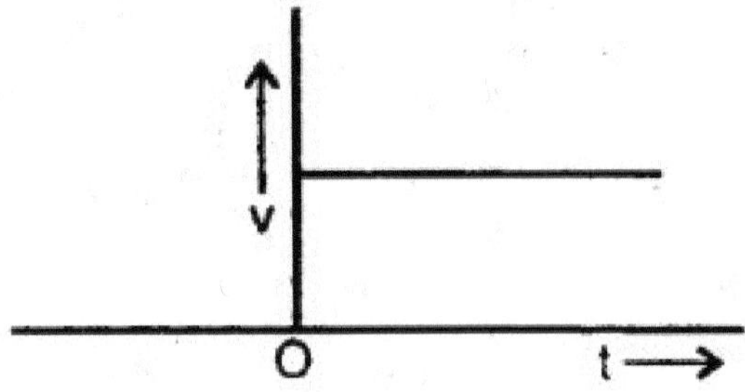

Answer 13: The line || to t – axis in fig. shows that the object is at rest t || t = 0. For t > 0, it shows that it is still at rest but at some another poi it at a distance XQ from the point for t < 0.

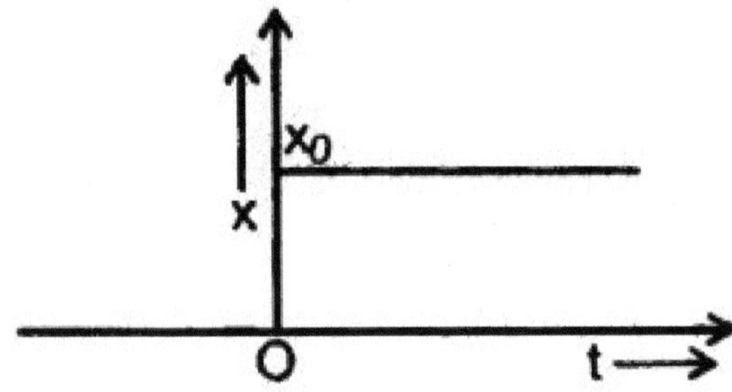

Answer 14: The motion of an object along a straight line in a fixed direction is called one-dimensional motion.

- The motion of an object in a plane is called two-dimensional motion
- The motion of an object in space is called three-dimensional motion

Answer 15: Statement (a) is true for displacement as it varies from starting

- Statement (b) is true for velocity as it is maximum at the time of projecting the ball and becomes zero at the highest point i.e. top.
- Statement (c) is true for acceleration as it is always constant throughout the course of the journey and is equal to 'g'.

Answer 16: $t = (2h/g)^{1/2}$

Answer 17: (a) and (b) as the distance moved by the bodies is much larger; the size of the body.

Answer 18: The origin of time is called zero time. The instant of time which is after the origin of time is called positive time and the instant of, which is taken before the origin of time is called negative time.

Answer 19: (a) When the displacement-time graph is parallel to the displacement axis, the velocity of the particle is infinity.

(b) When the displacement-time graph is parallel to the time axis, the velocity of the particle is zero as in this case $\Delta x = 0$.

Answer 20: The position of an object at any time t moving with a uniform velocity along a straight line is given by
$x = x_0 + vt$ ....(1)

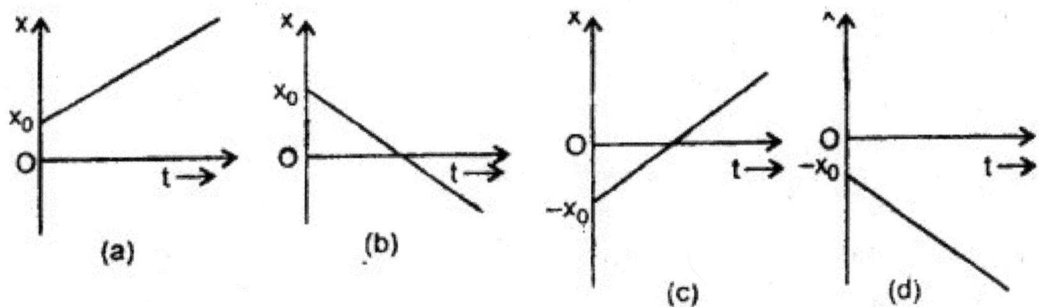

(a) If $X_0 > 0$, $v > 0$ i.e. both positive, then the position-time graph is as shown in Fig. (a).
(b) If X_0 = +ve, v = – ve, then the x – t graph is as shown in Fig. (b).
(c) If X_0 = – ve, v = +ve, then the x – t graph is as shown in Fig. (c).
(d) If both x_0 and v are – ve, then the x -t graph is as shown in Fig. (d).

Answer 21: It is defined as the change in the position of an object in a particular direction.

Characteristics of displacement:

1. It is a vector quantity.
2. It has units of length.
3. The magnitude of displacement is called distance.
4. The diode valve curve between voltage and current is quite like curve ABCD.

Answer 23: The following are some important points about the uniform motion:

1. The velocity in uniform motion does not depend upon the time interval (t_2 – 1,).
2. The velocity in uniform motion is independent of the choice of origin.
3. The average and the instantaneous velocities have the same value in uniform motion.
4. No force acts on the object having uniform motion.
5. Velocity is taken to be positive when the object moves toward the right of the origin and it is taken -ve if an object moves toward the left of the origin.

Answer 24: Initially, the graph will be parallel to the time axis and is represented by AB when the velocity is uniform. Thereafter it is accelerated and its velocity becomes v. The car will then move with this velocity represented by CD.

Answer 25: The motion of two objects moving along a straight line can be represented by two parallel lines on the position-time graph.

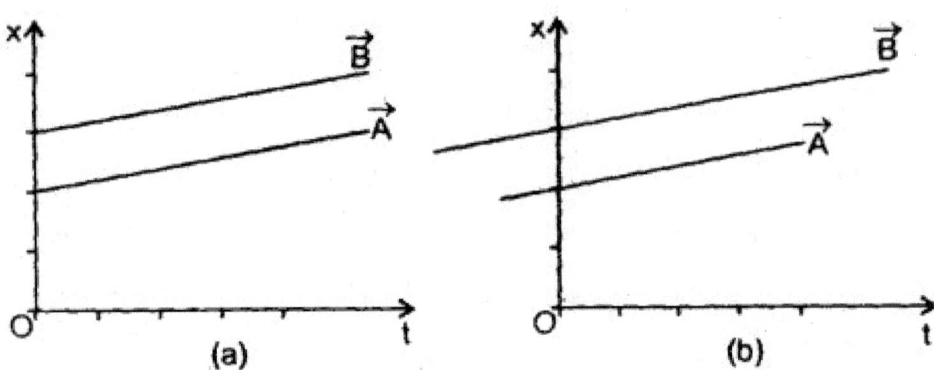

In case of zero relative velocity the two vectors $A^{\rightarrow}$ and $B^{\rightarrow}$ will have the same

magnitude as shown in fig. (a) and when the relative velocity is non-zero, the length of the two vectors i.e. the magnitude of vectors is different even though they are parallel and is shown in fig.(b).

Answer 26: i: net displacement = 0; ii: distance covered = 8πr. iii: Time taken = 5s;

Answer 27: Yes, when a body moves in a circular path, then the direction of the velocity is along the tangent to the point on the circle and the acceleration is always towards its centre.

Answer 28: No, because it is observed that only velocity and acceleration are sufficient to understand and explain the motion of a body.

Answer 29: This is because the relative velocity of the train in which the person is sitting w.r.t. the other train is zero.

Answer 30: Yes, both rest and motion are relative terms. A body at rest w.r.t. one object may be in motion w.r.t. another object, e.g. a person sitting in a moving train is at rest w.r.t. other passengers in the train but at the same time, he is in motion w.r.t. the surroundings (trees or buildings) on the side of the track.

Worksheet 6

1. What velocity will you give to a donkey and what velocity to a monkey so that both escape the gravitational field of Earth?

2. How does Earth retain most of the atmosphere?

3. Earth is continuously pulling the moon towards its center. Why does not then, the moon falls on the Earth?

4. Which is greater out of the following:

(a) The attraction of Earth for 5 kg of copper.

(b) The attraction of 5 kg copper for Earth?

5. Where does a body weigh more – at the surface of Earth or in a mine?

6. How is it that we learn more about the shape of Earth by studying the motion of an artificial satellite than by studying the motion of the moon?

7. If the Earth is regarded as a hollow sphere, then what is the weight of an object below the surface of Earth?

8. What is the formula for escape velocity in terms of g and R?

9. What is the orbital period of revolution of an artificial satellite revolving in a geostationary orbit?

10. Can we determine the mass of a satellite by measuring its time period?

11. Is it possible to put a satellite into an orbit by firing it from a huge canon?

12. What is the amount of work done in bringing a mass from the surface of Earth on one side to a point diametrically opposite on the other side? Why?

13. Name one factor on which the period of revolution of a planet around the Sun depends.

14. The gravitational potential energy of a body of mass m is -107 J. What is the energy required to project the body out of the gravitational field of Earth?

15. Does the force of friction and other contact forces arise due to gravitational attraction? If not, what is the origin of these forces?

16. Two satellites are at different heights. Which would have greater orbital velocity? Why?

17. How much energy is required by a satellite to keep it orbiting? Neglect air resistance? Why?

18. At noon the attractions of the Earth and Sun on a body on the surface of Earth are in opposite directions. But at midnight, they are in the same direction. Does a body weigh more at mid-night?

19. What is geodesic?

20. Why is G called a universal constant?

22. Where does a body weigh more at the pole or at the equator?

23. What is the relation between orbital and escape velocity?

24. The weight of a body is 20N, What is the gravitational pull of the body on the Earth?

25. Why Newton's law of gravitation is said to be universal- law?

26. A particle is to be placed, in turn, outside four objects, each of mass m;

(a) a large uniform solid sphere, (b) a large uniform spherical shell,

(c) a small uniform solid sphere, (d) a small uniform shell.

In each situation, the distance between the particle and the center of the object is d. Rank the objects according to the magnitude of the gravitational force they apply on the particle, greatest first.

27. Can we determine the mass of a satellite by measuring its time-period?

28. Does the gravitational force between two particles depend upon the medium between them?

29. Two artificial satellites of different masses are moving in the same orbit around the Earth. Can they have the same speed?

30. In an imaginary system, the central star has the same mass as our Sun but is much brighter so that only a planet twice the distance between Earth and the Sun can support life. Assuming biological evolution (including aging processes etc.) on that planet similar to ours, what would be the average life span of a 'human' on that planet in terms of its natural year? The average life span of a human on the Earth may be taken to be 70 years.

31. If the force of gravity acts on all bodies in proportion to their masses, then why does not a heavy body fall faster than a light body?

32. What is the weight of a body in a geostationary satellite?

33. A satellite does not need any fuel to circle around the Earth. Why?

34. What will be the effect on the weight of the bodies if Earth stops rotating about its axis?

35. Name the natural satellite of Earth.

36. Why a multi-stage rocket is required to launch a satellite?

37. Mention one difference between g and G.

38. When an apple falls towards the Earth, the Earth moves up to meet the apple. Is the statement true? If yes, why is the Earth's motion not noticeable?

39. Which of the following observations point to the equivalence of inertial and gravitational mass? Why?

(a) Two spheres of different masses dropped from the top of a long evacuated tube reach the bottom of the tube at the same time.

(b) The time period of a simple pendulum is independent of its mass.

(c) The gravitational force on a particle inside a hollow isolated sphere is zero.

(d) For a man in a closed cabin that is falling freely under gravity, gravity disappears.

(e) An astronaut inside a spaceship orbiting around the Earth feels weightless.

(f) Planets orbiting around the Sun obey Kepler's Third Law.

(g) Gravitational force on a body due to the Earth is equal and opposite to the gravitational force on the Earth due to the body.

40. How will the value of acceleration due to gravity be affected if the Earth begins to rotate at a speed greater than its present speed?

41. How do we choose zero levels of gravitational potential energy?

42. Is it possible to put an artificial satellite in an orbit in such a way that it always remains visible directly over New Delhi? Why?

43. A body is suspended with a spring balance attached to the ceiling of an elevator. The balance shows a reading of 5 divisions when the elevator is stationary. During the downward acceleration of the elevator, the balance shows zero reading. Do you think that the inertial mass and gravitational mass of the body are equal? Justify your answer.

44. Does a comet move faster at aphelion or perihelion?

45. Due to some unforeseen event, the planet of the I0 satellites of Jupiter does not pass through the center of Jupiter. Will the orbit of I0 be stable? Why?

46. Is it appropriate to describe the condition of weightlessness as the condition of masslessness? Why?

47. Define central force.

48. The angular momentum is always conserved in the motion under a central force. Name the two results that follow from this.

49. Why an astronaut has a sense of weightlessness in a satellite revolving around the Earth?

50. Why an astronaut in an orbiting spacecraft is not in zero-gravity although he is in a state of weightlessness?

Solutions:

1. We will give them the same velocity as escape velocity is independent of the mass of the body.
2. Due to force of gravity.
3. The gravitational force between the Earth and the moon provides the necessary centripetal force to the moon to move around the Earth. This centripetal force avoids the moon to fall onto the Earth.
4. Same.
5. At the surface of Earth, a body weighs more.
6. This is because an artificial satellite is closer to the Earth than Moon.
7. Zero.
8. --- .
9. It is 24 hours.
10. Yes.
11. Tins can be possible only if we can ignore air friction and technical difficulties.
12. The work done is zero. Because the gravitational potential difference is zero.
13. Mean distance of the planet from the Sun.
14. 107 J.
15. No. The contact forces have an electrical origin.
16. The satellite at the smaller height would have greater velocity.
17. This is because ----- (self study) .
18. No energy is required by a satellite to keep it orbiting. This is because the work done by the centripetal force is zero.
19. No. The weight of the body is due to the Earth's gravity only. What is the full form of the geostationary satellite APPLE? The full form of APPLE is the Ariane Passenger Pay Load Experiment.
20. It is the shortest distance between any two points.
21. G is called a universal constant because its value is the same everywhere.
22. It weighs more at the pole.
23. Self-study.
24. 20N.
25. It is called so because this law holds good irrespective of the nature of the interacting bodies at all places and at all times.
26. They all apply the same gravitational force and hence all will tie.
27. No.
28. No, it does not depend upon the medium between the two particles.
29. Yes, they can have the same speed as orbital speed is independent of the mass of the satellite.
30. 25 planet years.
31. Acceleration due to gravity is independent of the mass of the body.
32. The weight of a body is zero in a geostationary satellite.
33. The gravitational force between satellite and Earth provides the centripetal force required by the satellite to move in a circular orbit.
34. The weight of the bodies will increase.
35. Moon.
36. This is done to save fuel.
37. The value of 'G' remains the same throughout the universe while the value of 'g' varies from place to place.
38. Yes, the statement is true. The acceleration of Earth is very small as compared to that of apple as the mass of Earth is very large.
39. As bodies are in motion in observations (a), (b), (d), (e), (f), thus, these point to the equivalence of inertial and gravitational masses.
40. Acceleration due to gravity will decrease if the angular speed of rotation of Earth increases.
41. It corresponds to the infinite separation between two interacting masses.
42. It is not possible. This is because New Delhi is not in the equatorial plane.

43. Yes, they will be equal. The two masses differ only when the velocity of the lift approaches the velocity of light.
44. At the perihelion where it is close to Sun, the comet moves faster.
45. No. For a stable orbit, the plane of the orbit must pass through the center (equatorial plane) of the planet.
46. No. Weight and mass are different physical quantities. A body may have zero weight but never zero mass. So it is not appropriate to describe the condition of weightlessness as a condition of masslessness.
47. It is defined as the force which is always directed along the position vector of the point of application of the force w.r.t. the fixed point i.e. away or towards a fixed point.
48. (1) The motion of a particle under the central force is always confined to a plane.

    (2) The position vector of the particle w.r.t. the center of force has a constant areal velocity i.e. the position vector sweeps out equal areas in equal times as the particle moves under the influence of the central force.
49. For revolving around the Earth, the astronaut and the satellite require the centripetal force, and their weight is used up in providing the necessary centripetal force. So the astronaut feels weightlessness in space.
50. We know that acceleration due to gravity depends on the height, so there is some value of acceleration due to gravity at every point on the orbit of the spacecraft and his weight is used up in providing the necessary centripetal force for the orbital motion.

Enrichment Activity -----

Statement regarding metabolism:

I. Metabolism involves modification of chemicals (nutrients) in a living body for manufacturing and utilizing energy.

II. Photosynthesis is considered as Anabolism during which CO_2 binds to form six carbon molecule namely Carbohydrate (Glucose).

III. Respiration is a specific pathway of glucose catabolism. The final product of this pathway, the molecule that remains after every last drop of available energy has been squeezed out of the glucose, is carbon dioxide.

IV. Carbon Dioxide is a waste product of metabolism in which energy giving nutrients like sugar and fats are utiilised.

V. We dispose of harmful CO_2 through our lungs. A glucose molecule is made up of three sorts of atoms: carbon, hydrogen and oxygen. Carbon dioxide (as the name suggests) is made up of just two sorts of atoms, carbon and oxygen.

VI. During glucose catabolism, the hydrogen atoms have been removed. What happens to them? The mitochondria (remember these are the bacteria-sized structures involved in energy metabolism – the chocolates or cocktail sausages in the box model of chapter 3) turn them into water, which is another waste product.

On the basis of above mentioned statement two different types of metabolism are: ___________ and __________________ which moves opposite to each other in terms of the nature of chemical reactions. They jointly play a vital role in maintaining the balance of O_2 and CO_2 in nature.

Worksheet 7

1: Statement regarding Columnar Epithelium is as follows:

Simple columnar epithelium consists of a single layer of elongated cells. (a) Idealized representation of simple columnar epithelium. (b) Micrograph of a section through simple columnar epithelium. This tissue is composed of a single layer of cells with elongated nuclei located at about the same level, near the basement membrane **Cilia** extend from the free surfaces of the cells and move constantly. In the female reproductive tract, cilia aid in moving the egg cell through the uterine tube to the uterus.

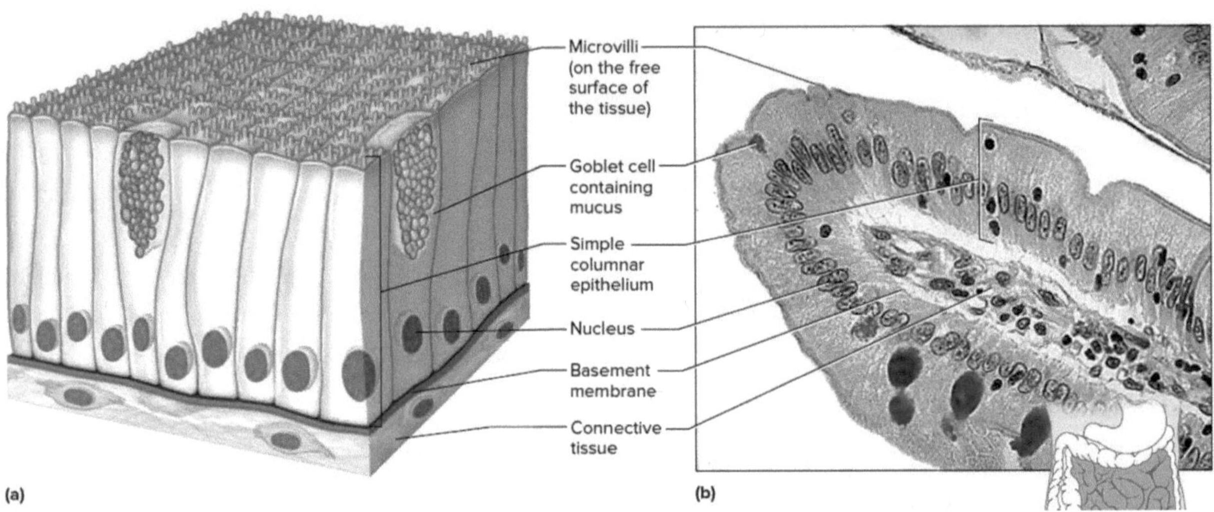

Complete the incomplete[13] statement as depicted below ---

I. Nonciliated simple columnar epithelium lines the uterus and portions of the digestive tract, including the stomach and the small and large intestines. Because its cells are tall, this tissue is thick, which enables it to protect underlying tissues.

II. Simple columnar epithelium also secretes digestive fluids and absorbs nutrients from digested food.

III. Simple columnar epithelial cells, specialized for absorption, often have many tiny, cylindrical processes, called microvilli, extending from their surfaces.

IV. These increase the surface area of the cell membrane where it is exposed to substances being absorbed.

V. Specialized flask-shaped glandular cells are scattered among the columnar cells of simple columnar epithelium.

VI. These cells, called, ___________ _________ secrete a protective fluid, popularly called ____________, onto the free surface of the tissue.

[13] *Source: McGraw-Hill Education/Dennis Strete, photographer*

2: Observe the following –

Simple cuboidal epithelium consists of a single layer of tightly packed, cube-shaped cells. (a) Idealized representation of simple cuboidal epithelium. (b) Micrograph of a section through simple cuboidal epithelium
Select the option which is not true:
I: Cells of this epithelium are mono-nucleated.
II: This epithelium covers the ovaries and lines most of the kidney tubules and the ducts of certain glands. In these tubules and ducts, the free surface faces the hollow channel or lumen.
IV: Cells of this epithelium also accommodates different water filled vacuoles.
V: In the kidneys, this tissue functions in the formation of urine.
VI: These epithelium also present in glands and plays a vital role in secretion of glandular products.

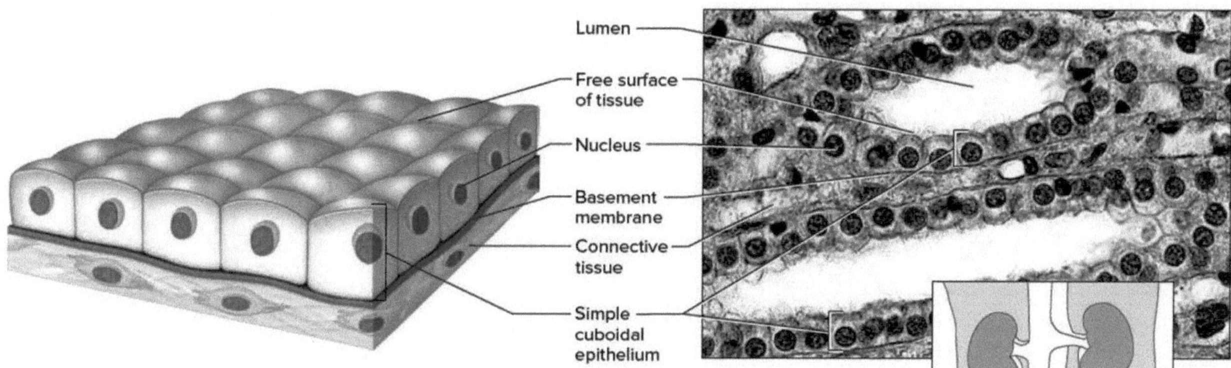

3: Complete the following statement ---

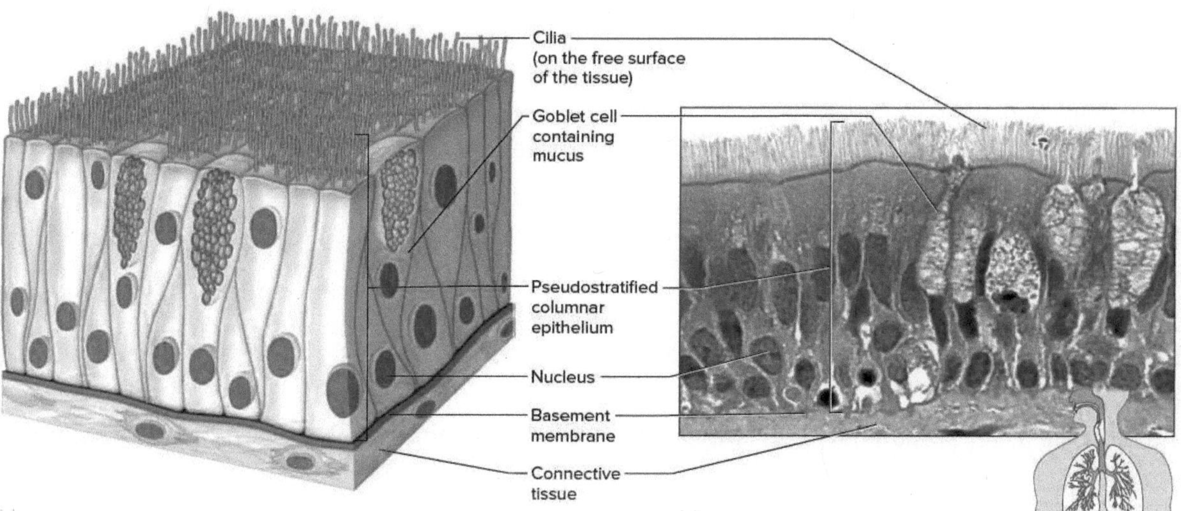

The ___________ ___________ linings are sticky and trap dust and microorganisms that enter with the air. The __________ move the mucus and its captured particles upward and out of the airways.

4: Identify this tissue: “The many cell layers of this tissue make it relatively thick. Cells divide in the deeper layers, and newer cells push older ones farther outward, where they flatten. These tissues are named for the shape of their top layer of cells.”

Option ____ is not correct.

Ans 1: goblet cells; mucus; 2: IV; 3: mucus-covered; cilia; 4: stratified squamous epithelium;.

Worksheet 8

1: Define force. Is force a scalar or a vector quantity?

2: State and define the unit of force in the S.I. system.

3: Define one newton. Write the relation between S. I. unit and C.G.S. unit of force.

4: Define 1 kgf., How is it related to the S.I. unit of force?

5: (i) Where is the centre of gravity of a uniform ring situated?

(ii) 'The position of the centre of gravity of a body remains unchanged even when the body is deformed.' State whether the statement is true or false.

6: Which of the following remains constant in uniform circular motion, Speed or Velocity or both?

7: Define 1 Dyne.

8: Define contact forces.

9: Define non-contact forces.

10: State the energy changes in the following devices while in use

(i) A loud speaker (ii) A glowing electric bulb

11: Give any two effects of a force on a non-rigid body.

12: Where does the position of centre of gravity lie for

(i) a circular lamina (ii) a triangular lamina

13: What is Gravitational force? Give gravitational units of force.

14: What is the work done by the gravitational force on the moon that revolves around the earth?

15: A coolie, with a load of 30 kg on his head, walks on the platform. If he walks a distance of 60 m, what is the work done by him?

16: A bullet fired against a window glass pane makes a hole in it without any cracks while a stone striking the same glass pane smashes it; explain with reason.

17: State one factor on which the magnitude of a non-contact force depends. How does magnitude of a non-contact force change along distance?

18: Under what condition will a set of gears produce

(i) a gain in speed (ii) a gain in torque.

19: Name the force required for uniform circular motion. State its direction.

20: A force is applied on (i) a non-rigid body and (ii) a rigid body. How does the effect of the force differ in the above two cases?

21: How does the distance of separation between two bodies affect the magnitude of the non-contact force between them?

22: In what way does an 'Ideal machine' differ from a 'Practical machine'?

23: Can a simple machine act as a force multiplier and a speed multiplier at the same time?

24: State two factors on which moment of force about a point depends.

25: State the units of moment of force.

26: State the principle of moments.

27: State when moment of force is positive and when it is negative.

28: Give the units of couple.

29: Two similar vehicles are moving with same velocity on the road, such that one of thus is loaded and the other one is empty which of the two vehicles will require larger force to stop?

30: What is meant by the term 'moment of force'? If the moment of force is assigned a negative sign then will the turning tendency of the force be clockwise or anti clockwise?

31: Define Uniform circular motion.
32: Define Translational motion.
33: Define Centripetal force.
34: Define the term momentum.
35: How is force related to the momentum of a body?
36: State the condition when the change in momentum of a body depends only on the change in its velocity.
37: With reference to their direction of action, how does a centripetal force differ from a centrifugal force?
38: Can the CG be situated outside the material of the body? Give an example.
39: Explain why It is easier to knock down a boy who is standing on one foot than one who is standing on two.
40: Explain why One leans forward while climbing up a hill.
41: Explain why a tight rope-walker, often holds a long pole in his hands when in action.
42: Explain why a ship loaded with light goods is more liable to be over turned than the one loaded with heavy goods.
43: Explain why Standing passengers are not allowed on the upper deck of a double decker bus.
44: Explain when we carry a weight on one hand, we bend on the other side.
45: What is the weight of a body placed at the centre of the earth?
46: What do you understand by work? Is work a scalar or a vector quantity?
47: In the following cases write yes, if the work is being done and no, if no work is being done.
(i) A man trying to push a wall, (ii) A man moving on the rough ground.
(iii) A coolie standing with a heavy load on his head, (iv) A boy climbing up a staircase.
48: State two conditions when the work done by a force acting on a body is zero.
49: (i) Define power.
(ii) Is power a scalar or vector quantity?
50: State the condition when the work done by force is (i) positive and (ii) negative.
51: A force F when acts on a body, displaces it by a distance d in a direction at an angle θ with the direction of force. Write down the expression for the work done by the force.
52: Can two agents, doing the same work, have different power?
53: When does a force do work? What is the work done by the moon when it revolves around the earth?
54: State the amount of work done by an object when it moves in a circular path for one complete rotation. Give a reason to justify your answer.
55: State two conditions for work to be done.
56: Why is less effort needed to lift a load over an inclined plane as compared to lifting the load directly?
57: What is the S.I. unit of work? Define it.
58: State S.I. unit of power and define it.
59: Justify the statement. “Power can be expressed as the product of force and velocity.”
60: State larger units of power.
61: State the practical unit mainly used in mechanical engineering and write down its

62: What happen to the power if the time for doing a work is reduced from t second to t/10

second?
63: What do you understand by the term energy? Is energy a scalar or vector? How is energy possessed by a body measured?
64: State the S.I. and C.G.S. units of energy. How are they related?
65: Write five forms of energy.

66: What do you understand by mechanical energy? What are the different forms of mechanical energy?
67: What do you understand by the potential energy of the body?
68: What do you understand by the kinetic energy of the body? Give three examples of bodies possessing kinetic energy.
69: How is kinetic energy possessed by a moving body measured?
70: A man climbs a slope and another walks same distance on level road. Which of the two

spends more energy and why?
71: Is it possible that a body may possess energy even when it is not in motion?
72: What kind of energy is possessed in the situations when?
(i) A cocked up spring of air gun. (ii) A stone lying on the top of roof.
(iii) A fish moving in water. (iv) A horse running along a level road,
(v) Water stored in dams. (vi) An electron spinning around nucleus.
(vii) A shooting arrow. (viii) A stone, in a strecthed catapult.
73: Relate 1 KWh (kilowatt hour) with joule.
74: Obtain an expression for the potential energy of a body of mass m at a height h above the ground.
75: When an arrow is shot from its bow, it has kinetic energy. From where does it get the kinetic energy?
76: What happens to the K.E. when (i) the mass of the body is doubled at constant velocity and (ii) the velocity of the body is doubled at constant mass?
77: Write the type of energy possessed in the following cases:
(i) A bent bow (ii) A falling apple
(iii) A wound up spring (iv) A moving cricket ball.
78: Give three examples of bodies possessing potential energy.
79: What is dissipation of energy?
80: State the energy changes which takes place in Electricity is obtained from solar energy.
81: What is the main energy transformation that occurs in:
(i) Photosynthesis in green leaves;
(ii) Charging of a battery.
82: A man climbs a slope and another walks same distance on level road. Which of the two expends more energy and why?
83: State the law of conservation of energy.
84: Name the two groups in which various sources of energy are classified?
85: Give two examples each of renewable and non-renewable sources of energy?
86: Why using wood as fuel is not advisable although wood is a renewable source of energy?
87: Name a device in which solar energy is converted into electricity state its two uses.
88: Name the material commonly used for manufacturing of solar cells.
89: Name two places in India where electricity is generated from nuclear power plants.
90: What should be the characteristic of a source of energy?
91: What is hydro-energy? Explain the principle of generating electricity from hydro-energy.
92: How much hydro-electric power is generated in India?
93: State two advantages and two disadvantages of using hydro-energy for producing electricity.
94: What is wind energy? Explain the principle of working of windmill for generating electricity.
95: State two advantages and disadvantage of using wind energy for producing electricity.
96: State two advantages and disadvantage of using nuclear energy for producing electricity.

97: State two ways for the judicious use of energy.

98: Explain, why submarines are able to dive under water as well as sail on the surface of water?

99: State the principle of conservation of energy.

100: Distinguish between work and power.

101: State the energy changes which takes place when:

a) A body released from rest from the top of a building.
b) A body thrown vertically upwards from the ground.
c) In a heat engine.
d) A bulb glows, when torch light is switched on.
e) A car moves up a hill.
f) A toy car spring is wound and car is made to run on level floor.
g) Water stored in dams rotates turbine connected to a dynamo.
h) An air gun is loaded and then fired.
i) A magnesium ribbon burns in air.
j) A stone projected vertically upwards, returns back to the thrower.
k) Water freezes in the freezing chamber of a fridge.
l) Photographic film is exposed to sunlight.
m) Food is digested by animals.
n) During electrolysis.
o) Burning of coal.
p) Petrol engine of a running motor car.
q) A battery lighting up a bulb.
r) Electricity obtained from nuclear energy.
s) Electricity obtained from solar energy.
t) Electricity obtained from wind energy.
u) Electricity obtained from hydro energy.

102: Give one example when:

a) Heat energy changes to kinetic energy.
b) Kinetic energy changes to heat energy.
c) Sound energy changes to electric energy.
d) Electric energy changes to sound energy.
e) Light energy changes to chemical energy.
f) Chemical energy changes to light energy.
g) Electric energy changes to mechanical energy .
h) Mechanical energy changes to electric energy.
i) Potential energy changes to electric energy.
j) Electric energy changes to potential energy.
k) Mechanical energy to heat energy.
l) Kinetic energy to potential energy.
m) Electrical energy to heat energy.
n) Chemical energy to electrical energy.

Solution:

1: A force is that cause which changes or tends to change the state of rest or of uniform motion of a body. Force is a vector quantity.

2: The unit of force in S. I. system is Newton (N). Newton is defined as the force which, when applied on a body of mass 1 kg produces in it an acceleration of 1 ms2.

3: One Newton: If a body of mass 1 kg moves with an acceleration of 1 m/s2 then force acting on the body is said to be one Newton. 1N = 105 Dyne.
Relation between S. I. and CGS unit of force is 1 Newton = 1 kg × 1 ms-2.

4: 1 kgf: It is the force due to gravity on a mass of 1kg. (kilogram), 1 kgf = 9.8 N.

5: (i) Centre of gravity of a uniform ring is at its centre.
(ii) False.

6: In uniform circular motion speed remains constant.

7: 1 dyne is that force which when acting on a body of mass 1 gram, produces an acceleration of 1 cm s-2 in it.
1 dyne = 1 g × 1 cm s-2.

8: The forces which are applied on a body through a connector, are called contact forces. Forces like Frictional force, Mechanical force etc., are the forces of contact.

9: The forces which act on a body without the help of any connector, are called non-contact forces or forces of distance. Gravitational force, Mechanical force etc., are non-contact forces.

10: (i) Loud speaker: Electric energy to sound.
(ii) Glowing electric bulb: Electric to heat energy to light energy.

11: Two effects of a force on a non-rigid body are:
(i) Force can change the state of rest or motion of the body
(ii) Force can change the size or shape of the body.

12: (i) Circular lamina – Centre of the lamina
(ii) Triangular lamina – Point of intersection of medians.

13: Earth exerts a force of attraction on each object. This force is due to gravity and its magnitude is directly proportional to the mass of the object. This force is known as gravitational force and its units are gravitational units.
In MKS system the gravitational unit of force is kilogramme force i.e., kgf. In CGS system it is gram force, gf.

14: The moon is revolving around the earth. In this process, the work done by the gravitational force is zero because the displacement of the moon is at right angle to the gravitational force.

15: The work done by the coolie is zero because there is no displacement of' the load in the direction of force, which he is applying vertically upwards.

16: When the bullet strikes the glass, the part of the glass coming in contact with the bullet, immediately shares the large velocity of the bullet and makes a hole in it while the rest of the glass pane, due to inertia of rest, remains at rest and so is not smashed. But when a stone strikes the same glass pan, the surrounding part of the glass gets time to share the comparatively low velocity of stone and so it is smashed.

17: The magnitude of a non-contact force depends on distance. If magnitude of a non-contact force increasing then distance decreasing.

18: (i) Gain in speed: When number of teeth in driving wheel is more than number of teeth in driven wheel.
(ii) Gain in torque: When number of teeth in driven gear is more than number of teeth in driving gear.

19: Force required for uniform circular motion is centripetal force. It is directed towards its centre i.e., centre of the circle.
A force is applied on (i) a non-rigid body and (ii) a rigid body. How does the effect of the force differ in the above two cases?

20: When force is applied on a non-rigid body it undergoes deformation i.e. change in size, shape and position where as a rigid body doesn't undergo change in shape, position and size.

21: Non-contact force decreases with the increase in separation.

22: Ideal machine has 100% efficiency i.e., work done on the machine = work done by the machine.

23: No.

24: Moment of force depends on two factors:
(i) Magnitude of force applied.
(ii) Distance of line of action of the force from the axis of rotation.

25: In CGS system, unit of moment of a force is Dyne-cm and in MKS system, unit of moment of a force is Newton-metre. The gravitational units in CGS and MKS system of measurement are gf cm and kg m respectively.

26: When number of forces acting on a body, keep it in equilibrium, then the sum total of clockwise moments about any turning point is equal to sum total of anticlockwise moments about the point.

27: If couple has a tendency to rotate the body in anti-clockwise direction then its moment is taken positive and if the tendency of rotation is clockwise then the moment is negative.

28: In MKS system, the unit of couple are Nm and kgf m.
In CGS system, the units of couple are Dyne cm and gf cm.

29: A large force is required to stop the loaded vehicle. It is because loaded vehicle has greater momentum than the empty vehicle as the mass of loaded vehicle is more than that of the empty one. So, it requires more force to stop.

30: It is equal to the product of the magnitude of the force and the perpendicular distance of the line of action of force from the axis of rotation. If moment of force is assigned a negative value, it means clockwise tendency of force.

31: When a particle moves with a constant speed in a circular path, its motion is said to be the uniform circular motion.

32: When a force acts on a rigid body which is free to move, the body starts moving in a straight line in the direction of force. This is called translational motion.

33: At each of circular path, the particle, instead of moving straight continuously, turns towards the centre. Therefore, the motion in circular path is under the action of a force which called the centripetal force.

34: The momentum of a body is the product of the mass of the body and its velocity, i.e. $p = mv$.

35: Force is equal to the rate of change of momentum.

36: If mass of the body m remains constant then the change in momentum of the body depends only on the change in its velocity.

37: Direction of centripetal force is towards the centre of the circle whereas centrifugal force is opposite to centripetal force.

38: The position of CG of a body depends on the distribution of mass in the body. It can be situated outside or inside the material of the body.
For example: The CG of a wire is at its mid-point but CG of a ring lies at the centre where there is no material.

39: It is easier to knock down a boy who is standing on one foot than one who is standing on two because boy standing on both feet has a larger base area and hence it has more stable equilibrium than a boy standing on one foot.

40: A person going uphill has to bend forward but while coming down has to bent backwards, this is to keep the CG at the centre of the body and between his feet.

41: A tight rope-walker carries a long stick in his hand to maintain the CG such that the vertical line passes through the rope.

42: A ship loaded with light goods is more liable to be over turned than the one loaded with heavy goods. This is because the CG in the former case is high and so a slight displacement due to water current may cause the vertical line passing through the CG to fall outside the base, thereby overturning the ship.

43: The centre of gravity is raised and on an inclined road the bus may topple.

44: This is to let our CG fall within the base of our support.

45: The weight of a body placed at the centre of the earth is zero as
$g = 0$
$\therefore W = mg$
$= 0$

46: Work is said to be done when a force displaces a body through some distance, in its own direction, i.e.,
Work = Force × Displacement
$W = F \times d$
Work is a scalar quantity.

47: (i) No. (ii) Yes. (iii) No. (iv) Yes.

48: (i) When there is no displacement by the force in the body.
(ii) When the displacement is normal to the direction of force.

49: (i) Power is defined as the rate of doing work or work done per second,
ICSE Solutions for Class 10 Physics - Force, Work, Power and Energy 1
(ii) Power is a scalar quantity.

50: (i) Work done by a force is positive when the displacement is in the direction of the force.
(ii) Work done by a force is negative when the displacement is in the direction opposite to the force.

51: Work done by the force, $W = Fd \cos \theta$.

52: Yes, since power = work/time the two agents can have different powers if they take different amounts of time to do the same work.

53: Work is said to be done if a body undergoes displacement due to applied force.
Work done = Force × Displacement
Work done is zero by the moon, as there is no displacement since it is moving in a circular path.

54: Amount of work done is equal to zero.
Work is said to be done only when there is displacement produced. In case of a body moving in a circular path, the body comes to its original place, therefore, there is no displacement and hence work is zero.

55: The two conditions are:

(i) Application of-force on the body.
(ii) Displacement of the body in the direction of force.

56: Less effort is required because for a given height 'h' as longer is the length 'l' of the inclined plane, smaller is the angle of inclination therefore, greater is the mechanical advantage, so lesser will be the effort required. As we know
Mechanical Advantage = l/h.

57: The S.I. unit of work is newton-metre or joule (J).
1 Joule = 1 N × 1 m.
1 J of work is said to be done by a force of 1 N if it displaces a body by 1 m in the direction of force.

58: S.I. unit of power is J/s or Js-1 (or watt W). The power is said to be 1 watt when 1 J of work is done in 1 sec.

59:
ICSE Solutions for Class 10 Physics - Force, Work, Power and Energy 2
(Since rate of change of displacement is velocity).

60: The larger units of power are:
1 Kilowatt = 1000 watt 103 W
1 Megawatt = 1000,000 W = 106 W.
equivalent in watt.

61: The practical unit of power used in mechanical engineering is 'Horse Power' (H.P,)
1 H.P. = 746 W = 0.746 KW.

62: The power becomes 10 times of its initial value. This is because power = work/time. Thus, power $\propto$ 1/time for a given work. Reducing the time by a factor of 10 thus increases the power 10 times.

63: Energy is defined as the capacity of a body to do work. Energy is a scalar quantity. The energy possessed by a body is measured by the amount of work done by a body while changing its state of rest or state of motion.

64: The S.I. unit of energy is joule (J) and C.G.S. unit is erg.
1J = 107 erg.

65: (i) Mechanical energy (ii) Chemical energy (iii) Solar energy
(iv) Heat energy (v) Light energy.

66: The energy possessed by body due to its state or its motion is called mechanical energy. Mechanical energy is of two forms: (i) potential energy, and (ii) kinetic energy.

67: The potential energy of a body is the energy possessed by body by virtue of its state or position.

68: The kinetic energy of a body is the energy possessed by body by virtue of its state of motion,
(i) A moving bullet (ii) A flowing river (iii) Wind.

69: The kinetic energy possessed by a moving body is measured by the amount of work done by an opposing force in bringing the body to rest from its present state of motion.

70: The man moving along the slope expends more energy. It is because, while moving along slope, he gains height and hence has extra potential energy.

71: Yes, the body may possess potential energy.

72: (i) P.E. (ii) P.E. (iii) K.E.
(iv) K.E. (v) P.E. (vi) K.E.
(vii) K.E. (viii) P.E.

73: 1 KWh = 1 KW × 1 h = 1000 W × 3600s = 36,00,000 J.

74: Force due to gravity on the body F = mg
Work done in lifting the body against the force of gravity to a height h above the ground
W = F × d = mg × h = mgh
Thus, potential energy of body = mgh.

75: A stretched bow possessed potential energy on account of a change in its shape. To shoot an arrow, the bow is released. The potential energy of the bow is converted into the kinetic energy of the arrow.

76: We have, K.E. = 1/2 mv2
Hence,
(i) On doubling the mass, at constant velocity, the K.E. becomes double of its original value.
(ii) On doubling the velocity, at constant mass, the K.E. becomes (2)2 i.e., 4 times its original value.

77: (i) A bent bow: Potential Energy
(ii) A falling apple: Kinetic Energy
(iii) A wound up spring: Potential Energy
(iv) A moving cricket ball: Kinetic Energy.

78: (i) An object kept at a height above the ground.
(ii) A compressed spring, and
(iii) A stretched catapult.

79: In transforming the mechanical energy if a part of it gets converted into another form of energy which cannot be utilised for useful work, this loss of energy is called the dissipation of energy.

80: Heat energy from sun is converted into electricity.

81: (i) Light energy of chemical energy.
(ii) Electric energy to chemical energy.

82: The man moving along the slope expends more energy. It is because, while moving along slope, he gains height and hence has extra potential energy.

83: According to law of conservation of mechanical energy, the sum of kinetic energy and potential energy always remains constant.

84: Renewable and Non-renewable sources of energy.

85: Renewable sources of energy: Solar energy and wind energy.
Non-renewable sources of energy: coal and oil.

86: It is not advisable to use wood as fuel even though it can be replenished because burning of wood produces smoke that causes pollution which results in environmental imbalance.

87: Solar cell. Its two uses are:
(i) All artificial satellites and space probes mainly depend upon electricity generated by solar cells.
(ii) Solar cells are used for lighting, operating water pumps, for running radio and television sets in remote areas and traffic signals etc.

88: Silicon and Gallium. Solar cell produces d.c. current. State whether a solar cell produces a.c. or d.c. current.

89: (i) At Kalpakkam in Tamil Nadu, and
(ii) At Narora, in Uttar Pradesh.

90: A good source of energy should have the following characteristics:
(i) It should do a large amount of work per unit mass or volume.
(ii) It should have high calorific value.
(iii) It should be easily accessible over a long period of time.
(iv) It should be economical and easy to store and transport.
(v) It should be Safe and convenient to use.

91: The energy possessed by the flowing water is called hydro-energy.
Principle: It works on the principle of conversion of kinetic energy of flowing water into electrical energy. When the stored water is allowed to fall from the top of dam on the blades of water-turbine, the potential energy of stored water is converted into kinetic energy which rotates the water turbine rapidly which in turn rotates the armature coil of generator and generates electricity.

92: At present, 23% of total electricity is generated in India using hydro-energy.

93: Advantages:
(i) When the electricity is generated, no greenhouse gases are made.
(ii) It is an inexhaustible source of energy.
Disadvantages:
(i) The dam is expensive to build.
(ii) By building a dam, the nearby area has to be flooded and this could affect nearby wildlife and Plants.

94: The blowing wind has kinetic energy is called wind energy.
Principle: It works on the principle of conversion of kinetic energy of blowing wind into electrical energy. When the blowing wind strikes across the blades of a windmill it exerts a force which rotates its blade. The turning of the blades would simultaneously cause the shaft to turn, which is connected to a generator. This makes the generator produce electricity.

95: Advantages:
(i) Wind is free and will not run out (renewable sources).
(ii) Wind energy does not create greenhouse gases.
Disadvantages:
(i) The wind farms can be established only at places near the coastal areas where wind blows around the year steadily with a speed not less than 15 Km h-1.
(ii) The establishment of wind farm is expensive.

96: Advantages:
(i) A very small amount of nuclear fuel produces huge amount of energy.
(ii) Nuclear fuel does not contribute harmful greenhouse gases to the atmosphere on burning.
Disadvantages:
(i) The waste that is produced when using nuclear fuel is radioactive and very harmful. It needs to be disposed of carefully.
(ii) World uranium supplies may run out in about 50 year.

97: (i) The wastage of energy should be avoided.
(ii) The excessive use of non-renewable resources such as coal, petroleum and natural gas should be reduced.

98: Submarines are provided with ballast tanks. When required to dive, the water is allowed to enter in the tanks. And when required to sail, the water is forced out by compressed air.
Work is a scalar quantity.

99: Principle of conservation of energy: It states that energy can neither be created nor be destroyed but can be transferred from one form to another form.

100: Work does not depend on time, while the power depends on time. Power is the work done in unit time.

101:

a) The potential energy changes to kinetic energy.
b) The kinetic energy changes to potential energy.
c) The heat energy changes to mechanical energy.
d) The chemical energy of cell changes to electric energy. The electric energy first changes to heat and finally to light energy.
e) The K.E. of moving car changes to potential energy.
f) The mechanical energy changes to potential energy during winding. The potential energy is then released in the form of kinetic energy.
g) P.E. of stored water changes to K.E. of flowing water, The K.E. of flowing water rotates turbine. The turbine in turn rotates the coil of generator and changes into electric energy.
h) During loading, the mechanical energy changes to potential energy of spring. On firing, the P.E. of spring changes to K.E. of bullet.
i) During burning of magnesium, chemical energy changes to heat and light energy.
j) The kinetic energy changes to potential energy when stone rises up. The potential energy then changes back to kinetic energy, when stone comes down.
k) The kinetic energy of water molecules is released in the form of heat energy.
l) The light energy changes to chemical energy?
m) The chemical energy changes into heat energy.
n) The electrical energy changes to chemical energy.
o) The chemical energy changes into heat energy.
p) The chemical energy changes into mechanical energy.
q) The electrical energy changes into heat energy and light energy.
r) The heat energy changes into electricity.
s) The heat energy changes into electricity.
t) The K. E. changes into electricity.
u) The Kinetic energy changes into electricity.

102:

a) In the automobile engine, heat energy changes to kinetic energy.
b) When two stones are rubbed against each other, kinetic energy changes to heat energy.
c) When we speak in front of microphone, sound energy changes to electric energy.
d) When a loudspeaker works, the electric energy changes to sound energy.
e) During photosynthesis, light energy changes to chemical energy.
f) During burning of magnesium, chemical energy changes to light energy.
g) In an electric motor, electric energy changes to mechanical energy.
h) In an electric generator, the mechanical energy changes to electric energy.
i) The P.E. of stored water in dams, changes to electric energy in generators.
j) When electrolysis is carried out, the electric energy changes to potential energy.
k) Rubbing of palms.
l) Throwing up a pebble from the ground.
m) Electric heater while in use.
n) Drawing current from an electric cell..

Worksheet 9

1: Answer the following.

Observe the stages of cell differentiation of a eukaryotic plant as displayed through a concept chart. Which parts of plant body are formed by the cork cambium?

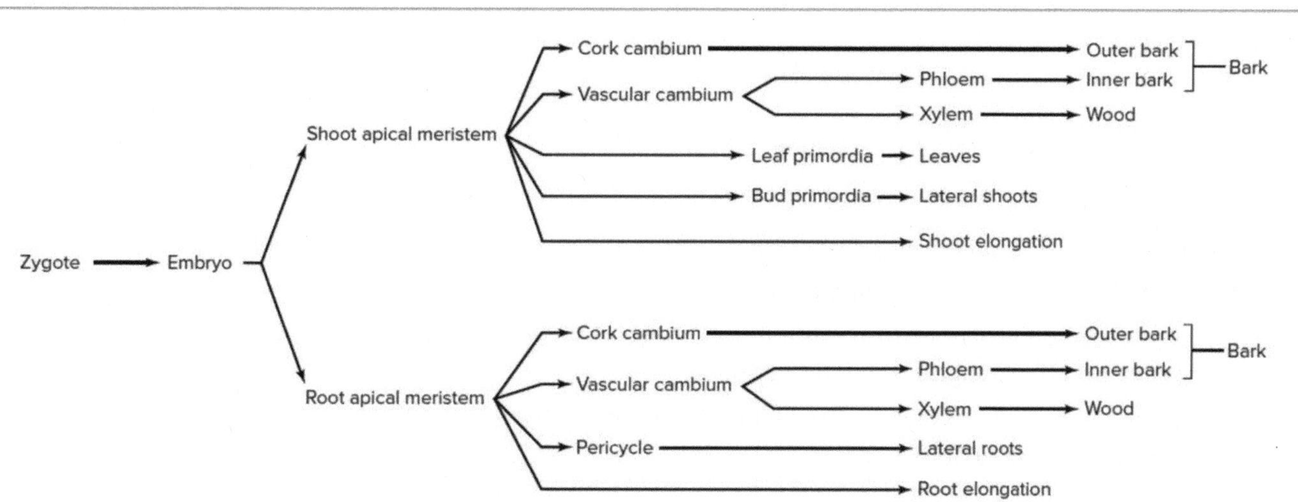

2: Identify the following --

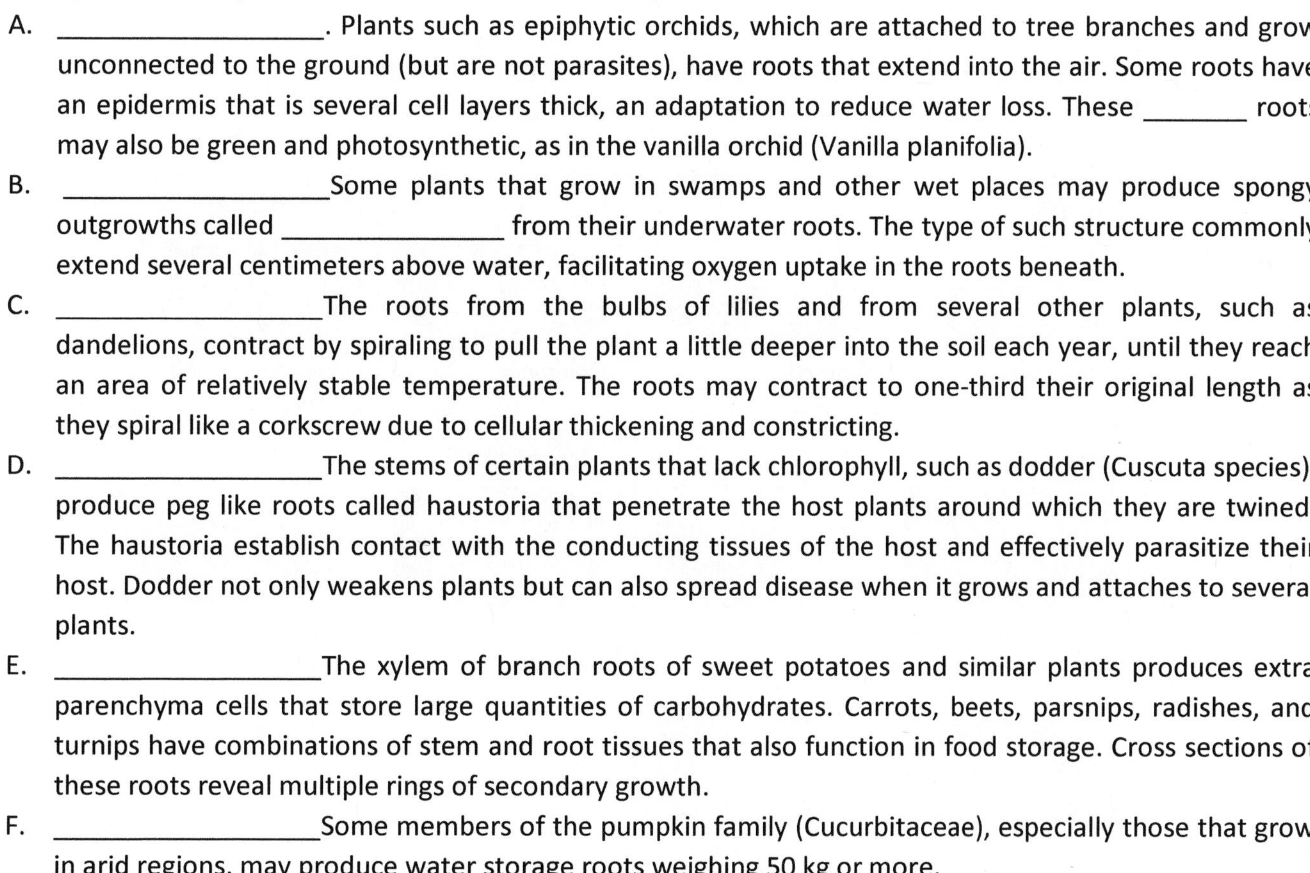

A. __________________. Plants such as epiphytic orchids, which are attached to tree branches and grow unconnected to the ground (but are not parasites), have roots that extend into the air. Some roots have an epidermis that is several cell layers thick, an adaptation to reduce water loss. These _______ roots may also be green and photosynthetic, as in the vanilla orchid (Vanilla planifolia).

B. __________________Some plants that grow in swamps and other wet places may produce spongy outgrowths called _______________ from their underwater roots. The type of such structure commonly extend several centimeters above water, facilitating oxygen uptake in the roots beneath.

C. __________________The roots from the bulbs of lilies and from several other plants, such as dandelions, contract by spiraling to pull the plant a little deeper into the soil each year, until they reach an area of relatively stable temperature. The roots may contract to one-third their original length as they spiral like a corkscrew due to cellular thickening and constricting.

D. __________________The stems of certain plants that lack chlorophyll, such as dodder (Cuscuta species), produce peg like roots called haustoria that penetrate the host plants around which they are twined. The haustoria establish contact with the conducting tissues of the host and effectively parasitize their host. Dodder not only weakens plants but can also spread disease when it grows and attaches to several plants.

E. __________________The xylem of branch roots of sweet potatoes and similar plants produces extra parenchyma cells that store large quantities of carbohydrates. Carrots, beets, parsnips, radishes, and turnips have combinations of stem and root tissues that also function in food storage. Cross sections of these roots reveal multiple rings of secondary growth.

F. __________________Some members of the pumpkin family (Cucurbitaceae), especially those that grow in arid regions, may produce water storage roots weighing 50 kg or more.

G. __________________Certain species of fig and other tropical trees produce huge roots toward the base of the trunk, which provide considerable stability.

3: Observe the table given below –

Measurement	Unit	Abbreviation
Force	dyne	dyne
Energy	erg	erg
Pressure	barye	ba
Electric current	biot	Bi
Magnetism	gauss	G
Electric charge	franklin	Fr

All these measurement units are in _____________ System of units.

4: Three layers of tissue are represented as follows ---

A: ____________________ : gives rise to the epidermis of the skin, lining of the mouth and nasal cavity, cornea, sweat and sebaceous glands, and mammary glands.

B: ____________________ : gives rise to the uriniferous tubules of the kidney, the lining of the reproductive and circulatory systems, and the lining of the body cavities.

C: ____________________ : gives rise to the lining of the gastrointestinal and respiratory systems and to the glands of the gastrointestinal system.

5: Answer the following:

Different epithelial tissues are displayed in the following diagram.
Which of the following tissue forms the inner lining of ova?

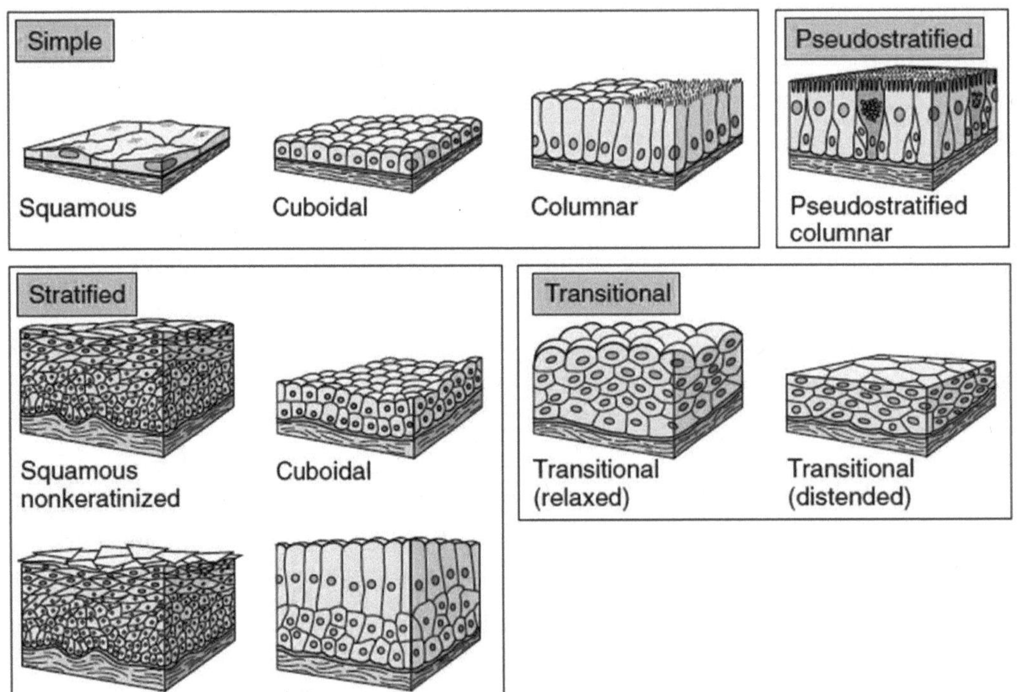

6: Structure and function of a group of tissue given below –

A: Cartilage, bone, tendons, ligaments, and capsules of organs provide structural support.
B: Blood, lymph, and connective tissue proper act as a medium for exchange by delivering nutrients, waste products, and signalling molecules to and from cells of the body.
C: Certain cells that travel in the bloodstream leave the blood and enter connective tissue proper to defend and protect the body from potentially deleterious agents.
D: Adipose cells store lipids and congregate to form adipose tissue serving as local storage depots of fat.
All these tissues resemble some functional similarity. All these tissue belongs to ____________ Tissue.

7: Complete the following:

All of the following types of cells duly originated from undifferentiated mesenchymal cell will take part in the formation of ______________ Tissue.

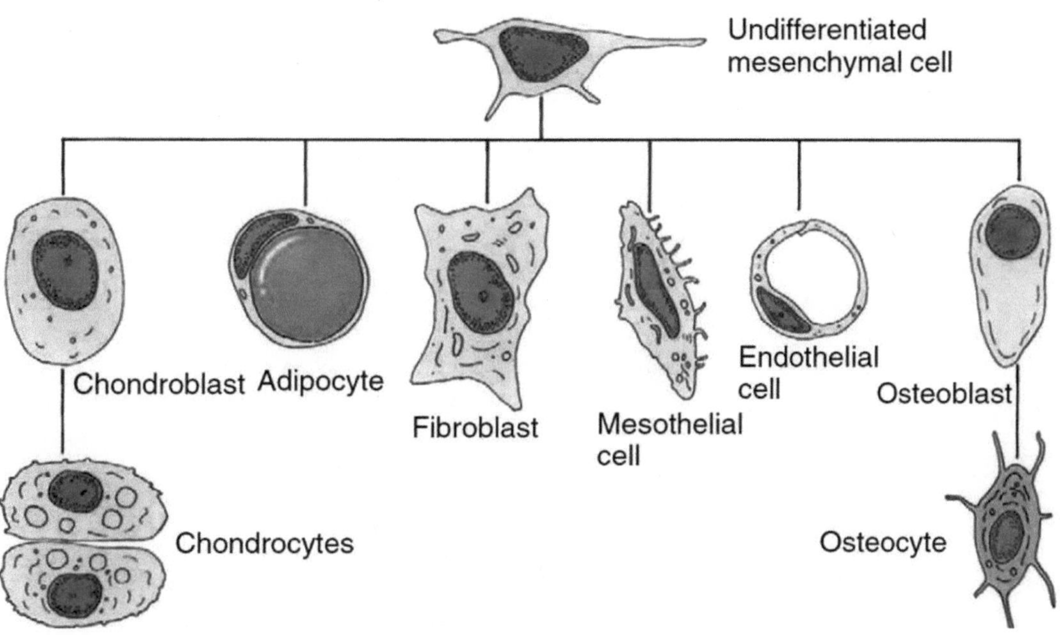

8: Fibroblasts may be modified to become _________________ in regions of wound healing. They possess characteristics of fibroblasts and smooth muscle cells, but in contrast to smooth muscle, they do not have any attachment of an external lamina. _______________ function in wound contraction, and as resident cells of the periodontal ligament. They may assist in tooth eruption.

Solution:
1: Outer and inner bark; 2: A = Aerial roots; B = Pneumatophores.; C = Contractile roots; D = Parasitic roots; E = Food storage roots ; F = Water storage roots ; G = Buttress roots ; 3: CGS;
4: A= Ectoderm; C =Endoderm; B = Mesoderm; 5: Simple columnar; 6: Connective; 7: Connetive ;
8: myofibroblasts;

Worksheet 10

1: Complete the following –

All of the following types of cells duly originated from undifferentiated Hematopoietic Stem cell will take part in the formation of a special type ______________ Tissue namely ________.

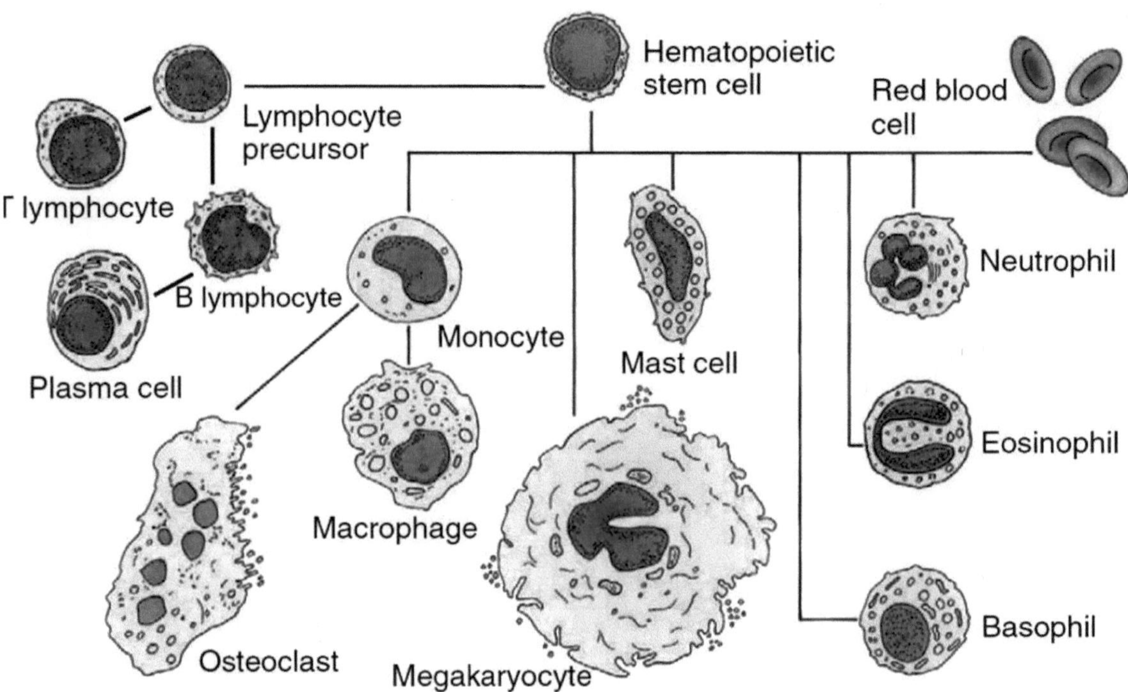

2: Which of the following gland has an additional endocrine part?

Spleen, Ovary, Liver, Pancreas;

3: Blood and bones are ______________ tissues.

4: A free falling object takes 4 seconds to touch ground if it is falling from a height where the object was at rest. Find the speed of this object just before touching ground.

5: Anita measured displacement of an object as 600 m in first 40 second and 480 m in rest of 32 s. Find the average speed of the object.

Solutions:

1: Connective; Blood; 2: Pancreas; 3: connective; 4: 40m /s; 5: Average speed = (1080 m/72 s) = ______m/s; .

Worksheet 11

1: The acceleration due to gravity on a planet is 1.96 ms-2. If it is safe to jump from a height of 2m on the Earth, what will be the corresponding safe height on the planet?

Compare Assertion and Reason.

Select the correct statement:

A: Both Assertion and Reason are correct and Reason is the correct explanation for the Assertion.

B: Assertion is correct the Reason is not the correct explanation.

C: Both Assertion and Reason are wrong.

D: Assertion itself is wrong.

2: Assertion: we are living at the bottom of a gravitational well.

Reason: The gravitational force varies with distance from the center of Earth as shown in the adjoining figure below. The graph clearly shows a minimum zone at a definite point on the surface of Earth. On the basis of such observation it can be ascribed that we are living at the bottom of a gravitational well.

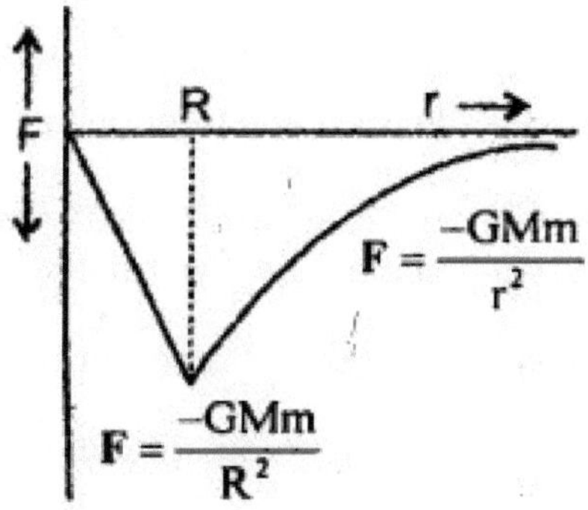

3: Assertion: Atmosphere of Jupiter contains light gases (generally hydrogen in greater percentage) whereas the Earth's atmosphere has little hydrogen gas.

Reason: The escape velocity of Jupiter is much larger than the escape velocity of Earth. So to escape from the surface of Jupiter, a very large velocity is required. It is observed that the thermal velocity of hydrogen gas molecules is lesser than the escape velocity of Jupiter. Because of that reason hydrogen can't overcome the force of gravity implied by the gas giant Jupiter on it.

4: Assertion: An astronaut uses a simple pendulum clock in a satellite revolving around the Earth.

Reason: Acceleration due to gravity is zero inside a satellite therefore the time period of vibration of the simple pendulum $T = 2\pi(l/g)^{1/2}$. So the pendulum will do not vibrate inside the satellite and hence the clock will not work.

5: At what height from the surface of Earth will the value of g be reduced by 36% from the value at the surface? The radius of Earth, R = 6400 km.

6: If the Earth has a mass 9 times that of Mars and a radius twice that of the planet Mars, calculate the minimum velocity required by a rocket which is required to pull out of the gravitational force of Mars. Escape velocity on the surface of Earth is 11.2 km s^{-1}.

Solution: 1: h_e = 2m and h_p = 10m; 2: A; 3: A; 4: D ; the correct Assertion is -- Astronaut does not use a simple pendulum clock in a satellite. 5: h =1600 km; 6: 5.279 km s^{-1}

Worksheet 12

1: Mathematical expression of force of gravity $F = G\, m_1 m_2 r^{-2}$; G stands for universal Gravitation constant.

Explanation related to Acceleration due to Gravity as proposed by Newton:

a) The law is a direct outcome of the study of acceleration of bodies. Newton wondered how Moon revolves around the Earth or other planets revolve around the Sun. His calculations showed that the Moon is accelerated by the same amount as does any other object towards the Earth.

b) His famous narration of the apple falling from the tree and noticing every other object fall towards Earth led to the announcement of his famous law of gravitation about 50 years later in his book 'Principia'.

c) Out of the known forces in nature, the Gravitational force is the strongest.

d) It is the most apparent one as it acts for long distances and between objects which are visible to us.

e) The law of gravitation has been used to determine the mass of heavenly bodies. It has been used to study the atmosphere of planets. Man-made satellites remain in the orbits due to gravitation.

Which of the above statement is supporting the universal law of the force of gravity?

2: The period of the moon around Earth is 27.3 days and the radius of its orbit is 3.9 × 105 km. Find the mass of Earth, G = 6.67 × 10-11 Nm2 Kg^{-2}. [Hints: $v^2 = GM/r$ and $T = 2\pi r/v$]

3: Find the percentage decrease in weight of a body when taken 16 km below the surface of Earth. Take the radius of Earth = 6400 km.

4: Consider an Earth's satellite so positioned that it appears stationary to an observer located on Earth and serves the purpose of a fixed relay station for the purpose of intercontinental transmission of television and other communications. What should be the height at which the satellite must be positioned and what would be the direction of its motion? (Radius of Earth R = 6400 km.)

Solution: 1: option c is wrong ; 2: $M = 6.31 \times 10^{24}$ kg ; 3: 0.25%; 4: $h = 35.9 \times 10^6$ m;

Solution outline for problem 4:

$$(R + h) = \left[\frac{t^2 R^2 g}{4\pi^2}\right]^{\frac{1}{3}}$$

Here, $R = 6.4 \times 10^6$ m, $T = 24 \times 60 \times 60$s, $g = 9.8$ ms^{-2}

$$\therefore \quad R + h = \left[\frac{(86400\text{s})^2 \times (6.4 \times 10^6\text{m})^2 \times 9.8\text{ms}^2}{4 \times 9.87}\right]^{\frac{1}{3}}$$

$$= 42.3 \times 10^6 \text{ m}$$

or

$$h = 42.3 \times 10^6 \text{ m} - 6.4 \times 10^6 \text{ m}$$

$$= 35.9 \times 10^6 \text{ m.}$$

Most of satellites launched by space research organisation are of geostationary types. They also serve as a vital instrument for relaying different types of signals.

8. Selected Sheets of Activities

Activity Sheet I

1: Statements regarding Gravity are as follows –

a. According to Newton's law of gravitation, every particle of this universe attracts every other particle with a force that is inversely proportional to the square of the distance between them. When we move our fingers, the distance between the particles changes, and hence the force of attraction changes which in turn disturbs the whole universe.

b. The value of acceleration due to gravity is lesser on hills than on the plains, so the weight of the tennis ball at hills is lesser than that on the plains and hence it re-bounces more. In other words, the force with which the Earth attracts the ball on hills will be lesser than that on the plains.

c. The escape velocity of some of the planets is very small as compared to that on the surface of Earth.

d. Percentage of hydrogen in the atmosphere of the earth is more than that of the percentage in the atmosphere of Jupiter.

e. Most of gases have their root mean square (r.m.s.) velocities more than the escape velocity on these planets and hence they have escaped from the surface of these planets and hence the atmosphere is rarer on some of the planets than on Earth.

Statement _____ is not correct as per the universality of the force of Gravity is concerned.

2: Neglecting the presence of other planets and satellites, calculate the binding energy of the Sun-Earth system. Mass of Earth ME = 6 × 1024 kg, mass of Sun = 1.98 × 1030 kg, Orbital radius of Earth R= 1.5 × 1011 m.

3: The linear velocity of a particle moving on the circumference of the circle is equal to the velocity acquired by a freely falling body through a distance equal to one-fourth the diameter of the circle. What is the centripetal acceleration of the particle moving along the circle?

4 (a): A body is moving with uniform velocity. Can it be said to be in equilibrium? Why?

4 (b): Why Newton's second law of motion is not applicable to the motion of a rocket?

5: A ball is thrown up at a speed of 36 ms^{-1} by a thrower. If the ball returns to the thrower with the same speed. Will, there be any change in: (a) Momentum of the ball? (b) Magnitude of the momentum of the ball?

6: When a high jumper leaves the ground, where does the force which accelerates the jumper upward comes from?

7: Name the forces which are in equilibrium in each of the following situations:

(a) a book resting on a table. (b) a cork floating on water. (c) a pendulum bob suspended from the ceiling with the help of a string.

Solution: 1: d is wrong; 2: 52.8 X 10^{32} J; 3: g;

4: a: Yes, it can be said to be in equilibrium when it moves with uniform velocity as no acceleration i.e. no net force acts on the body.

4 b: Newton's second law i.e. F = ma is applicable only if the mass (m) of the body remains constant. In the case of the rocket, the mass continuously decreases and hence F = ma is not applicable.

5 a: There will be a change in the direction of the momentum of the ball.

5 b: There is no change in the magnitude of the momentum of the ball.

6: The high jumper after taking a short run presses the ground hard, the ground, in turn, reacts on him and provides the necessary upward accelerating force to the jumper. Thus, the reaction of the ground on the jumper is the required force.

7 a: The gravitational force on the book and a force of reaction of the table.

7 b: The gravitational force on the cork and an upward thrust or buoyant force of water.

7 c: The gravitational force on the bob and the tension in the string.

Outline Solution 2:

The binding energy effectively working in between Earth and Sun is equal to the amount of energy spent in bringing the Earth-Sun system from infinity to the distance R. In other words, this is equal to the energy required to separate them to infinity hence it is equal to (P.E.)g

$$E = \frac{-GM_S M_E}{R}$$

Here,

$$M_s = 1.98 \times 10^{30} \text{ kg}$$
$$M_E = 6 \times 10^{24} \text{ kg}$$
$$R = 1.5 \times 10^{11} \text{m}^{-2}$$
$$G = 6.67 \times 10^{-11} \text{Nm}^2 \text{ kg}^{-2}$$

$$\therefore \quad E = -\frac{6.67 \times 10^{-11} \text{Nm}^2 \text{kg}^{-2} \times 1.98 \times 10^{30} \text{kg} \times 6 \times 10^{24}}{1.5 \times 10^{11} \text{m}}$$

$$= -\frac{6.67 \times 1.98}{1.5} \times 10^{32}$$

or

$$E = -52.8 \times 10^{32} \text{ J.}$$

Activity Sheet II

1. (a) Why do we beat dusty blankets with a stick to remove dust particles?

(b) A stone when thrown on a glass window smashes the window pane to pieces. But a bullet fired from a gun passes through it making a hole. Why?

2. (a) If you jerk a piece of paper from under a book quick enough, the book will not move, why?

(b) Passengers sitting or standing in a moving bus fall in forward direction when the bus suddenly stops. Why?

3. (a) Why passengers are thrown outward when a bus in which they are travelling suddenly takes a turn around a circular road?

(b) Is any force required to move a body with constant velocity?

4. (a) Why a one rupee coin placed on a revolving table flies off tangentially?

(b) Why mud flies off tangentially to the wheel of a cycle?

5. (a) When the electric current is switched off, why the blades of a fan keep on moving for some time?

(b) Why the passengers fall backward when a bus starts moving suddenly?

6. (a) A body of mass m is moving on a horizontal table with constant velocity. What is the force on the table?

(b) Name a factor on which the inertia of a body depends.

7. (a) Rocket works on which principle of conservation?

(b) Is the relation F→=ma→ applicable to the motion of a rocket?

8. (a) Will a person while firing a bullet from a gun experiences a backward jerk? Why?

(b) A bomb explodes in mid-air into two equal fragments. What is the relation between the directions of their motion?

9. (a) What happens to the acceleration of an object if the net force on it is doubled?

(b) An electron moving with a certain velocity collides against a stationary proton and sticks to it. Is the law of conservation of linear momentum true in this case?

10. (a) According to Newton's third law of motion, every force is accompanied by an equal (in magnitude) and opposite (in direction) force called reaction, then how can a movement take place?

(b) You can move a brick easily by pushing it with your foot on a smooth floor, but, if you kick it, then your foot is hurt. Why?

11. (a) Why does a swimmer push the water backward?

(b) Why does not a heavy gun kick so strongly as a light gun using the same bullets (i.e. cartridges)?

12. (a) Can a rocket operates in free space?

(b) In a game of tug of war, two opposing teams are pulling the rope with equal (in magnitude) but the opposite force of 1000 kg wt at each end of the rope. What is the tension in the rope if a condition of equilibrium exists?

13. (a) Which of Newton's laws of motion are involved in rocket propulsion?

(b) Action and reaction are equal in magnitude and opposite in direction, then why do not they cancel/balance each other?

14. (a) A passenger sitting in a bus at rest pushes it from within. Will it move? Why?
(b) How would you explain the motion of a motorcyclist in a globe of death in a circus?
15. Can a body in linear motion be in equilibrium? why?

Solution:
1 a: It is done due to inertia of rest.
1 b: This is due to the inertia of rest.
2 a: It is due to the inertia of rest.
2 b: This is due to the inertia of motion.
3 a: This is due to the inertia of direction.
3 b: No.
4 a: This is due to the inertia of direction.
4 b: This is due to the inertia of direction.
5 a: This is due to the inertia of motion.
5 b: This is due to the inertia of rest.
6 a: mg i.e. equal to the weight of the body.
6 b: Mass.
7 a: Law of conservation of linear momentum.
7 b: No.
8 a: Yes, it is due to the law of conservation of linear momentum.
8 b: The two fragments will fly off in two opposite directions.
9 a: As a = Fm i.e. $a \propto F$, so acceleration will be doubled when m the force is doubled.
9 b: Yes, it is true.
10 a: As the action and reaction never act on the same body, so the motion is possible.
10 b: As Ft remains constant, so if t is reduced, then F will be increased and hence hurt our foot.
11 a: So as to get forward push according to Newton's third law of motion.
11 b: The recoil speed of the gun is inversely proportional to its mass. So the recoil speed of the heavy gun is lesser than that of the light gun.
12 a: Yes.
12 b: 1000 kg wt.
13 a: Newton's third law of motion.
13 b: They don't balance each other as they act on different bodies.
14 a: No, internal forces are unable to produce motion in a system.
14 b: It is a case of motion in a vertical circle.
15: Yes, it will be in equilibrium if the vector sum of the forces acting upon the body is zero.

Activity Sheet III

1: Sometimes we need to increase friction. Why? Given an example.

2: Vehicles stop applying brakes. Does this phenomenon violate the principle of conservation of momentum?

3: True/ False—Two surfaces if made extremely smooth, will have a very low value of friction between them.

Compare the following [4 to 8]

A: Both Assertion and Reason are correct and Reason is the correct explanation for the Assertion.

B: Assertion is correct the Reason is not the correct explanation.

C: Both Assertion and Reason are wrong.

D: Assertion itself is wrong.

4: Assertion: force of friction increases when the two surfaces in contact are made extremely smooth.

Reason: When the two surfaces in contact are made extremely smooth, then they come in intimate contact with each other. So the force of adhesion comes into play- Due to this force, the motion of one surface over the other surface becomes retarding and hence causes an increase in the friction.

5: Assertion: small amount of water spread on a marble floor causes slipping.

Reason: Water fills the grooves in the floor and makes it less smooth thus increasing friction and it causes slipping.

6: Assertion: A body moving over the surface of another body suddenly comes to rest.

Reason: The force of friction will be present only so long as there is relative motion between the two bodies and it automatically disappears as soon as the relative motion ceases to exist.

7: Assertion: one should take long steps rather than short steps while walking on ice

Reason: There is a danger of slipping if one walks on ice by taking long steps because of friction implied by the surface on the person is comparatively less.

8: Assertion: A cricket player lowers his hands while catching a cricket ball.

Reasons: He has to apply retarding force to stop the moving ball which is approaching his hands. If he catches the ball abruptly, then he has to apply a large retarding force within a short time period. So he gets hurt. On the other hand, if he moves his hands backward then the player applies the force for a longer time to bring the ball to rest. During such instance, he has to apply less retarding force and thus will not get hurt. Thus to avoid injuries to his hands, the player lowers his hands while catching a cricket ball.

9: "Buffers are provided between the bogies of a train to reduce shocks or jerks by reducing the impulse or impact of a force. Springs of buffers increase the time of contact in the collision of bogies and thus the force acting on the bogies will become small and hence the passengers sitting inside the train will feel lesser jerks than the original one." Is this statement explaining the applicability of the laws of motion properly?

10: It is more difficult to catch a cricket ball than to catch a tennis ball moving with the same velocity. Explain the reason.

11: A body of mass 125 g is moving with a constant velocity of 5 ms^{-1} on a horizontal frictionless surface in a vacuum. What is the force acting on the body?

12: A bird is sitting on the floor of a wire cage and the cage is in the hand of a girl. The bird starts flying in the cage without maintaining contact with the floor. Will the girl experience any alteration in the weight of the cage?

13: A woman stands on a spring scale placed on an elevator. In which case will the scale record the minimum reading and the maximum reading?

(i) elevator stationery, (ii) elevator cable breaks, free fall,

(iii) elevator accelerating upward and (iv) elevator accelerating downward.

14: Two bodies of different masses m1 and m2 are falling from the same height. If resistance offered by the air be the same for both the bodies, then will they reach the Earth simultaneously? Assume m1 > m2?

Solution:

1: Sometimes friction between two surfaces decreases to such an extent that it becomes difficult to move on that surface properly. So friction needs to be increased. For example, vehicles can't move on a road covered with snow. In such cases, we have to throw sand on the road to increase the friction.

2: The law of conservation of momentum is not violated by stopping vehicles by applying brakes. Some retarding force is being applied due to brakes and the vehicle ultimately comes to rest such that the total loss of its momentum is equal to the impulse of the applied force. Thus the law of conservation of momentum is not violated in this case.

3: False; Reason -- the force of frictions increased when the surfaces in contact are made highly smooth.

Examples: In factories, the conveyer belt is made smooth by rubbing it with wax or resin. The wheel over which the belt is to move is also made extremely smooth. Due to the increased force of friction between the belt and the wheel, slipping does not take place. The wheels of the railway train and the surfaces of the railway tracks are also made very smooth.

4: A; 5: B; 6 A: 7: D; 8: A; 9: Yes;

10: The mass of a cricket ball is comparatively greater than the mass of a tennis ball that is why the change in momentum of the cricket ball is more than that of the tennis ball. For that reason greater force is required to catch the cricket ball than that required for catching a tennis ball.

11: No Force; 12: the cage will appear lighter;

13: I = actual weight; ii= weightlessness; iii= maximum; less than the actual;
Change of weight depends on the acceleration of the elevator;
The reading of the scale is recorded minimum when the elevator falls freely and the reading of the scale is maximum when the elevator accelerates upwards.
14: body having larger acceleration will reach earlier, that is why the body of larger mass will reach the earth earlier than the body of smaller mass.

Activity Sheet IV

1: Mark different parts of the plant cell.

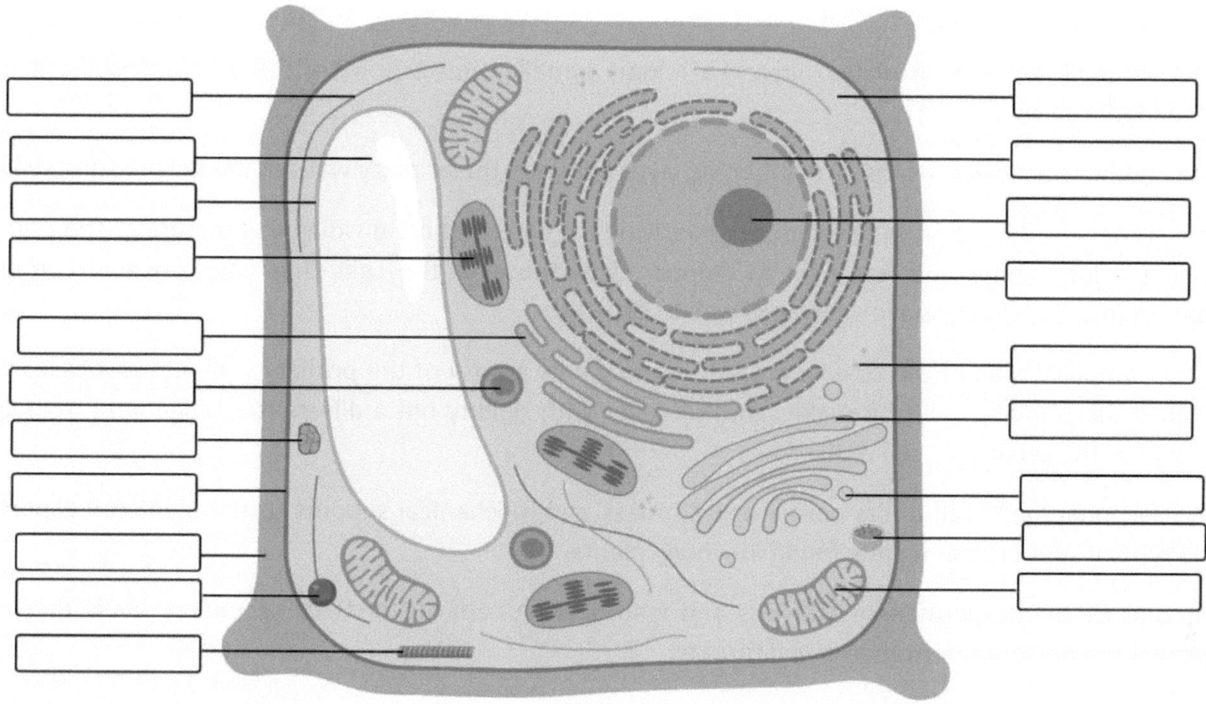

2: Complete the following..

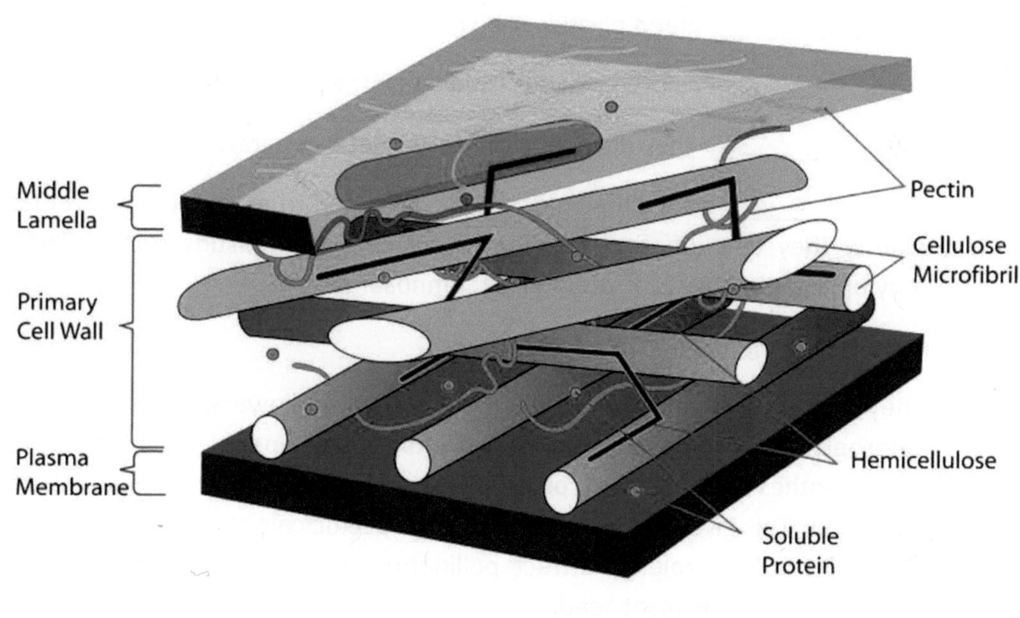

There are _______________ layers in a cell wall. Cellulose microfibrils present in _____________ Cell Wall.

3: Statement regarding structure of a Plant Cell –

A. There is a specialized matrix that covers the surface of the plant cell. Most of the plant cells have a rigid protective covering namely cell wall which is a major distinguishing factor between a plant cell and an animal cell.

B. The cell wall is made up of two layers, a middle lamella, and a primary cell wall and sometimes a secondary cell wall.

C. The middle lamella acts as the strengthening layer between the primary walls of the neighboring cells.

D. The primary wall is made up of cellulose underlying the cells that are dividing and maturing. The primary wall is a lot thinner and less rigid as compared to those of the cells that have reached complete maturation. The thinness allows the cell wall to expand.

E. After complete span of the cellular growth, some plants get rid of the primary wall. In most cases they thicken the primary wall or it makes another layer with rigidity but a different arrangement, popularly known as the secondary cell wall.

F. The secondary cell wall offers permanent stiffness and mechanical support to the plant cell especially the type of support and rigidity found in woody plants.

G. In contrast to the permanent stiffness and load-bearing capacity of thick secondary walls they also protect the protoplasm from external threats.

Statement _______ is not correct.

4: Identify the following ---

A. ______________– green plastids used in photosynthesis

B. ______________– colored plastids used to synthesize and store plant pigments

C. ______________ – they dismantle photosynthetic apparatus during aging of plants

D. ______________ – they are colorless plastids used to manufacture terpene substance that protects the plants. they can differentiate, forming specialized plastids performing a variety of functions. i. e amyloplast. elaioplasts. proteinoplast, tannosomes.

5: Statement regarding function of a Plastid ---

a) They give distinctive colors to plant parts such as flowers, fruits, roots, and leaves. Differentiation of chloroplast to chromoplast makes the fruits of plant ripen.
b) They synthesize and store plant pigments such as yellow pigments for xanthophyll, orange for carotenes. This gives the plant and its parts specific color.
c) They play a vital role to attract pollinators by the colors they produce. It helps indirectly in the reproduction of the plant seed.
d) These types of plastids found in roots enable the accumulation of water-insoluble elements especially in tubers such as carrots and potatoes.
e) They contribute to a great extent in the process of color change during plant aging of flowers, fruits, and leaves.

All these are the functions of ______________________.

Activity Sheet V

1: Identify following types of tissues –

A. _________ tissue – this tissue lies on the surface of plants and is made up of epidermal cells that protect the plants from losing water.

B. _________ tissue – This makes up the root vascular and epidermal system majorly made up of parenchyma, collenchyma, and sclerenchyma cells responsible for plant photosynthesis, storage of water and food, and the plant support system.

C. _________ tissue – this tissue is made up of xylem, phloem, parenchyma, and cambium cells, with its functions including transportation of water (xylem), transportation of food (phloem), minerals, hormones in the parts of the plant cells.

2: Identify the following three types of cartilages—

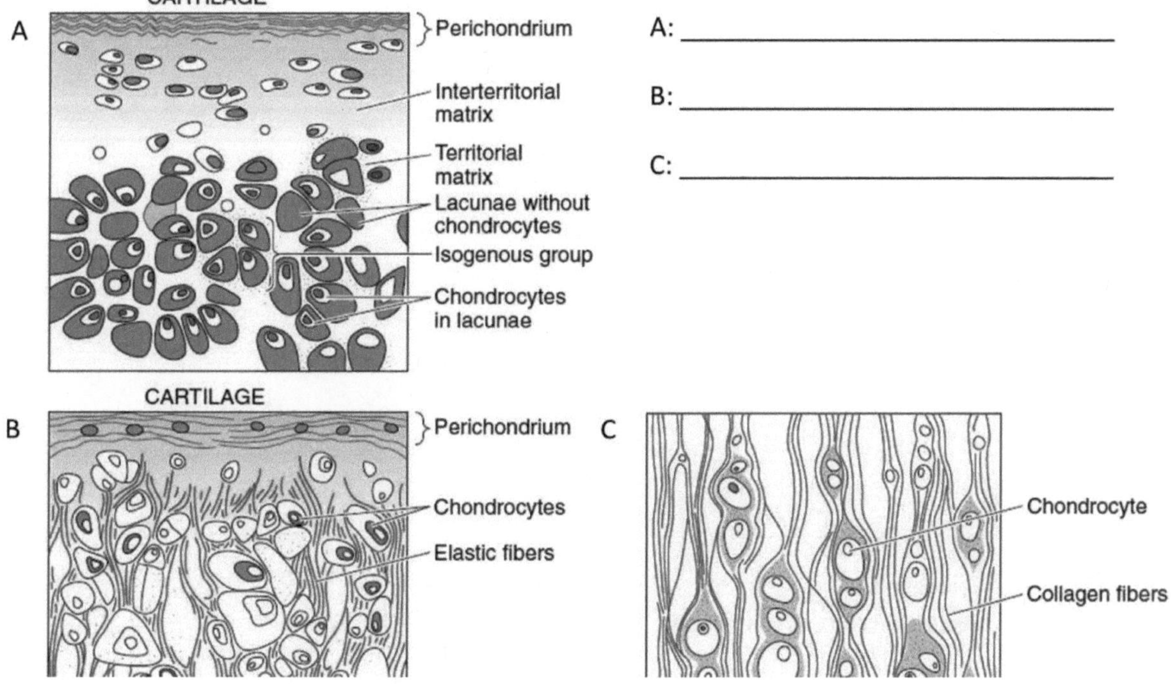

A: ______________________________

B: ______________________________

C: ______________________________

3: Which of the following is not a function of a parenchyma?

a) Parenchyma cells are closely linked to the surface epidermal cells which contribute largely to light penetration and absorption and regulate gas exchange.

b) The permeable cell wall allows the transportation of small molecules between the cells and the inernally enclosed cell cytoplasm.

c) The palisade parenchyma combined with spongy mesophyll cells found below the layer of the epidermis tissue assists in light absorption used in photosynthesis.

d) Ray parenchyma cells are found in wood rays which transport materials along the plant stem.

e) The parenchyma cells are also found in good numbers within the xylem and the phloem of vascular plants, helping in the transportation of water and food materials in the plant.

f) These tissues offer flexibility and tensile strength to plant organs, allowing the plants to bend differently.

g) Some of these tyeps of tissues are also involved in the biochemical secretion of nectar and manufacturing secondary elements that act as protective materials from herbivores' feeding.

h) Those parenchyma cells found in root tubers (specially modified stem for the storage of food) such as potatoes, leguminous plants, help in the storage of food.

Option _________ is not correct.

4: Identify the following anomaly:

_________________results from a genetic defect in which osteoclasts are formed that are unable to resorb bone because they cannot form a ruffled border. Patients with osteopetrosis present with very dense bones and possibly anaemia because of a reduced volume of marrow cavity. These individuals are also susceptible to blindness, deafness, and cranial nerve anomalies as a consequence of narrowing of the foramina through which cranial nerves exit the skull.

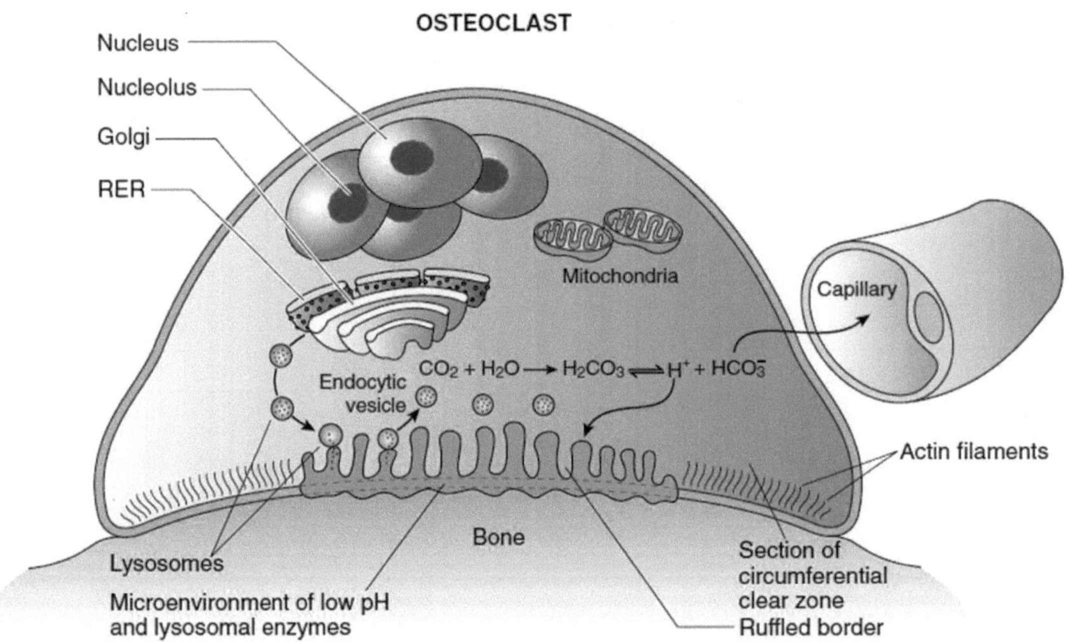

5: The xylem cells are also combined with fibers and parenchyma cells hence they have a primary cell wall combined with a lignified cell wall, forming rings and looped networks with pits known as __________ _____for conduction.

6: Major function of this tissue is too transport water and mineral from soil and pass on the same to leaves. Identify this tissue.

Solution 4: Osteopetrosis; 5: bordered pits; 6: Xylem;

9. Off the School Enrichment

Activity P

Provide Key Words for the following --

1. : lipid storage cells
2. : specialized areolar tissue rich in stored fat
3. : mechanically attaches adjacent cells to each other or to the basement membrane
4. : that part of a cell or tissue which, in general, faces an open space
5. : release of a substance along with the apical portion of the cell
6. : programmed cell death
7. : (also, loose connective tissue) a type of connective tissue proper that shows little specialization with cells dispersed in the matrix
8. : star-shaped cell in the central nervous system that regulates ions and uptake and/or breakdown of some neurotransmitters and contributes to the formation of the blood-brain barrier
9. : loss of mass and function
10. : thin extracellular layer that lies underneath epithelial cells and separates them from other tissues
11. : in epithelial tissue, a thin layer of fibrous material that anchors the epithelial tissue to the underlying connective tissue; made up of the basal lamina and reticular lamina
12. : heart muscle, under involuntary control, composed of striated cells that attach to form fibers, each cell contains a single nucleus, contracts autonomously
13. : point of cell-to-cell contact that connects one cell to another in a tissue
14. : cells of the cartilage
15. : also called coagulation; complex process by which blood components form a plug to stop bleeding
16. : flexible fibrous proteins that give connective tissue tensile strength

17. : connective tissue that encapsulates organs and lines movable joints

18. : Connective tissue containing a viscous matrix, fibers, and cells.

19. : type of tissue that serves to hold in place, connect, and integrate the body's organs and systems

20. : skin; epithelial tissue made up of a stratified squamous epithelial cells that cover the outside of the body

21. : connective tissue proper that contains many fibers that provide both elasticity and protection

22. : outermost embryonic germ layer from which the epidermis and the nervous tissue derive

23. : type of cartilage, with elastin as the major protein, characterized by rigid support as well as elasticity

24. : fibrous protein within connective tissue that contains a high percentage of the protein elastin that allows the fibers to stretch and return to original size

25. : groups of cells that release chemical signals into the intercellular fluid to be picked up and transported to their target organs by blood

26. : innermost embryonic germ layer from which most of the digestive system and lower respiratory system derive

27. : tissue that lines vessels of the lymphatic and cardiovascular system, made up of a simple squamous epithelium

28. : epithelium attached to a layer of connective tissue

29. : type of tissue that serves primarily as a covering or lining of body parts, protecting the body; it also functions in absorption, transport, and secretion

30. : group of epithelial cells that secrete substances through ducts that open to the skin or to internal body surfaces that lead to the exterior of the body

31. : most abundant cell type in connective tissue, secretes protein fibers and matrix into the extracellular space

32. : tough form of cartilage, made of thick bundles of collagen fibers embedded in chondroitin sulfate ground substance

33. : less active form of fibroblast

34. : specialized cells that circulate in a watery fluid containing salts, nutrients, and dissolved proteins

35. : allows cytoplasmic communications to occur between cells

36. : unicellular gland found in columnar epithelium that secretes mucous

37. : fluid or semi-fluid portion of the matrix

38. : chemical compound released by mast cells in response to injury that causes vasodilation and endothelium permeability

39. : microscopic study of tissue architecture, organization, and function

40. : release of a substance caused by the rupture of a gland cell, which becomes part of the secretion

41. : most common type of cartilage, smooth and made of short collagen fibers embedded in a chondroitin sulfate ground substance

42. : response of tissue to injury

43. : (singular = lacuna) small spaces in bone or cartilage tissue that cells occupy

44. : areolar connective tissue underlying a mucous membrane

45. type of connective tissue proper that shows little specialization with cells dispersed in the matrix

46. : extracellular material which is produced by the cells embedded in it, containing ground substance and fibers

47. : release of a substance from a gland via exocytosis

48. mesenchymal cell: adult stem cell from which most connective tissue cells are derived

49. : embryonic tissue from which connective tissue cells derive

50. : middle embryonic germ layer from which connective tissue, muscle tissue, and some epithelial tissue derive

51. : simple squamous epithelial tissue which covers the major body cavities and is the epithelial portion of serous membranes

52. : specialized loose connective tissue present in the umbilical cord

53. : group of cells that secrete mucous, a thick, slippery substance that keeps tissues moist and acts as a lubricant

54. : tissue membrane that is covered by protective mucous and lines tissue exposed to the outside environment

55. : type of tissue that is capable of contracting and generating tension in response to stimulation; produces movement.

56. : layer of lipid inside some neuroglial cells that wraps around the axons of some neurons

57. : muscle cells

58. : accidental death of cells and tissues

59. : type of tissue that is capable of sending and receiving impulses through electrochemical signals.

60. : supportive neural cells

61. : excitable neural cell that transfer nerve impulses

62. : neuroglial cell that produces myelin in the brain

63. : functional cells of a gland or organ, in contrast with the supportive or connective tissue of a gland or organ

64. : edges of a wound are close enough together to promote healing without the use of stitches to hold them close

65. : tissue that consists of a single layer of irregularly shaped and sized cells that give the appearance of multiple layers; found in ducts of certain glands and the upper respiratory tract

66. : fine fibrous protein, made of collagen subunits, which cross-link to form supporting “nets” within connective tissue

67. : matrix containing collagen and elastin secreted by connective tissue; a component of the basement membrane

68. : type of loose connective tissue that provides a supportive framework to soft organs, such as lymphatic tissue, spleen, and the liver

69. : neuroglial cell that produces myelin in the peripheral nervous system

70. : wound healing facilitated by wound contraction

71. : group of cells within the serous membrane that secrete a lubricating substance onto the surface

72. : type of tissue membrane that lines body cavities and lubricates them with serous fluid

73. : tissue that consists of a single layer of column-like cells; promotes secretion and absorption in tissues and organs

74. : tissue that consists of a single layer of cube-shaped cells; promotes secretion and absorption in ducts and tubules

75. : tissue that consists of a single layer of flat scale-like cells; promotes diffusion and filtration across surface

76. : usually attached to bone, under voluntary control, each cell is a fiber that is multinucleated and striated

77. : under involuntary control, moves internal organs, cells contain a single nucleus, are spindle-shaped, and do not appear striated; each cell is a fiber

78. : tissue that consists of two or more layers of column-like cells, contains glands and is found in some ducts

79. : tissue that consists of two or more layers of cube-shaped cells, found in some ducts

80. : tissue that consists of multiple layers of cells with the most apical being flat scale-like cells; protects surfaces from abrasion

81. : alignment of parallel actin and myosin filaments which form a banded pattern

82. : type of connective tissue that provides strength to the body and protects soft tissue

83. : connective tissue membrane that lines the cavities of freely movable joints, producing synovial fluid for lubrication

84. : forms an impermeable barrier between cells

85. : thin layer or sheet of cells that covers the outside of the body, organs, and internal cavities

86. : group of cells that are similar in form and perform related functions

87. : embryonic cells that have the ability to differentiate into any type of cell and organ in the body

88. : form of stratified epithelium found in the urinary tract, characterized by an apical layer of cells that change shape in response to the presence of urine

89. : widening of blood vessels

90. : process whereby the borders of a wound are physically drawn together.

Solution:

1. adipocytes
2. adipose tissue
3. anchoring junction
4. apical
5. apocrine secretion
6. apoptosis
7. areolar tissue
8. astrocyte
9. atrophy
10. basal lamina
11. basement membrane
12. cardiac muscle
13. cell junction
14. chondrocytes
15. clotting
16. collagen fiber
17. connective tissue membrane
18. connective tissue proper
19. connective tissue
20. cutaneous membrane
21. dense connective tissue
22. ectoderm
23. elastic cartilage
24. elastic fiber
25. endocrine gland
26. endoderm
27. endothelium
28. epithelial membrane
29. epithelial tissue
30. exocrine gland
31. fibroblast
32. fibrocartilage
33. fibrocyte
34. fluid connective tissue
35. gap junction
36. goblet cell
37. ground substance
38. histamine
39. histology
40. holocrine secretion
41. hyaline cartilage
42. inflammation
43. lacunae
44. lamina propria
45. loose connective tissue: (also, areolar tissue)
46. matrix
47. merocrine secretion
48. mesenchyme
49. mesoderm
50. mesothelium
51. mucous connective tissue
52. mucous gland
53. mucous membrane
54. muscle tissue
55. myelin
56. myocyte
57. necrosis
58. nervous tissue
59. neuroglia
60. neuron
61. oligodendrocyte
62. parenchyma
63. primary union
64. pseudostratified columnar epithelium
65. reticular fiber
66. reticular lamina
67. reticular tissue
68. Schwann cell
69. secondary union
70. serous gland
71. serous membrane
72. simple columnar epithelium
73. simple cuboidal epithelium
74. simple squamous epithelium
75. skeletal muscle
76. smooth muscle
77. stratified columnar epithelium
78. stratified cuboidal epithelium
79. stratified squamous epithelium
80. striation
81. supportive connective tissue
82. synovial membrane
83. tight junction
84. tissue membrane
85. tissue
86. totipotent
87. transitional epithelium
88. vasodilation
89. wound contraction

Activity Q

1: Identify different levels of organisation depicted in the following chart.

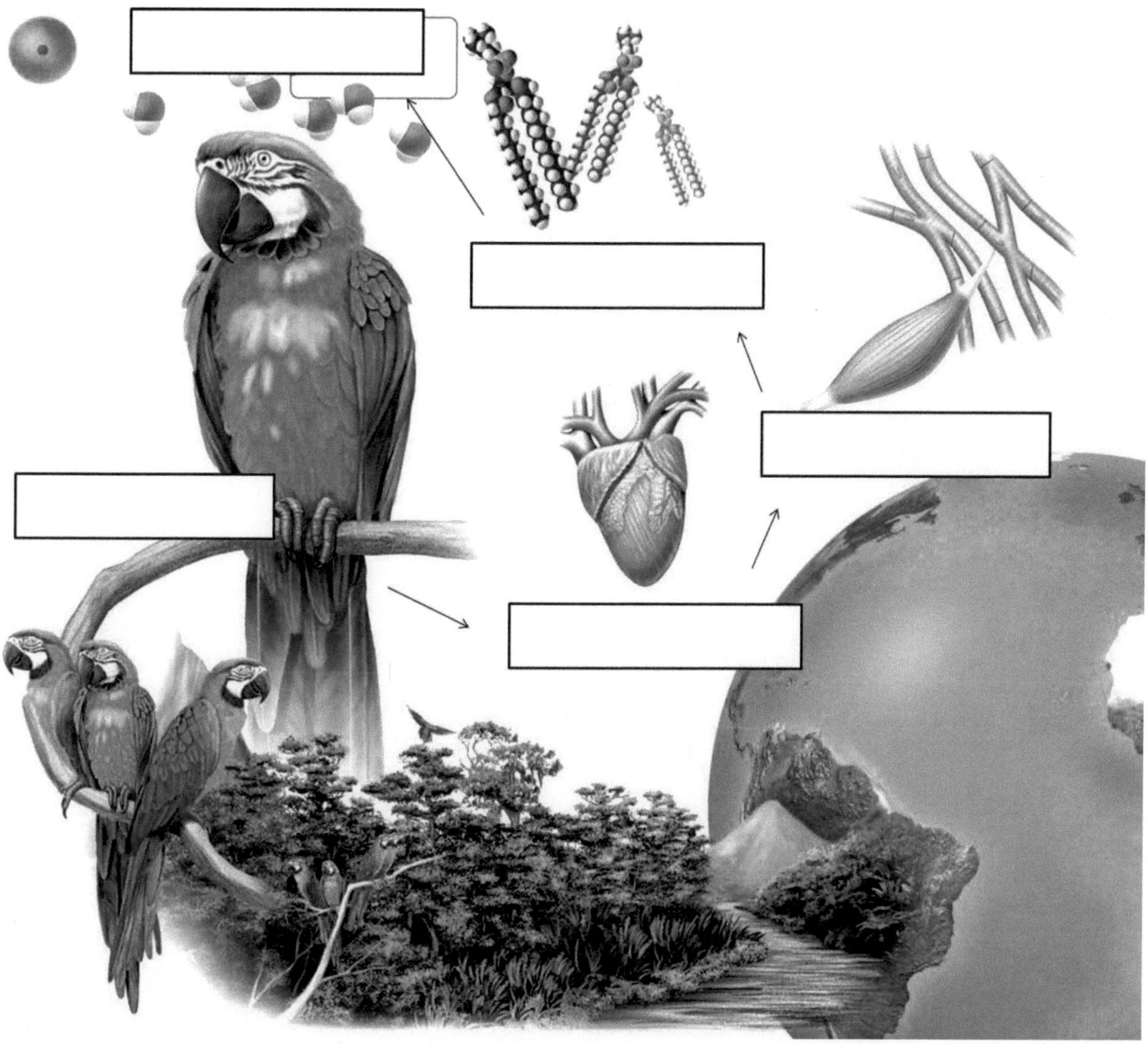

2: Which of the following distance-time graph displays a graph of uniform motion?

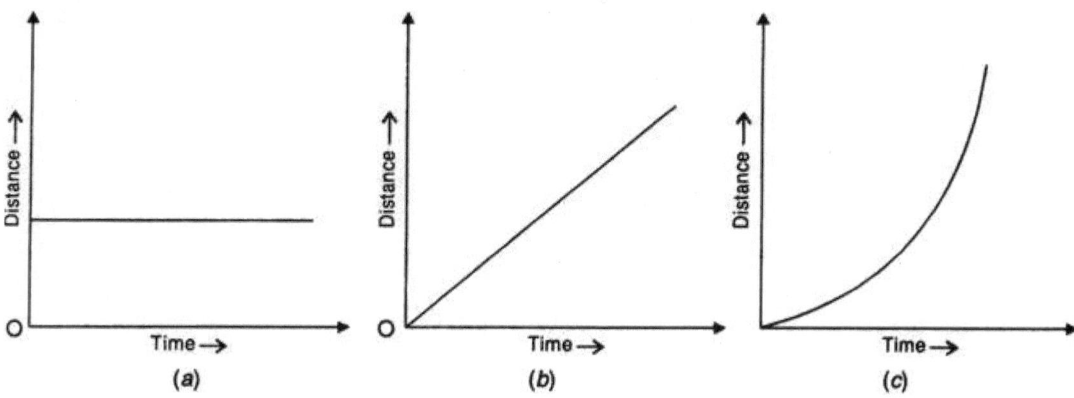

3: Identify the wrong statement ---

Most leaves are specialized systems for photosynthesis.

a) There are two types of mesophyll cells.
b) Both types contain chloroplasts
c) Palisade mesophyll absorbs sunlight.
d) Spongy mesophyll connects to stomata.

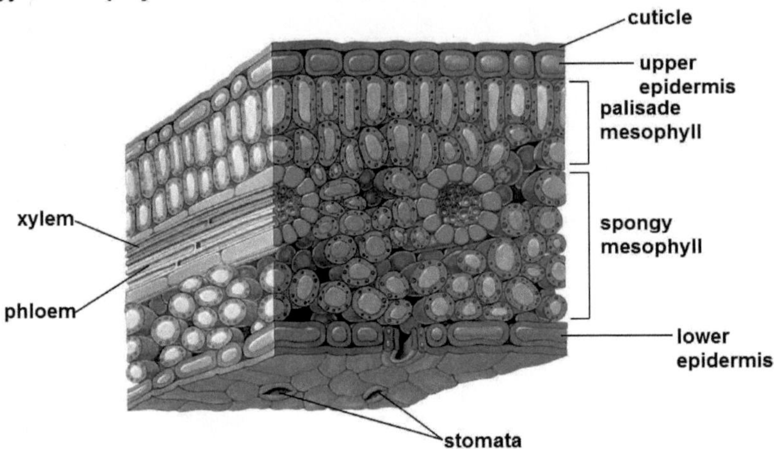

4: Complete the following –

Cells present in tissues interact with the immediate external environment for accomplishing different vital functions.
These diagrams resemble the process of _______________ in both plant and animal cells.

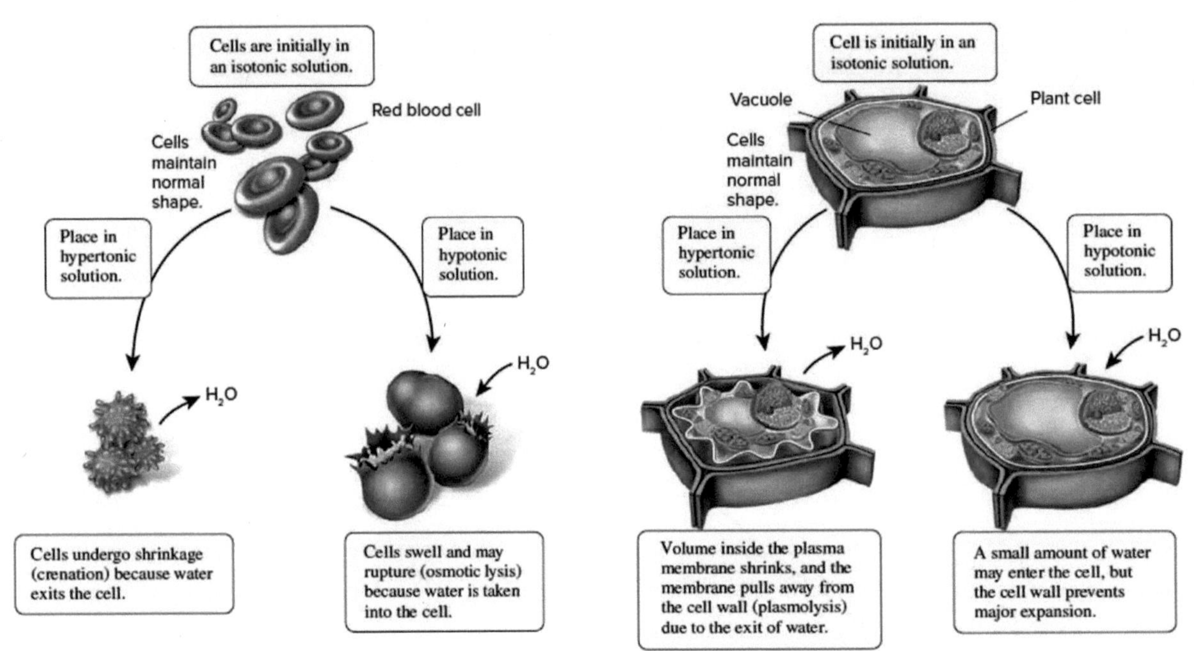

5: Cells taking art in the formation of tissue follows certain biological process for accomplishing certain vital functions.

These steps of biological process resembles ___________ through which cells liberate secretory materials in the external environment.

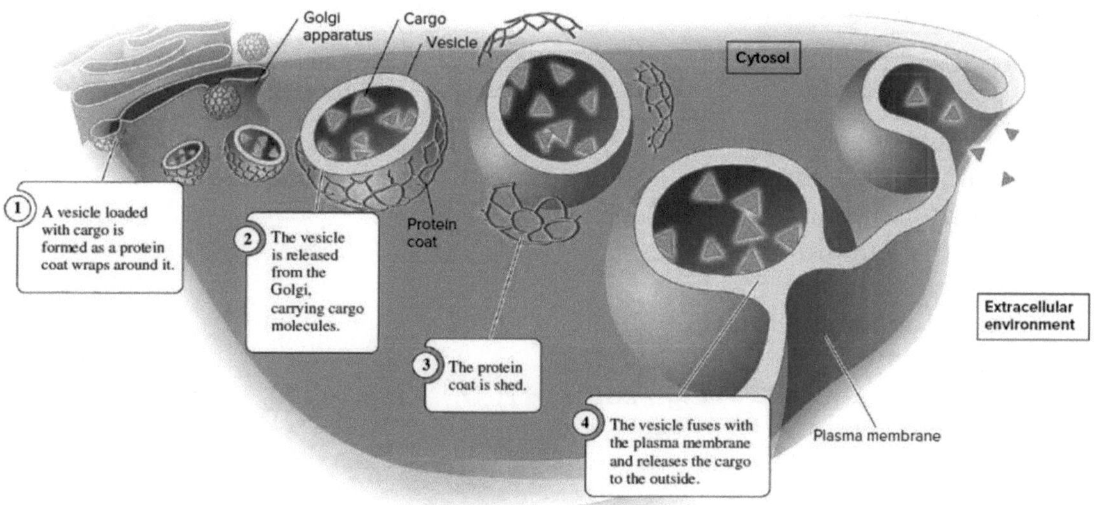

6: Identify the process:

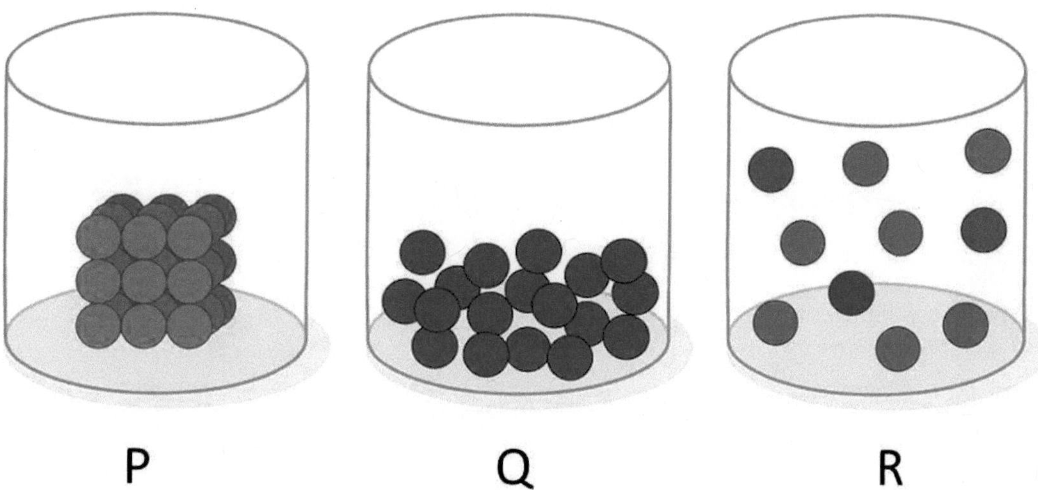

P Q R

Three containers represent three different states of matter. There is one spepcific change during which P state directly changes to R without involvement of any intermediate state of Q.
This process is _________________.

7: Complete the following chart ...

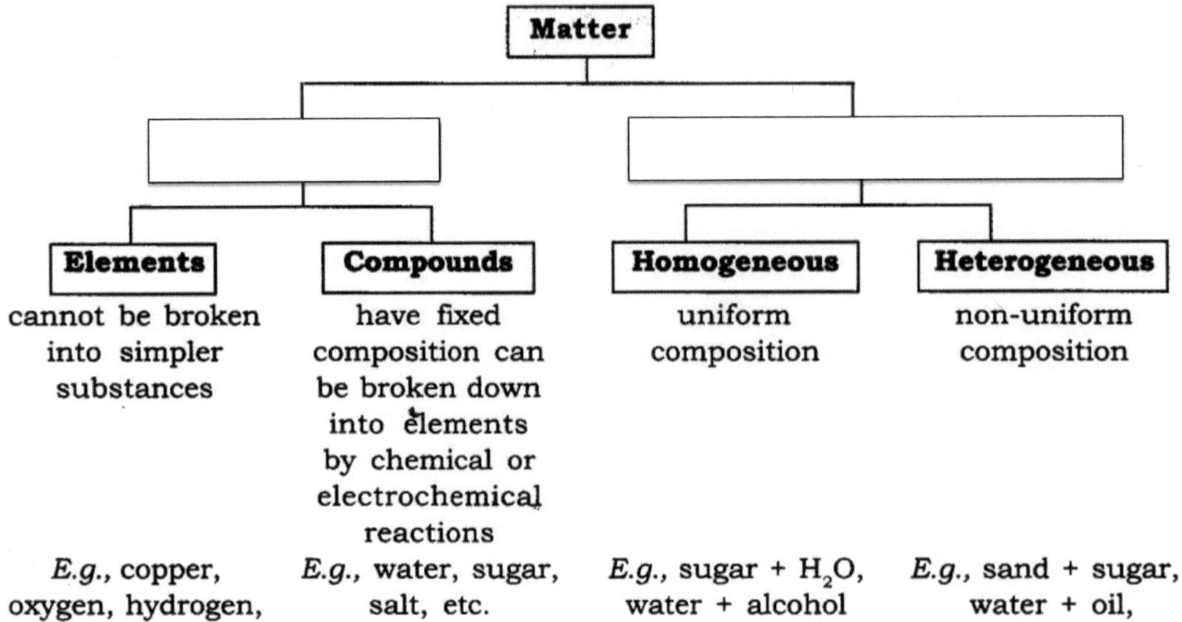

8: We have different forces acting on the particles of matter. Gravitational force, electrostatic force and magnetic forces are three different types of non-contact forces. Among the known type of forces in nature, the gravitational force is the weakest. Why then does it play a dominant role in the motion of bodies on the terrestrial, astronomical, and cosmological scale?

9: Answer the following—

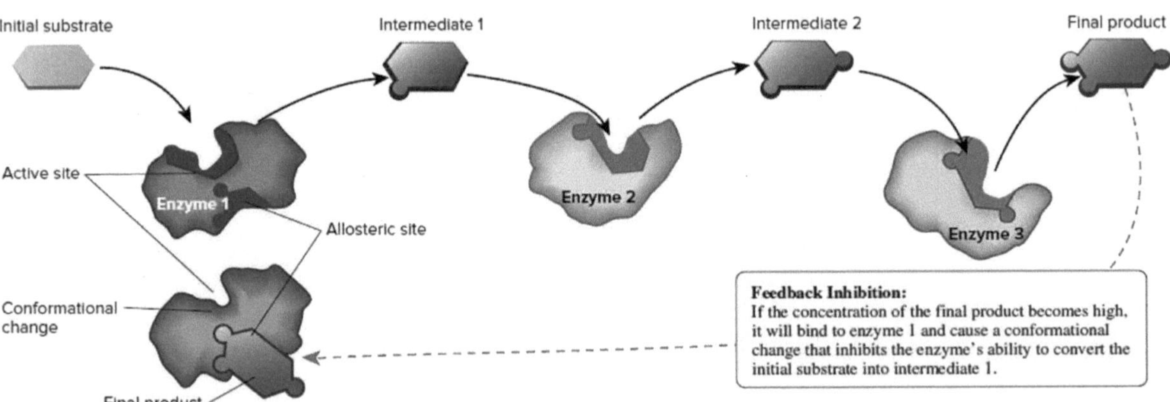

Living Organisms Maintain Homeostasis. In this example, feedback inhibition prevents the formation of too much product of a metabolic pathway.. In this process, the final product of a metabolic pathway inhibits an enzyme that functions in the pathway, thereby preventing the overaccumulation of the product.

What is Feedback Inhibition? Write its mechanism.

10: The thermal speed of hydrogen is comparatively much larger than oxygen. Therefore a large number of hydrogen molecules are able to acquire escape velocity than that of oxygen molecules with much easiness. What will be result of the fact mentioned above?

11: The feeling of upward and downward sense of motion is due to the gravitational force of attraction between the body and the earth. In a spaceship, the gravitational pull force is counter-balanced by the centripetal force needed for mobility of the satellite to move around the Earth in a definite orbit. What will be the feeling of the person on board?

12: Identify –

How many active phases are there in the following reaction?
Mention the site of all these reactions.

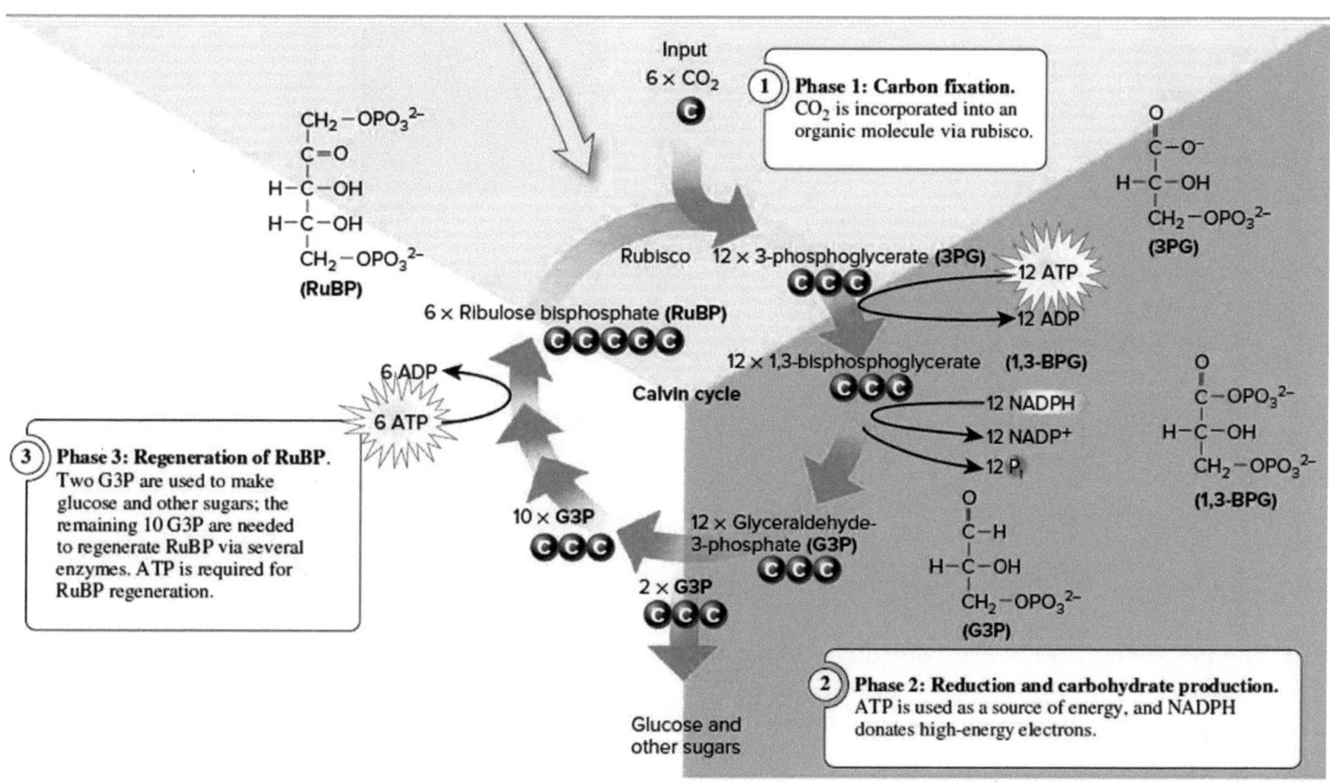

13: Assertion: In most cases the space rockets are generally launched from west to east.

Reason: Since the Earth revolves from west to east around the Sun, so when the rocket is launched from west to east, the relative velocity of the rocket should be equal to sum total of launching velocity of rocket and linear velocity of Earth. Thus the velocity of the rocket increases which helps it to rise without much consumption of the fuel. The linear velocity of Earth is maximum in the equatorial plane.

Compare assertion and reason.

14: Complete the following statement...

All these three types of diagrams represent tissue level organisation of glands. On the basis of structural similarities all these three glands are of similar types.

They all are _______________ glands. They never release their secretion directly into blood.

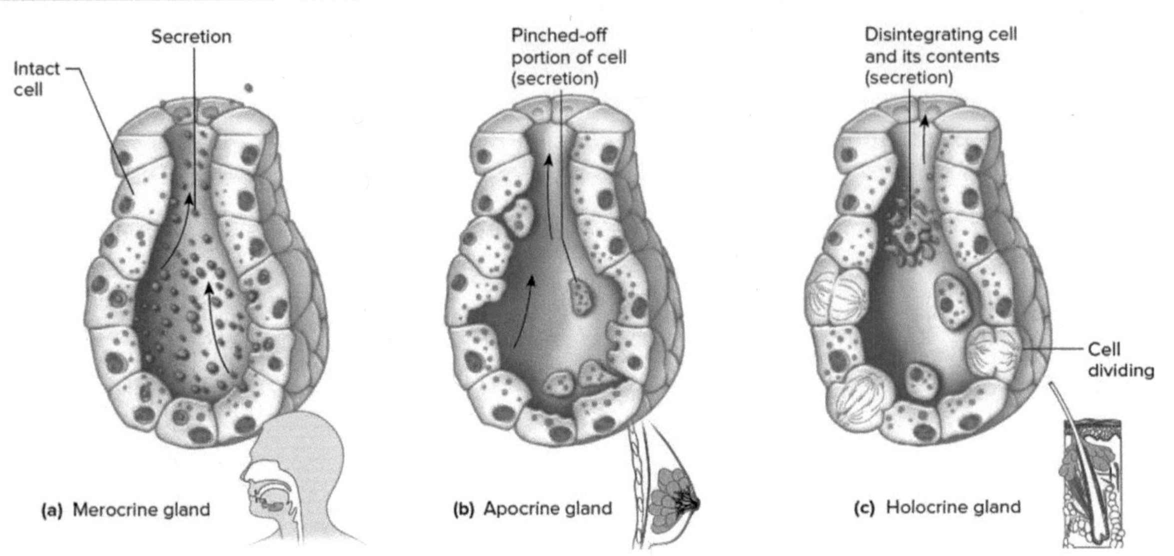

Answer 8: Gravitational forces act on celestial bodies from farthest distance. Combination of all gravitational pull makes a particle moving in space. Part of this force is utilized to maintain the motion of a body. That is why it appears feeble in some cases.

Answer 10: Hydrogen will escape the environment of earth than compared to oxygen.

Ans 11: The person may not feel up and down motion of the space-ship.

Ans 13: Both assertion and reason are true and reason is the correct explanation of assertion.

10. Test Papers

You can replace this text with the fourth chapter of the book here.

Test Paper A

1: Statement regarding some important tissues is as follows:

a) Sometimes, too much granulation tissue grows over a wound, leaving an excess of bumpy, shiny, red tissue called "proud flesh". Other terms to describe proud flesh include hyper granulation, hyperplasia of granulation, and exuberant granulation. If too much granulation tissue forms, this can actually hinder the healing process and lead to a long-lasting wound. Proud flesh can be "healthy", i.e. an overgrowth of normal granulation tissue, or "unhealthy" if it becomes infected. It can be treated with foam dressing, antimicrobials, antibiotics, tapes, creams, silver nitrate, or as a last resort, surgical removal.

b) There are four main types of wound tissues as described by clinicians: granulating, necrotic, sloughy, and epithelizing. In contrast to granulating tissue, necrotic tissue is dead tissue. Necrotic tissue occurs when cells in or around a wound die from infection or simply old age. Since skin cells only live for three weeks at most, a wound that has been kept under a bandage for weeks will naturally have some necrotic tissue around it.

c) Sloughy tissue is stringy necrotic tissue that is separating from the site of the wound. If there is a lot of sloughy tissue forming around a wound, it is often removed.

d) When granulating tissue forms, it grows over and replaces necrotic tissue. Likewise, epithelizing (or epithelializing) tissue grows over granulating tissue. It is a layer of densely packed keratinocytes and other skin cells. When a wound first forms, it will have a lot of necrotic and sloughy tissue. As it heals, granulating tissue will appear. Then, granulating tissue is replaced by epithelizing tissue. When a wound has a lot of epithelizing tissue, it is well on its way to healing.

_______________ tissue forms a protective guard around a wound which is not exposed to air or water.

2: Provide Key Terms

a) – The most common type of connective tissue cell in the body; it produces collagen and fibers.

b) – A protein that is found in skin and connective tissue; it is the most common protein in the human body.

c) – White blood cells.

d) – The formation of blood vessels.

3. What type of tissue forms over granulation tissue when a wound is healing?

A. Necrotic B. Epithelizing C. Sloughy D. Proud flesh

4. Why is granulation tissue red?

A. The formation of the wound has exposed blood vessels beneath the skin.

B. Vascularization is occurring to provide nutrients to the newly forming tissue.

C. It is composed of keratinocytes. D. Type III collagen produced by fibroblasts is red.

5. What other term is "proud flesh" known as?

A. Hypergranulation B. Hyperplasia of granulation C. Exuberant granulation; D. All of the above

6: Complete the following –

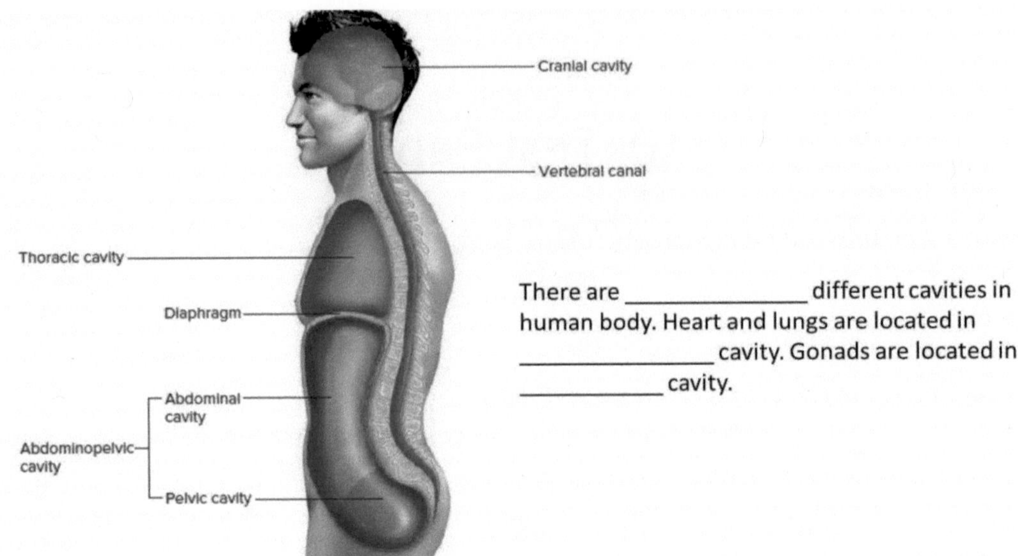

There are ______________ different cavities in human body. Heart and lungs are located in ______________ cavity. Gonads are located in ____________ cavity.

7: Structural orientation of a Tendon[14]: Components of type I collagen fibre. The arrangement of the gap and overlap regions of the adjoining _____________molecules gives rise to the characteristic 67-nm cross-banding noted in electron micrographs

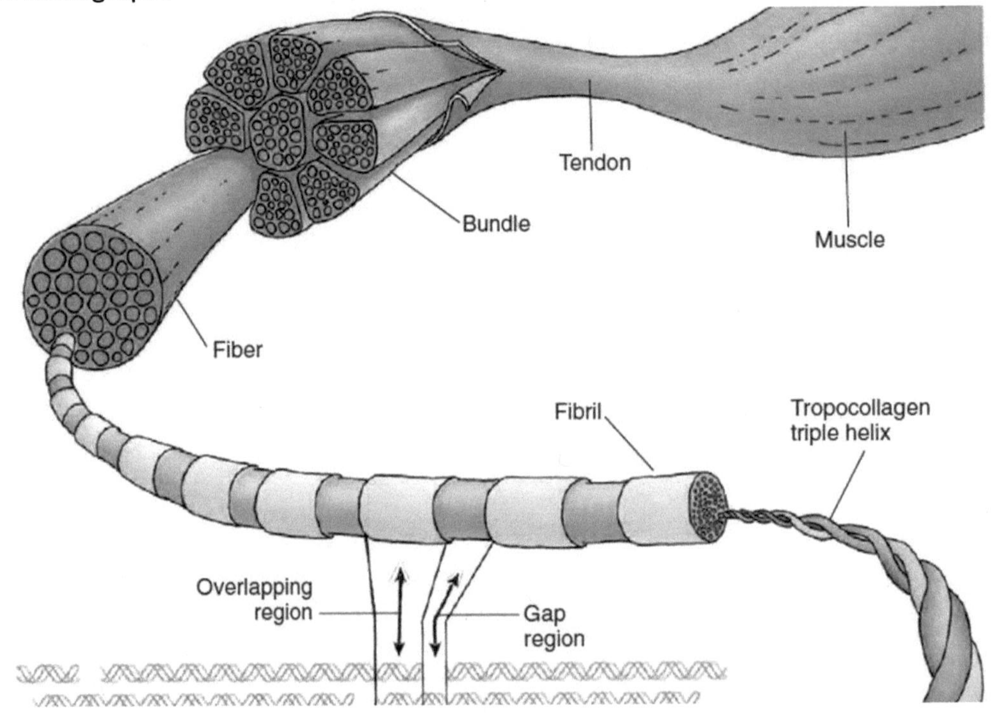

Solution :

1: sloughy; 2: Fibroblast ; Collagen; Leukocytes; Vascularization;

3: B is correct. Epithelizing tissue is a layer of densely packed cells that forms over granulation tissue during the wound healing process. It indicates that a wound is healing properly.

4: B is correct. Granulation tissue has a reddish color because vascularization, the formation of new blood vessels, is taking place. Blood vessels are full of red blood cells that provide oxygen and nutrients to the newly forming tissues.

5: D is correct. Proud flesh is the overabundance of granulation tissue around a wound, and it is also known by all of these terms.

Ans 6: five; Thoracic; Pelvic; Ans 7: tropocollagen; .

---

[14] *From Gartner LP, Hiatt JL: Color Textbook of Histology, 3rd ed. Philadelphia, Saunders, 2007, p 74.*

Test Paper B

1: Write structural features of Apical Meristem.

2: Define Parenchyma.

3: What type of animal tissue is called Parenchyma?

4: Statement regarding function of Parenchyma --

a) Because "parenchyma" is an umbrella term for all cells that perform non-structural biological functions, the functions of parenchymal cells are many. Here are a few.
b) In plants, parenchymal cells with thin cell walls and the ability to reproduce fulfill functions including: Photosynthesis, Gas exchange, Food storage , Wound repair and new growth, Secretion of sap.
c) This type of tissue provides flexibility to shoots and helps in different types of bending during motion.
d) Other specialized functions in certain plants, such as buoyancy control in aquatic plants.
e) In animals, "parenchymal" cells refer to the functional cells in every organ. That means that almost every function performed in an animal's body is performed by parenchymal cells. There are too many of these functions to count in total, but some examples are:
f) Perception, thinking, information storage and processing (nervous system), Gas exchange (lungs), Producing immune cells (lymphatic system), Secreting hormones (pancreas, various reproductive , organs, brains, adrenal glands), Filtering blood (kidneys), Breaking down toxins (liver)

Which of the function is not performed by Parenchyma?

5: _____________ is the complex tissue, which acts as a transport system for soluble organic compounds within vascular plants. The _____________ is made up of living tissue, which uses turgor pressure and energy in the form of ATP to actively transport sugars to the plant organs such as the fruits, flowers, buds and roots; the other material that makes up the vascular plant transport system, the xylem, moves water and minerals from the root and is formed of non-living material.

6: Function of a special type of tissue in plant body:

"Through the system of translocation, the phloem moves photoassimilates, mainly in the form of sucrose sugars and proteins, from the leaves where they are produced by photosynthesis to the rest of the plant. The sugars are moved from the source, usually the leaves, to the phloem through active transport. The next step, translocation of the photoassimilates, is explained by the pressure flow hypothesis. When there is a high concentration of organic substance (in this case sugar) within the cells, an osmotic gradient is created. Water is drawn passively from the adjacent xylem over the gradient to create a sugar solution and a high turgor pressure within the phloem. The high turgor pressure causes the water and sugars to move through the tubes of the phloem, in to the 'sink tissues' (e.g. the roots, growing tips of stems and leaves, flowers and fruits)."

Identify the tissue type.

7: Identify the wrong statement ---

a) Transpiration: As the water moves up and into the leaves, some of it is needed to dissolve the sugars created by photosynthesis and carry them back down the plant. Remember that photosynthesis creates glucose, which the plant will use as energy.
b) The plant combines glucose molecules to create sucrose, a temporary storage sugar. The root cells, and other cells in the stems and leaves, do not create their own glucose and rely on the plant to provide them energy.
c) The xylem cells work to transport this created energy all throughout the plant from source cells, like leaves, to sink cells, such as those in the roots.
d) The vascular tissue is also responsible for controlling the flow of nutrients when the plant is creating flowers and fruits, which drastically affects the process.
Farmers have learned to manipulate the vascular system of plants in various ways to modify their crops in various ways. For instance, by damaging the vascular tissue below a fruit on a branch, the sugars will be translocated to the fruit.
e) While the roots may suffer, the fruit will become much larger as a result. This is called girdling, and is one of many techniques used to alter the flow of nutrients within a plant by modifying the vascular tissue.

8. Which of the following is NOT a vascular tissue?

A. Xylem B. Phloem C. Meristem

9. Why is phloem made of living cells, while xylem is made of dead cells?

A. No reason

B. Phloem is involved in active transport, Xylem is not

C. Phloem is a newer tissue, Xylem has simply died

10. Why can vascular plants be much taller than non-vascular plants?

A. They can transfer nutrients higher B. They need less water

C. They need less sunlight

11: Complete the following.

The ______ ___________ and _____________ ___________are connected via plasmodesmata, a microscopic channel connecting the cytoplasm of the cells, which allows the transfer of the sucrose, proteins and other molecules to the sieve elements. The ___________ _____ are thus responsible for fuelling the transport of materials around the plant and to the sink tissues, as well as facilitating the loading of sieve tubes with the products of photosynthesis, and unloading at the sink tissues. Additionally, the ___________ ________ generate and transmit signals, such as defense signals and phytohormones, which are transported through the phloem to the sink organs.

12: Identify the special type of tissue --- The ____________ is a collection of cells, which makes up the 'filler' of plant tissues. They have thin but flexible walls made of cellulose. Within the phloem, their main function is the storage of starch, fats and proteins as well tannins and resins in certain plants.

13: "The ______________ is the main support tissue of the phloem, which provides stiffness and strength to the plant. Sclerenchyma comes in two forms: fibres and Sclereids; both are characterized by a thick secondary cell wall and are usually dead upon reaching maturity. The bast fibres, which support the tension strength while allowing flexibility of the phloem, are narrow, elongated cells with walls of thick cellulose, hemicellulose and lignin and a narrow lumen (inner cavity)."

The above mentioned property signifies a type of plant tissue called ________________.

14: Identify Key Terms

A. – One of two types of transport tissue within vascular plants, xylem is responsible for the transport of water from the roots to the leaves and shoots.
B. – The process which most plants use to convert energy from the sunlight, water and carbon dioxide into oxygen and carbohydrates.
C. – The biological compounds (usually energy-storing monosaccharaides) which are produced by photosynthesis.
D. – Adenosine triphosphate is the high-energy molecule that transports energy for metabolism within cells.
E. -- These are slightly shorter, irregularly shapes cells, which add compression strength to the phloem, although somewhat restrict flexibility. Sclereids act somewhat as a protective measure from herbivory by generating a gritty texture when chewed.

15. What is the main function of the phloem?

A. Transporting nutrients from a source to a sink

B. Transporting nutrients from a sink to a source

C. Transporting water from a sink to a source

D. Transporting water from a source to a sink

16. What service does the companion cell not provide to the sieve element?

A. Providing energy B. Communication between cells

C. Physical rigidity D. Unloading photoassimilates to sink tissues

17. What does the P-protein do?

A. Increases the rate of metabolism within the companion cell

B. Builds the sieve plates

C. Forms a clot over a sieve plate when the phloem is damaged

D. Works within the phloem to transport sap

18: What is organ Parenchyma?

19:Tumor Parenchyma

20. Which of the following is NOT made up mostly of parenchymal tissue?

A. The leaves of a tree B. A kidney C. A large cancerous tumor D. Tree bark

21. What might be one reason for having multiple definitions of the term "parenchyma?"

A. Scientists are easily confused and imprecise with their language.

B. Scientists began using the term when tissue types were described based on superficial similarities, and attempts were made to draw similarities between tissue types in different living organisms.

C. Scientists from one discipline sometimes "borrow" terms that were originally developed by another discipline to describe a similar concept in their own field.

D. B & C

22. Which of the following organisms would you NOT expect to have parenchymal cells?

A. Tree B. Daisy C. Bacteria D. Human

23: ______________ is responsible for the transport of processed food from leaves of an autotrophic green flowering plant to rest of the body parts.

24 : Comment on regulation in the Apical Meristem

25. What is the difference between an apical meristem and an intercalary meristem?

A. No difference B. The apical meristem is at the tip C. Intercalary meristems can be apical

26. How can the apical meristem be manipulated to increase the harvest of a crop?

A. They can be cut to create a bushy plant; B. More meristems means more fruit; C. They can't be manipulated

27. How is the apical meristem similar to stem cells in a human foetus?

A. Both have the ability to differentiate ; B. They are completely different;

C. They divide in the same way

28 : Write functions of Lateral Meristem.

29. What type of meristem is responsible for the production of shoots and leaves?

A. Axillary Meristem; B. Shoot Apical Meristem; C. Lateral Meristem; D. Root Apical Meristem

30. What kind of tissue is not found in the apical meristem?

A. Protoderm B. Ground meristem C. Procambium D. Cork cambium

31. What is apical dominance?

A. When the presence of apical meristem prevents growth from the lateral meristem.

B. When the presence of an apical bud prevents growth from the lateral meristem.

C. When the presence of an apical bud prevents growth from the lateral bud.

D. When the presence of an apical meristem prevents growth from the lateral bud.

Solutions:

Ans 1: The apical meristem is located just below the root cap in the roots, as seen in the image below. The actual apical meristem is a cluster of densely packed and undifferentiated cells. From these cells will come all of the various cell structure the plant uses. An undifferentiated apical meristem cell will divide again and again, slowly becoming a specialized cell.

In the root apical meristem, the cells are produced in two directions. In the shoot apical meristem, cells are only created in one direction. The shoot apical meristem may exist at the tips of plants, as in many dicots, or may start slightly below the soil and generate leaves which grow upward, like most monocots. However, in both groups the shoot apical meristem is the growth center of all above ground growth.

Interestingly, the shoot apical meristem in most plants is capable of producing an entire plant, whereas the root apical meristem cannot. Scientists have used the ability of the shoot apical meristem to clone many species of plant. By simply cutting off the apical meristem and transferring it to an appropriate growth medium, the apical meristem will develop roots and differentiate into a whole new plant. As an added benefit, more apical meristems form on the plant, and can be harvested for more clones. In this way, a desirable plant can be replicated almost indefinitely.

Ans 2: Parenchyma is a term used to describe the functional tissues in plants and animals. This tissue is "functional" – performing tasks such as photosynthesis in plants or storing information in the human brain – as opposed to "structural" tissues like wood in plants or bone in animals.

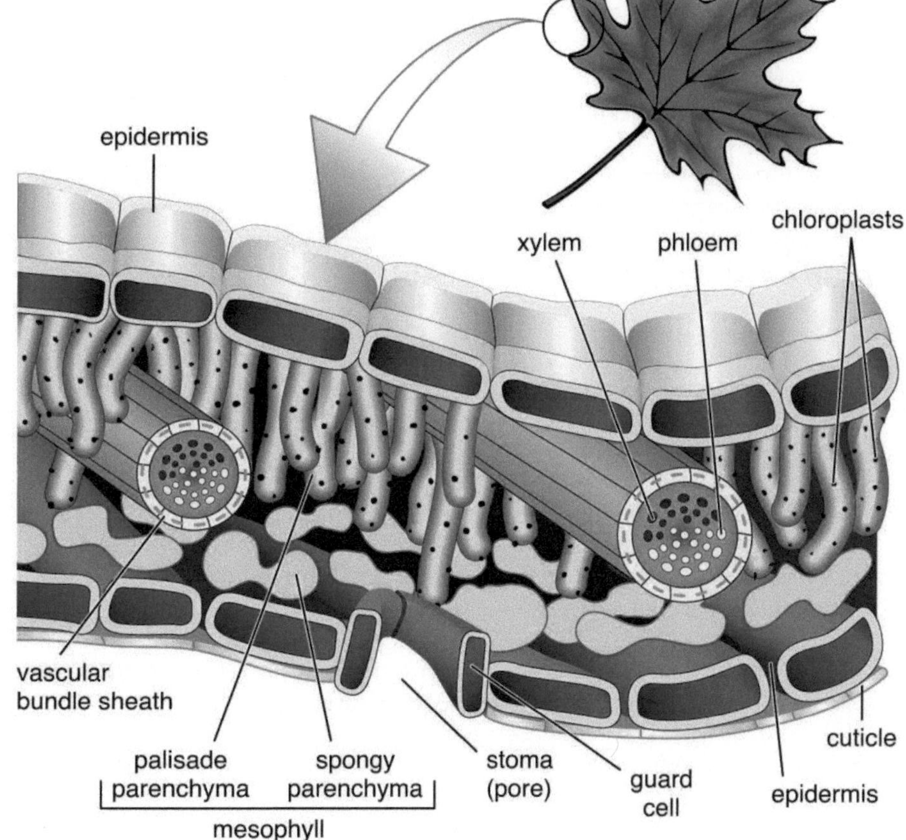

In plants, parenchyma refers to a specific type of ground tissue with thin cell walls and the ability to grow and divide.

Parenchyma makes up most of the cells within leaves, flowers, and fruits. Hard, structural features such as bark, outer coverings, and major veins in these structures are "structural" rather than "parenchymal" tissue.

Ans 3: In healthy animals, "parenchyma" is much more varied. It refers to the cells that perform the biological function of the organ – such as lung cells that perform gas exchange, liver cells that clean blood, or brain cells that perform the functions of the brain.

Another definition of "parenchyma" is a definition applied to cancer and other growths. When discussing growths, the "parenchyma" is the pathological tissue of the growth which is capable of growing and reproducing.

The last definition of "parenchyma" refers to the spongy, connective tissue in certain invertebrates such as flatworms. In most animals, connective tissues are not considered "parenchyma," but because some simple invertebrates do not have highly differentiated tissues, their connective tissue may also be parenchymal.

Ans 4: Option c is not performed by Parenchyma.

Types of Parenchyma: The term "parenchyma" has been used to describe several different types of plant and animal tissues. Here are the most common uses of the word "parenchyma."

Plant Parenchyma: In plants, "parenchyma" refers to a distinct tissue type that has thin cell walls and the ability to grow and divide. Plant parenchyma cells make up the bulk of leaves, flowers, and the growing, dividing inner parts of stems and roots. They perform functions such as photosynthesis, food storage, sap secretion, and gas exchange.

Ans 5: Phloem;

Ans 6: Function of Phloem;

Ans 7: Option c is wrong

Ans 8: C is correct. The meristem is the tissue which is actively dividing in a plant. While it may give rise to vascular tissue, it has not yet differentiated as is not currently serving that function.

Ans 9: B is correct. The cells of the vascular tissue in phloem must actively transport sugar molecules, which do not diffuse well through the cell membrane or the cell wall. To do this quickly, the cells must stay alive. In fact, they are supported by companion cells to help them survive. Xylem, on the other hand, only transports water and nutrients easily carried within water. These substances can move more quickly through hollow tubes of dead cells.

Ans 10: A is correct. While they need the same amount of water, sunlight, and nutrients to grow, vascular plants are capable of directing the water where they need it. Some trees can transport water to hundreds of feet, using only transpiration in the leaves and absorption through the roots. Therefore, the vascular tissue allows them to grow much taller, and the supporting cells of the vascular tissue can provide rigidity and strength.

Ans 11: sieve tube; companion cells

Ans 12: Parenchyma;

Ans 13: Sclerenchyma;

Ans 14: Xylem; Photosynthesis; Photoassimilates; ATP; Sclereids

Ans 15: A is correct. The main function of the phloem is to transport nutrients from the source where they are produced (e.g. the leaves through photosynthesis) to the sink (e.g. flowers and fruits) where they are used.

Ans 16: C is correct. The companion cell is important for providing energy, transferring materials and transmitting signals. The parenchyma and sclerenchyma provide strength and rigidity to a plant.

Ans 17: C is correct. When the phloem is damaged, the P-protein, which is produced in the sieve element lumen, accumulates on the sieve plate to prevent loss of nutrient rich sap.

Ans 18: In animals, the bulk of functional cells in any organ are called the "parenchyma." This distinguishes the cells which perform the organ's primary function from "structural" cells that serve mainly to protect or give form to the parenchyma. That means that virtually all functions performed within an animal's body, except for structural and protective functions, are performed by parenchymal cells. Examples of "structural" cells in animals include the hard, calcified cells in bones and the protective membranes around most organs.

Ans 19: When talking about cancer or other growths, the term "functional" is again useful for discussing parenchyma. The parenchyma of a tumor or other growth is considered to be the "neoplastic" part which is capable of cell division. This allows the parenchyma to serve the pathological "function" of allowing the tumor to keep spreading and growing.

Ans 20: D is correct. Tree bark is made up primarily of structural tissue, while the other three are made primarily of "functional" tissue of various types.

Ans 21: D is correct. Both B & C are reasons why the same term might be used in different ways in different fields of biology or medicine.

Ans 22: C is correct. "Parenchyma" refers to tissues found in both plants and animals. However, single-celled organisms like bacteria, by definition, cannot have parenchymal cells.

Ans 23: Phloem;

Ans 24: Diversification of cells in the apical meristem is a complex process controlled by a number of genes. In effect, these genes determine the shape and structure of a plant. As the apical meristem grows, it branches of smaller meristem locations, which will develop into branches of the stems and roots. The timing and number of these events are controlled by a series of genes within plants. The various expressions of these genes lead to different forms, some of which are more successful than others. The interaction between these genes and the growth of the apical meristem has led to the millions of different species of plants which exist today.

The variety of forms in plants is attributable almost solely to the differences in how their apical meristem functions. Some plants, like bushes, branch continuously and equally, while plants like pine trees have a single main branch. The root apical meristem is likewise responsible for root development. Roots can be deep, and focused on a single branch, such as tap-root, common to many weeds. Corn and bamboo, on the other hand, has much more dispersed and fibrous root system, which depends on lots of branching and lateral roots.

Ans 25: B is correct. The term apical simply means at the tip. A meristem is simply a portion of the organism with stem cells. Intercalary describes the space between apical meristems, in which smaller branches form.

Ans 26: B is correct. While it might also create a bushy plant, most fruits and vegetables are the product of a fertilized flower. Flowers typically form at a meristem. Therefore, if clipping the apical meristem means more meristems, more flowers can be created.

Ans 27: A is correct. Both sets of cells are totipotent, in that they can differentiate into an entire organism. While the apical meristem may stay totipotent, the stem cells in humans typically reduce the stem cells to multipotent, able to only transform into a handful of related cell types. This is one reason it is much harder to clone a human.

Ans 28: While the apical meristem is responsible for vertical growth, the lateral meristem is responsible for lateral growth, or growth in diameter. This type of growth is known as secondary growth because it is growth around an already established stem. In all woody plants and some herbaceous plants, there are two types of lateral meristems: the vascular cambium and the cork cambium. Similar to the procambium of the apical meristem, the vascular cambium produces secondary xylem and phloem; however, the procambium is also accountable for the development of wood that increases the girth of a plant. The cork cambium gives rise to the periderm, which is similar to the protoderm. While the protoderm produces the primary epidermis growth of a plant, the periderm replaces that epidermis to produce bark. The bark acts like a shield for the plant, barring it from physical damage and preventing water loss via a waxy substance called suberin.

Ans 29: B is correct. An axillary bud is the site of leaf growth, and is found on the lateral parts of the shoot apical meristem. The lateral meristem is responsible for lateral growth. The root apical meristem is responsible for root growth.

Ans 30: D is correct. The cork cambium is found in the lateral meristem and contributes to secondary growth rather than primary growth.

Ans 31: C is correct. Apical dominance is defined as dormancy at the lateral buds because of inhibiting factors received from the apical bud. The lateral meristem contributes to secondary growth and is not relevant in apical dominance.

Enrichment:

1. Which of the following is not a plant tissue?
A. Parenchyma B. Cork C. Leaf
2. What is the main different between Parenchyma and Sclerenchyma plant tissues?
A. Parenchyma are protective cells B. Sclerenchyma plant tissue photosynthesizes
C. Parenchyma cells have thinner walls and remain living
3. In your high-tech laboratory, you carefully cut part the epidermis from the top of a plant's leaf. What will happen to the leaf?
A. It will dry out and die B. It will keep photosynthesizing, but not regrow the epidermis
C. It will regrow the epidermis and survive
4. What is the difference between a parenchyma and sclerenchyma cell?
A. Parenchyma cells typically don't die at maturity B. They are essentially the same
C. Parenchyma cells provide more structural support
5. What is the difference between a parenchyma and chlorenchyma cell?
A. Chlorenchyma cells are internal, without chloroplasts ; B. Parenchyma cells do not have chloroplasts
C. Chlorenchyma cells are a type of parenchyma cells, which contain chloroplasts
6. Could a plant survive without parenchyma cells?
A. No B. Yes, if you water it C. Yes under all circumstances

Solutions:

Answer to Question #1 : C is correct. A leaf is a plant organ. An organ has many different tissue types and can have different functions. The leaf is the main source of photosynthesis and transpiration for the plant.
Answer to Question #2: C is correct. Parenchyma cells are sometimes considered the most important plant tissue, because they do much of the work of moving, creating, and storing the products the plants need. However, the other tissues provide the support and strength the plants needs to survive.
Answer to Question #3: C is correct. This leaf will die, as the water will escape too quickly from the surface of the exposed leaf. The parenchyma cells, when damaged, will become meristematic and begin producing epidermis cells to heal the wound, in a very similar process to how a human wound heals.
Answer to Question #4: A is correct. Sclerenchyma cells typically have very thick walls, embedded with structural proteins like lignin. When these tissues die, they form rigid, tough structural support. Parenchyma cells stay alive, typically helping produce and store nutrients. They constitute the majority of most plants.
Answer to Question # 5: C is correct. Chlorenchyma cells differentiate from parenchyma cells, and produce chloroplasts. To say that parenchyma cells do not have chloroplasts is false, because chlorenchyma cells are a type of parenchyma cell.
Answer to Question #6: A is correct. The parenchyma cells form a majority of the living cells in the plant. They carry out most of the metabolism reactions, and conduct most of the activities which constitute life, such as growth and photosynthesis. Without the parenchyma cells, a plant would be a hollow shell of mostly structural cells. Without chloroplasts or an ability to transport nutrients, they would be useless.

.

11. Notes and References

Solved Paper Set I

Question 1. (a) Why do we beat dusty blankets with a stick to remove dust particles?

(b) A stone when thrown on a glass window smashes the window pane to pieces. But a bullet fired from a gun passes through it making a hole. Why?
Answer 1: (a) It is done due to inertia of rest. (b) This is due to the inertia of rest.

Question 2. (a) If you jerk a piece of paper from under a book quick enough, the book will not move, why?

(b) Passengers sitting or standing in a moving bus fall in forward direction when the bus suddenly stops. Why?
Answer 2: (a) It is due to the inertia of rest. (b) This is due to the inertia of motion.

Question 3. (a) Why passengers are thrown outward when a bus in which they are travelling suddenly takes a turn around a circular road?

(b) Is any force required to move a body with constant velocity?
Answer 3: (a) This is due to the inertia of direction. (b) No.

Question 4. (a) Why a one rupee coin placed on a revolving table flies off tangentially?
Answer 4 a:
This is due to the inertia of direction.

(b) Why mud flies off tangentially to the wheel of a cycle?
Answer 4 b:
This is due to the inertia of direction.

Question 5. (a) When the electric current is switched off, why the blades of a fan keep on moving for some time?
Answer 5 a: This is due to the inertia of motion.

(b) Why the passengers fall backward when a bus starts moving suddenly?
Answer 5 b: This is due to the inertia of rest.

Question 6. (a) A body of mass m is moving on a horizontal table with constant velocity. What is the force on the table?
Answer 6 a: mg i.e. equal to the weight of the body.

(b) Name a factor on which the inertia of a body depends.
Answer 6 b: Mass.

Question 7. (a) Rocket works on which principle of conservation?
Answer 7 a: Law of conservation of linear momentum.

(b) Is the relation F→=ma→ applicable to the motion of a rocket?
Answer 7 b: No.

Question 8. (a) Will a person while firing a bullet from a gun experience a backward jerk? Why?
Answer 8 a: Yes, it is due to the law of conservation of linear momentum.

(b) A bomb explodes in mid-air into two equal fragments. What is the relation between the directions of their motion?
Answer 8 b: The two fragments will fly off in two opposite directions.

Question 9. (a) What happens to the acceleration of an object if the net force on it is doubled?
Answer 9 a: As a = Fm i.e. a ∝ F, so acceleration will be doubled when m the force is doubled.

(b) An electron moving with a certain velocity collides against a stationary proton and sticks to it. Is the law of conservation of linear momentum true in this case?
Answer 9 b: Yes, it is true.

Question 10. (a) According to Newton's third law of motion, every force is accompanied by an equal (in magnitude) and opposite (in direction) force called reaction, then how can a movement take place?
Answer 10 a: As the action and reaction never act on the same body, so the motion is possible.

(b) You can move a brick easily by pushing it with your foot on a smooth floor, but, if you kick it, then your foot is hurt. Why?
Answer 10 b: As Ft remains constant, so if t is reduced, then F will be increased and hence hurt our foot.

Question 11. (a) Why does a swimmer push the water backward?
Answer 11 a: So as to get forward push according to Newton's third law of motion.

(b) Why does not a heavy gun kick so strongly as a light gun using the same bullets (i.e. cartridges)?
Answer 11 b: The recoil speed of the gun is inversely proportional to its mass. So the recoil speed of the heavy gun is lesser than that of the light gun.

Question 12. (a) Can a rocket operate in free space?
Answer12 a: Yes.

(b) In a game of tug of war, two opposing teams are pulling the rope with equal (in magnitude) but the opposite force of 1000 kg wt at each end of the rope. What is the tension in the rope if a condition of equilibrium exists?
Answer 12 b: 1000 kg wt.

Question 13. (a) Which of Newton's laws of motion is involved in rocket propulsion?

Answer 13 a:
Newton's third law of motion.

(b) Action and reaction are equal in magnitude and opposite in direction, then why do not they cancel/balance each other?
Answer 13 b: They don't balance each other as they act on different bodies.

Question 14. (a) A passenger sitting in a bus at rest pushes it from within. Will it move? Why?
Answer 14 a: No, internal forces are unable to produce motion in a system.

(b) How would you explain the motion of a motorcyclist in a globe of death in a circus?
Answer 14 b: It is a case of motion in a vertical circle.

Question 15. Can a body in linear motion be in equilibrium? why?
Answer 15 :
Yes, it will be in equilibrium if the vector sum of the forces acting upon the body is zero.

Question 16. Is the law of conservation of momentum valid for a system consisting of more than two particles?
Answer 16: Yes, the law of conservation of momentum is a general law that is applicable to all systems.

Question 17. Which is greater out of the following
(i) The attraction of 1 kg lead for Earth,
(ii) the attraction of Earth for 1 kg of lead? Why?
Answer 17: Both are equal, the forces of action and reaction are always equal and opposite in direction according to Newton's third law of motion.

Question 18. Mention the conditions for the maximum and minimum pull of a lift on a supporting cable.
Answer 18:
The pull of the cable is minimum (zero) when the lift is falling freely.
The pull of the cable is maximum when the lift is moving up with the same acceleration.
Question 19. A man is at rest in the middle of a pond on perfectly frictionless ice. How can he get himself to the shore of the pond?
Answer 19 : He can get himself to the shore if he throws away his shirt or anything in his possession in a direction opposite to the desired direction of motion or by spitting in the forward direction or by blowing air from his mouth.

Question 20. Suppose you are seated in a cabin that has no doors, no windows, etc., and is also soundproof. Shall it be possible to detect the uniform velocity with which this cabin is moving? Why?
Answer 20: No, this is because when the cabin is. moving with uniform velocity, there will be no net unbalanced force.

Question 21. (a) Why do we pull the rope downwards for climbing up?
Answer 21 a: When we pull the rope downwards, an upward reaction helps us to rise up.

(b) Why is it easier to roll than to pull a barrel along a road?
Answer 21 b: It is due to the fact that rolling friction is less than sliding friction.

Question 22. (a) Why are the lubricants used in machines?
Answer 22 a: Lubricants are used in machines so as to reduce friction.

(b) Friction is independent of the area, but brakes of a very small contact area are not used. Why?
Answer 22 b: This is done so as to avoid wear and tear.

Question 23. Mention a factor on which coefficient of friction depends.
Answer 23: The coefficient of friction depends upon the nature of the surfaces in contact.

Question 24. Carts with rubber tires are easier to ply than those with iron tires. Why?
Answer 24: The coefficient of friction between the rubber tires and the road is lesser than the coefficient of friction between iron and steel.

Question 25. Why are wheels made circular? Explain.
Answer 25: Circular wheels roll without sliding on the road. Since rolling friction is less than sliding friction, so they move easily.

Question 26. (a) What do you mean by dry friction?
Answer 26 a: When both the bodies in contact are solids, then the force of friction is called dry friction.

(b) A soda water bottle is falling freely. Will the bubbles of the gas rise in the water of the bottle?
Answer 26 b: A freely falling soda water bottle is in a state of weightlessness. Thus the bubbles of the gas will not rise in the water of the bottle rather they remain floating.

Question 27. What do you mean by liquid or fluid or wet friction?
Answer 27: It is defined as the friction which conies into play between a surface and a liquid or fluid.

Question 28. "Friction is a self-adjusting force." Is this statement correct?
Answer 28: This statement is correct only so long as the friction is static friction. Up to the limiting friction, the force of friction is equal (in magnitude) and opposite to the applied force.

Question 29. (a) Several forces act simultaneously on a body. In which direction will it move?
Answer 29 a:
It will move in the direction of the net force.

(b) Name the physical quantity which is a measure of inertia of a body?
Answer 29 b: Inertial mass.

Question 30. Can a force change only the direction of the velocity of an object keeping its magnitude constant?
Answer 30 : Yes, a force can only change the direction of the velocity of an object keeping its magnitude constant.

Question 31. (a) Two objects having different masses have some momentum. Which one of them will move faster?
Answer: 31 –a The object with a smaller mass will move faster.

(b) A table is lying on the floor of a room. Is some force of friction acting on it?
Answer: 31-b No.

Question 32. (a) A book is lying on an inclined plane. Is some force of friction acting on the book?
Answer: 32-a -- Yes

(b) Name the physical quantity which can be found from the area under the force-time graph.
Answer: 31-b -- Impulse

(c) Will the body be in equilibrium under the action of three non-coplanar forces.
Answer: 31—c-- No.

Question 33. (a) Write the S.I. units of force, momentum, and impulse.
Answer 33-a --: S.I. units of force, momentum, and impulse are newton (N), kg ms-1, and Ns (Newton-second).

(b) Why should the hammer be heavier to push the nail deeper into the wooden blocks?
Answer 33-b: It should be heavier so as to increase the impact of force i.e. more force applied for a shorter time.

Question 34. (a) Why rockets are given conical shapes?
Answer 34 -a: The rockets are given conical shapes so as to reduce atmospheric friction.

(b) How does air friction affect the maximum height of a projectile?
Answer 34-b: The maximum height of a projectile is reduced due to air friction.

Question 35. (a) Explain why jet planes cannot move in air-free space but rockets can move?
Answer 35-a:
Jet planes use atmospheric oxygen to foil their fuel but rockets carry their own fuel and don't depend on atmospheric oxygen.

(b) Is it correct to state that a body always moves in the direction of the net force acting on it?
Answer 35-b: The statement is true only for bodies at rest before the application of force.

Question 36. At which place on Earth, the centripetal force is maximum?
Answer 36: The centripetal force is maximum at the equator.

Question 37. What provides the centripetal force in the following cases?
(i) Electron revolving around the nucleus.
Answer 37-i: It is provided by The electrostatic force of attraction between the electron and the nucleus.

(ii) Earth revolving around the sun.
Answer 37-ii: The gravitational force of attraction between Earth and Sun.

(iii) Car taking a turn on a banked road.
Answer 37-iii: A component of the reaction of the road.

Question 38. (a) What is the direction of the angular velocity of the minute hand of a wall-clock?
Answer 38-a: The direction of the angular velocity of the minute hand of a wall- clock is perpendicular to the wall and directed inwards.

(b) What is the difference between 'Newton' and 'newton'?
Answer 38-b: Newton is the name of a scientist but newton is the S.I. unit of force named after the scientist Newton.

Question 39. (a) Is it possible that a particle moving with a constant velocity may not have a constant speed?
Answer 39-a: No.

(b) For uniform circular motion, does the direction of centripetal force depend on the sense of rotation {i.e. clockwise or anti-clockwise)?
Answer 39-b: No. It is always radial irrespective of the sense of rotation.

Question 40. Why chinaware crockery is wrapped in paper or straws?
Answer 40: Paper or straw provides a cushion between the° pieces of crockery.
In case of any jerk (impulse), these will prolong the time of impact and reduce its effect, the crockery will thus be saved.

Question 41. AH, vehicles are provided with springs and shockers, why?
Answer 41: To reduce the impact of force on the vehicle as shockers and springs break the impact of force and increase the time of action of force thus reduce the impulse and save the vehicle from shock.

Question 42. A body falls from a single-story building roof on a muddy floor and another boy falls from the same height on a stone, who is likely to survive out of them and why?
Answer 42: The boy who falls on a muddy floor will survive due to the reduction of the impact of force by prolonging the time of reduction of force from maximum to zero.

Question 43. What is the effect on the direction of centripetal force when the revolving body reverses its direction of motion?
Answer 43: The centripetal force will be directed towards the center of the circle. This fact does not depend upon the sense of the rotation of the circle.

Question 44. Is it correct to say that the banking of roads reduces the wear and tear of the tires of automobiles? If yes explain.

Answer 44: Yes, if the road is not banked, then the necessary centripetal force will be provided by the force of friction between tires and the road. On the other hand; when the road is banked, a component of the normal reaction provides the necessary centripetal force, which reduces wear and tear.

Question 45. The linear velocity of a particle moving on the circumference of the circle is equal to the velocity acquired by a freely falling body through a distance equal to one-fourth the diameter of the circle. What is the centripetal acceleration of the particle moving along the circle?
Answer 45:g;

Question 46. (a) A body is moving with uniform velocity. Can it be said to be in equilibrium? Why?
Answer 46-a:
Yes, it can be said to be in equilibrium when it moves with uniform velocity as no acceleration i.e. no net force acts on the body.
(b) Why Newton's second law of motion is not applicable to the motion of a rocket?
Answer 46-b: Newton's second law i.e. F = ma is applicable only if the mass (m) of the body remains constant. In the case of the rocket, the mass continuously decreases and hence F = ma is not applicable.

Question 47. (a) A thief jumps from the upper story of a house with a load on his back. What is the force of the load on his back when the thief is in the air?
Answer 47-a: When the thief is in the air, he is in the state of free fall, and hence in the state of weightlessness. So the force of the load on his back is zero.
(b) When a body falls to the Earth, the Earth also moves up to meet it. But the motion of Earth is not noticeable. Why?
Answer 47-b: We know that acceleration is the ratio of the applied force to the mass of the body. As the mass of Earth is very large, so its acceleration is very small.

Question 48. What are the different effects a force is capable of producing?
Answer 48: Force can cause the following
Circular motion
Translatory motion
Deformations in the body on which it is applied.

Question 49. A ball is thrown up at a speed of 36 ms-1 by a thrower. If the ball returns to the thrower with the same speed. Will, there be any change in:
(a) Momentum of the ball? (b) Magnitude of the momentum of the ball?

Answer 49: (a) There will be a change in the direction of the momentum of the ball. (b) There is no change in the magnitude of the momentum of the ball.

Question 50. When a ball falls from a height its momentum increases. What causes the increase in the momentum of the ball?
Answer 50: The gravitational force acting in the direction of motion increases the velocity and hence momentum of the ball.

Question 51. When a high jumper leaves the ground, where does the force which accelerates the jumper upward comes from?
Answer 51: The high jumper after taking a short run presses the ground hard, the ground, in turn, reacts on him and provides the necessary upward accelerating force to the jumper. Thus, the reaction of the ground on the jumper is the required force.

Question 52. Name the forces which are in equilibrium in each of the following situations:
(a) a book resting on a table. (b) a cork floating on water. (c) a pendulum bob suspended from the ceiling with the help of a string.

Answer 52: a : The gravitational force on the book and a force of reaction of the table. b: The gravitational force on the cork and an upward thrust or buoyant force of water. c: The gravitational force on the bob and the tension in the string.

12. Achiever Section

1: Answer the following:

Vitamins play a vital role in the development of joints and other associated structures of skeletal system. Which vitamin plays a definite role in erotion of cartilage colums without letting the number of cells to increase?

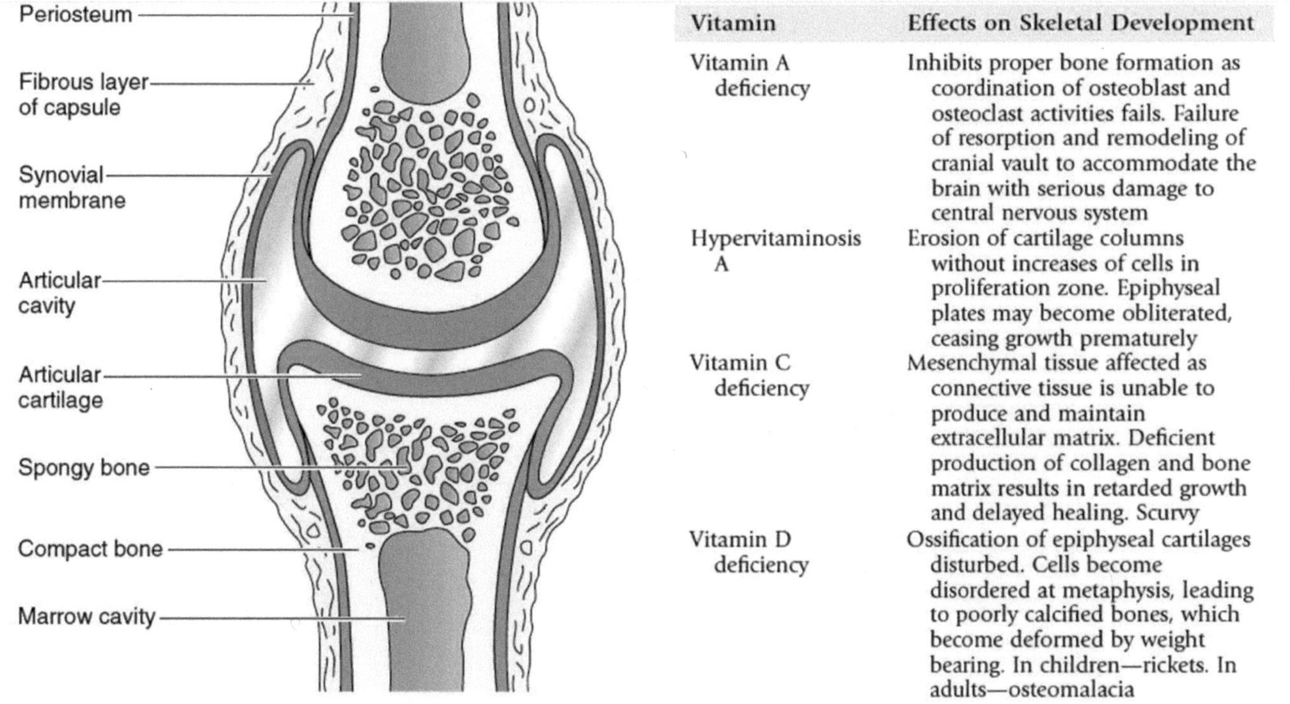

Vitamin	Effects on Skeletal Development
Vitamin A deficiency	Inhibits proper bone formation as coordination of osteoblast and osteoclast activities fails. Failure of resorption and remodeling of cranial vault to accommodate the brain with serious damage to central nervous system
Hypervitaminosis A	Erosion of cartilage columns without increases of cells in proliferation zone. Epiphyseal plates may become obliterated, ceasing growth prematurely
Vitamin C deficiency	Mesenchymal tissue affected as connective tissue is unable to produce and maintain extracellular matrix. Deficient production of collagen and bone matrix results in retarded growth and delayed healing. Scurvy
Vitamin D deficiency	Ossification of epiphyseal cartilages disturbed. Cells become disordered at metaphysis, leading to poorly calcified bones, which become deformed by weight bearing. In children—rickets. In adults—osteomalacia

2: Answer the following question –

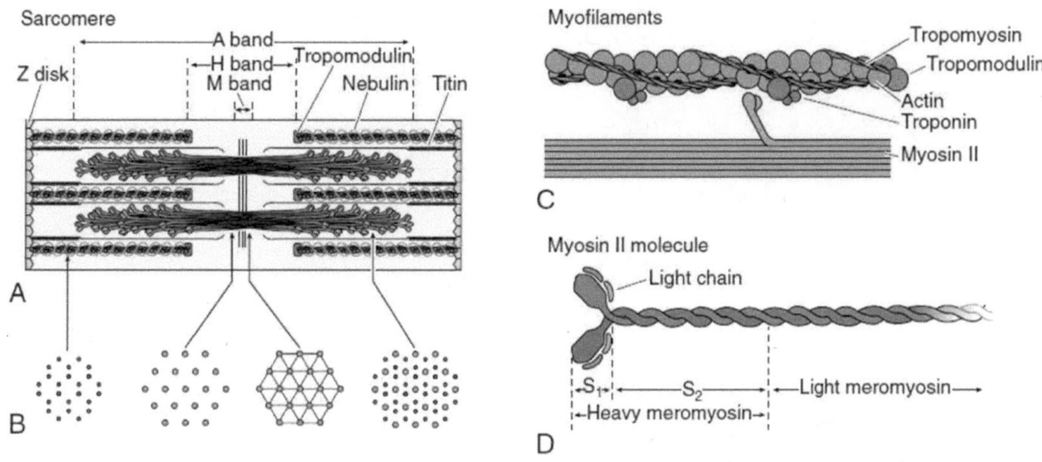

The give structures as displayed in figure A to D are associated to which tissue system?

3: Complete the following ---[15]

The diagram displayed below resembles the details of a skeletal muscle.

Organization of ____________ and ___________________ of skeletal muscle fibers are represented in the given diagram.

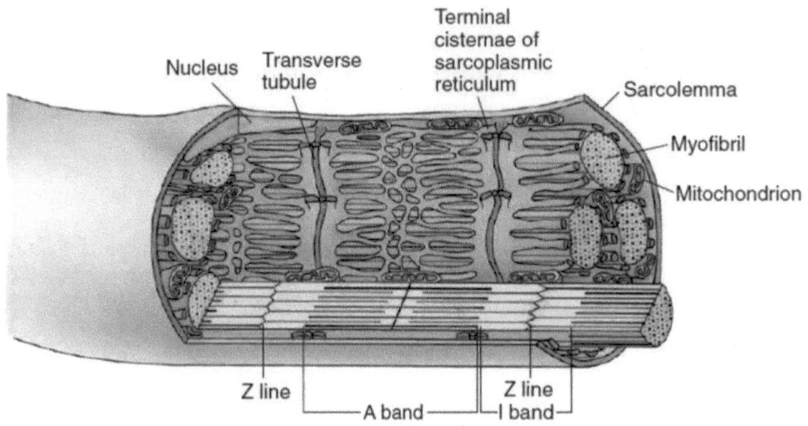

4: Identify the structures marked as P, Q and R .

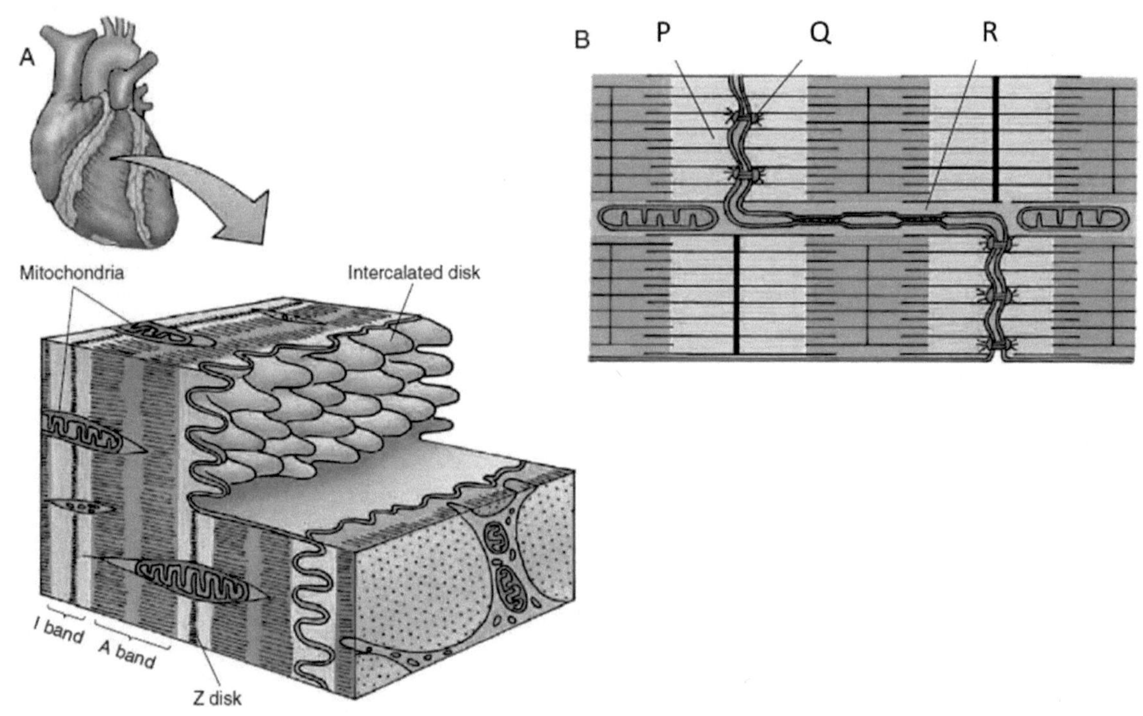

5: This property of solid is defined as _____________ _____________. It is the ratio of maximum load to which the wire is less than subjected to the original cross-sectional area.

6: ______________ and ______________ are two types of derivatives we often find in a nerve cell.

[15] *From Gartner LP, Hiatt JL: Color Textbook of Histology, 3rd ed. Philadelphia, Saunders, 2007, p 162*

7: Identify the marked structures as displayed in the following drawing.

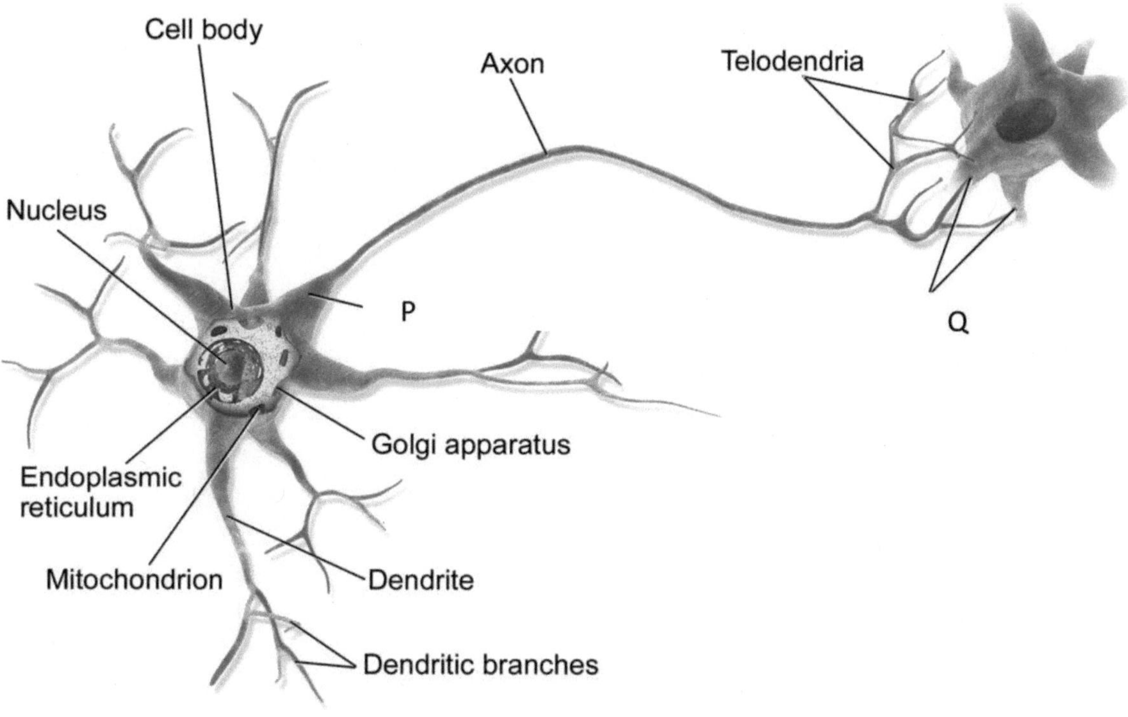

8: Statements related to functions and structural properties of a definite type of tissue is as follows:

A. The fibres present in phloem are called______________ ______________. They are also called as _________ fibres. They are long and narrow with pointed ends. They overlap with each other at different places.

B. These are generally absent in the primary tissue but are generally found in the secondary tissue.

C. The kind of structures have lignified walls.

D. The walls show simple pits. Rarely bordered pits may be present. These structures may be living or dead.

E. These structures often store food materials.

F. At maturity, these parts lose their protoplasm and become dead. At that condition these parts of tissue provide rigidity and mechanical support to the plant body.

G. Such parts of jute, flax and hemp are used commercially.

H. The primary structure of this tissue consists of narrow sieve tubes and is referred to as protophloem and the in later situation this structure has bigger sieve tubes and is referred to as metaphloem.

9: The kinetic energy of a particle of mass 1 kg is 200J. Find its velocity.

10: Identify the missing part ---

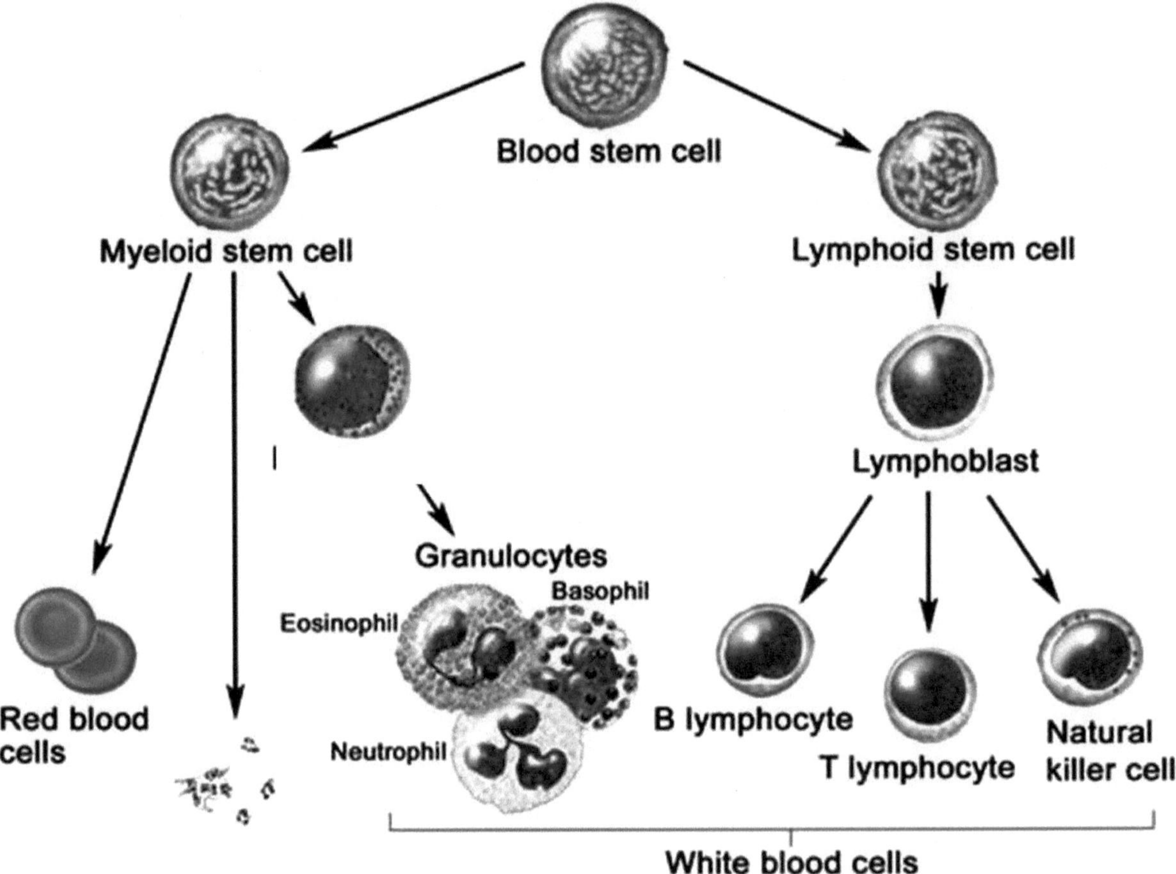

Solutions: ---

1: Vitamin A; 2: Skeletal muscle; 3: triads; 4:sarcomeres; P = Fascia adherens; Q = Desmosome; R = Gap junctions;

5: Breaking Stress; 6: Axon; Dendron; 7: P = Axon Hillock; Q = Synaptic Terminals; 8: phloem fibers; bast; 9: 10 ms^{-1} ;

10: P = Platelets; Q = Myeloblast;

.

Printed by Libri Plureos GmbH in Hamburg,
Germany